Mission and Evangelism in a Secularizing World

Evangelical Missiological Society Monograph Series

Mark Kreitzer, Edward L. Smither, Allen Yeh, and Anthony Casey
SERIES EDITORS

A Project of the Evangelical Missiological Society
www.emsweb.org

Mission and Evangelism in a Secularizing World

Academy, Agency, and Assembly Perspectives from Canada

Edited by
Narry F. Santos
and **Mark Naylor**

Foreword by Enoch Wan

☙PICKWICK *Publications* · Eugene, Oregon

MISSION AND EVANGELISM IN A SECULARIZING WORLD
Academy, Agency, and Assembly Perspectives from Canada

Evangelical Missiological Society Monograph Series 2

Copyright © 2019 Wipf and Stock Publishers. All rights reserved. Except for brief quotations in critical publications or reviews, no part of this book may be reproduced in any manner without prior written permission from the publisher. Write: Permissions, Wipf and Stock Publishers, 199 W. 8th Ave., Suite 3, Eugene, OR 97401.

Pickwick Publications
An Imprint of Wipf and Stock Publishers
199 W. 8th Ave., Suite 3
Eugene, OR 97401

www.wipfandstock.com

PAPERBACK ISBN: 978-1-5326-7598-0
HARDCOVER ISBN: 978-1-5326-7599-7
EBOOK ISBN: 978-1-5326-7600-0

Cataloguing-in-Publication data:

Names: Santos, Narry F., editor. | Naylor, Mark, editor.

Title: Mission and evangelism in a secularizing world : academy, agency, and assembly perspectives from Canada / edited by Narry F. Santos and Mark Naylor.

Description: Eugene, OR: Pickwick Publications, 2019 | Evangelical Missiological Society Monograph Series 2 | Includes bibliographical references.

Identifiers: ISBN 978-1-5326-7598-0 (paperback) | ISBN 978-1-5326-7599-7 (hardcover) | ISBN 978-1-5326-7600-0 (ebook)

Subjects: LCSH: Missions, Canadian.

Classification: BV2121 M4 2019 (print) | BV2121 (ebook)

Manufactured in the U.S.A.   02/04/19

Contents

Permissions | vii

Contributors | ix

Tables and Figures | xi

Foreword | xiii
—Enoch Wan

Preface | xv
—Narry F. Santos

Introduction: Canadian Perspectives on Mission and Evangelism in a Secularizing World | xvii
—Mark Naylor

Part 1: Mission Perspectives from the Agency, Assembly, and Academy

1. Doing Things We Have Never Done Before | 3
—Sam Chaise

    Response to "Doing Things We Have Never Done Before" | 13
—Minho Song

2. Returning to Ancient Paths | 16
—Connie denBok

    Response to "Returning to Ancient Paths" | 27
—Michael Krause

3. Connecting with Secular Muslims through History and Film: The Case Study of "Augustine: Son of Her Tears" | 31
—Edward L. Smither

Response to "Connecting with Secular Muslims through History and Film" | 38
—John Franklin

Part 2: Mission to the Next Generation

4 Infidels in the Temple of Secularism | 45
—Johnson Hsu

5 The Exodus of Generation Xs and Millennials from Canadian Churches: Implications for Evangelism in a Secular Multicultural Context | 64
—David Cheung

6 Millennial Islam and Secularization: Witness Among the Next Generation of Muslims (Some Preliminary Thoughts) | 93
—Matthew Friedman

Part 3: Mission in Global Christianity

7 How Africa Might Save Global Christianity | 105
—Glenn Martin

8 Do Missionaries Destroy Culture? | 119
—Joanne Pepper

Part 4: Mission and Strategy for a Changing Context

9 Tentmaking: Creative Mission Opportunities within a Secularizing Canadian Society | 131
—James W. Watson and Narry F. Santos

10 Technology as Loose Cannon on the Deck of Secularization's Ship | 149
—Glenn Martin

11 Their Eyes Were Opened: A Holistic Epistemology for Missional Discipleship | 163
—Steven Shetterly and Rhonda M. McEwen

Conclusion: Next Steps for Mission and Evangelism in a Secularising World—Canadian Perspectives | 177
—Narry F. Santos

Permissions

Unless otherwise indicated, all Scripture references are taken from English Standard Version, ESV® Bible (The Holy Bible, English Standard Version®), copyright © 2001 by Crossway, a publishing ministry of Good News Publishers. Used by permission. All rights reserved.

Scripture references marked NIV are taken from New International Version, ESV®, NIV® Copyright ©1973, 1978, 1984, 2011 by Biblica, Inc.® Used by permission. All rights reserved worldwide.

Scripture references marked NLT are taken from New Living Translation, copyright © 1996, 2004, 2015 by Tyndale House Foundation. Used by permission of Tyndale House Publishers Inc., Carol Stream, Illinois 60188. All rights reserved.

Scripture references marked RSV are taken from Revised Standard Version of the Bible, copyright © 1946, 1952, and 1971 National Council of the Churches of Christ in the United States of America. Used by permission. All rights reserved worldwide.

Contributors

Sam Chaise, Executive Director of the Christie Refugee Welcome Centre in Toronto.

David Cheung, President Emeritus of Asian Theological Seminary and Senior Pastor at Immanuel Christian Reformed Church in Richmond, BC.

Connie denBok, Lead Minister of the Alderwood United Church in Toronto.

John Franklin, Executive Director of Imago and Adjunct Professor at Trinity College University of Toronto.

Matthew Friedman, Professor of Intercultural Studies and Global Ministry Program Director at Kingswood University.

Johnson Hsu, Chaplain at the University of Toronto, Greater Toronto Area Director for International Student Ministries Canada, and Pastor to two English congregations at the Toronto China Bible Church network.

Michael Krause, R.J. Bernardo Family Assistant Professor of Leadership and Ministry and Coordinator of the Doctor of Ministry Leadership Track at Tyndale University College and Seminary.

Glenn Martin, Managing Editor of *Glocal Conversations* Journal with the University of the Nations.

Rhonda McEwen, Associate Professor, Education and Culture, and Director of The Calling Initiative at the Regent College in Vancouver, BC.

Joanne Pepper, Associate Professor and Coordinator, Intercultural Studies at Trinity Western University and ACTS Seminaries.

Steven Shetterly, MDiv student at Regent College in Vancouver, BC, and Director of Local and Global Outreach at Bellingham Covenant Church in Washington State.

Edward Smither, Professor of Intercultural Studies and History of Global Christianity and Dean of the College of Intercultural Studies at Columbia International University.

Minho Song, Senior Pastor of the Young Nak Korean Church of Toronto and Adjunct Professor in Pastoral Ministry at Tyndale University College and Seminary.

James Watson, Corps Health and Planting Consultant for The Salvation Army.

Tables and Figures

List of Tables

Table 1: Religious Self-Identification among Canadians (%), 1945–2000

Table 2: Religious Self-Identification among Canadians, 2001–2011

Table 3: Weekly Religious Attendance among Canadians (%)

Table 4: Canadian Religious Service Attendance

Table 5: Birth Years of Generation Xs and Millennials

Table 6: Weekly Attendance by Age Group (%), 1991

Table 7: Canadian Teens (%)

Table 8: Decline in Weekly Church Attendance (%)

Table 9: Religious Identification in Childhood Retained in Young Adulthood (%)

Table 10: Religious Nones by Generation (%), 1971–2011

Table 11: Survey Question: "In your view, what is it about Canada that you think most deserves to be celebrated on its 150th birthday?," 2010

Table 12: Religious Self-Identification, 1945–2000

Table 13: Religious Self-Identification, 2001, 2011

Table 14: Religious Self-Identification among Canadians (%), 1971–2011

Table 15: Other-Religions and No-Religions, 1991–2011

List of Figures

Figure 1: Religious Self-Identification among Canadians (%), 1945–2000

Figure 2: Survey Question Result: Canada's Multicultural Makeup Is One of the Best Things about this Country, 2002

Figure 3: Canadian Perception of Multiculturalism in Relation to National Identity, 2008

Foreword

Enoch Wan

Secularization is a massive wave from Europe sweeping across the globe. It came to North America by way of Canada, southward, toward the United States of America. With the combination of multiculturalism, pluralism, and postmodernism, the impact of secularization on Canadian socio-cultural fabric is epic and extensive.

This volume is a collection of multiple contributors and a record of the conversation between representatives from agency, assembly, and academy. The publication of this volume is a contribution to the relevant literature on secularization with a unique perspective: Canadian missiological research and reflection on secularization. The contributors recognize their historical and contextual situation in Canada and share a theoretical assumption that secularization is a movement of an anthropocentric ideology toward dominance that contrasts or opposes theocentric tradition or religious worldviews.

As a fellow Canadian and former Evangelical Missiological Society (EMS) president for two terms, the publication of this volume is a celebration of the recent and exciting regional conference under the leadership of Narry Santos and the vibrancy of the conversation held regionally, with video-conferencing from other locations within Canada.

The collection of multi-author contributions in this volume is a visible sign that the Canadian chapter of EMS is gaining *momentum* and interest in many centers across Canada. The changes initiated by Mark Naylor (regional VP of EMS in Canada for more than one term) have been helpful along with partnerships with other agencies and institutions. I personally participated in the Canadian regional conference repeatedly with a dual-role: contributor and cheerleader to Mark. Therefore, it is a privilege for me to write the foreword to this celebratory publication with reflection and rejoicing.

Preface

Narry F. Santos

WHILE SECULARISM AND SECULARIZATION have been discussed, dissected, and debated for many years, this volume adds significantly to the conversation from a missiological perspective as the contributors make sense of and respond to the complexities and uncertainties of a secularizing world. The title of the book, *Mission and Evangelism in a Secularizing World,* comes from the 2018 theme (with the same title) of the Evangelical Missiological Society (EMS) regional and national meetings in North America. The subtitle *Academy, Agency, and Assembly Perspectives from Canada* indicates the breadth of perspective from three major segments of Canadian Evangelical Christianity today.

On April 6, 2018, EMS Canada gathered the academy (seminaries and Bible colleges), agency (parachurch and mission groups), and assembly (local churches) at its annual regional meeting that met simultaneously in five Canadian centers: Trinity Western University and ACTS Seminaries in Langley, BC; Jaffray Centre at Ambrose University in Calgary, AB; Providence University College and Theological Seminary in Otterburne, MB; Tyndale University College and Seminary in Toronto, ON; and Kingswood University in Sussex, NB. Each of the three EMS Canada 2018 plenary speakers and respondents to the speakers represented one of academy, agency, or assembly (3As). The 3As were also adequately represented around the tables for group discussion and reflection after each plenary session.

In its September 2018 meeting, the EMS National Board approved the special publication of the EMS Canada 2018 Regional Meeting plenary and paper presentations to be part of the EMS Monograph Series. The board approval means that for the first time in EMS history, the papers from Canada would not be incorporated in the annual compendium from the EMS National Meeting proceedings—though Canadian papers were still presented at the national meeting in Dallas, Texas on September 12–14, 2018.

This first-ever edited Canadian volume is grouped into four parts: part 1, "Mission Perspectives from the Agency, Assembly, and Academy," includes the three plenary essays and the corresponding responses to them; part 2, "Mission to the New Generation," contains three papers that focus on international students, the Generation X and Millennials, and second-generation secularized Muslims; part 3, "Mission in Global Christianity," has two papers that deal with African Christianity and the role of missionaries in culture change; and part 4, "Mission and Strategy for a Changing Context," covers three papers that discuss bivocational (or tentmaking) ministry, technology's relation to secularization and mission, and missional discipleship. For parts 2–4, each of the eight essays (chapters 4–11) ends with three reflection questions that motivate the reader to relate the chapter insights to their walk or work, ministry or mission. In addition, the whole book is framed with an overview in the introduction and a set of next steps in the conclusion.

As co-editors, we—Narry Santos (EMS Canada VP) and Mark Naylor (former EMS Canada VP)—are privileged to put this volume together. We sense that the theme of the book resonates with the 3As in Canadian Christianity and beyond. We are also thankful to Edward Smither (EMS President) for seeing the value of this Canadian volume, to Enoch Wan (EMS VP Publications) for writing the book's foreword, and the EMS Board for supporting and believing in EMS Canada. Further, we extend our gratitude to Chris Spinks (Wipf and Stock editor) for graciously helping us throughout the publishing process.

We would also like to express appreciation to all who presented the eleven EMS papers in Canada and those who gave their responses to them, especially the chapter contributors who diligently edited their papers into essay form. Finally, we thank God for his graciousness toward the EMS Canada team that faithfully and diligently planned, promoted, and coordinated the simultaneous 2018 Regional Meeting in their own centers—Mark Naylor, Timothy Stabell, Daryl Climenhaga, Robert Cousins, Charles Cook, Lauren Goldbeck, Matthew Friedman, and Alexander Best. Thank you all for your labor of love!

Introduction

Canadian Perspectives on Mission and Evangelism in a Secularizing World

Mark Naylor

When asked if the Jewish people, occupied and oppressed by the powerful Roman Empire, should pay taxes to Caesar or not, Jesus asked to see a Roman coin. Indicating Caesar's inscription, Jesus stated, "Give to Caesar what belongs to Caesar, and give to God what belongs to God" (Mark 12:17 NLT). Rightly or wrongly, this saying has been used to indicate a distinction between the sacred and the secular and to support the principle of the separation of church and state. There are duties to be paid toward God and distinct and separate duties toward the state, it is argued. A more nuanced exegesis may recognize that in Jewish and Christian thought, the "image" belonging to God is humanity itself, and therefore all powers are subject to the supreme Creator and King. Nonetheless, the Enlightenment did usher in influential philosophical reflections that displaced the creator God with humanity at the center of life and meaning. The global influence of this shift in Western thought—from a theological to an anthropological orientation of life—together with considerations of an appropriate missiological response, is the subject of this volume.

In order to put these academic papers into their correct context, clarity is important. What do we mean by "secularization"? What is mission and evangelism? What are the implications of the phrase "secularizing world" that makes this a relevant and significant contribution to the participation of evangelicals in God's global mission?

What Is "Secularization"?

Hibbert helps us address the first question by asking, "Is secularism a matter of neutrality in matters of religion . . . or is secularism, by definition, hostile toward religious belief of all kinds?"[1] He goes on to suggest that there are "multiple interpretations of secularism, some of which are consistent with expressions of religion in public life," while acknowledging that other interpretations are hostile to religions as "competing visions."[2] Nonetheless, even when a secular society provides an inclusive environment for religious thought, the understanding of what constitutes an appropriate worldview and a healthy vision for society will clash. In light of this, he adopts Clifford Geertz's definitions of "irreligious" and "ecumenical" secularism. Irreligious secularism is driven by a "competing intellectual and moral vision" with the aim of eliminating religion from society, while ecumenical secularism seeks neutrality for religion and belief, rather than opposition and hostility.[3]

Although a neutral secular state, inclusive of all beliefs and not invested in an ideology of its own, can be envisioned in theory, the reality is quite different. All cultures and societies are inevitably influenced by and constantly negotiating their worldview, beliefs, and values. In particular, neutrality and equity are not possible where there are contrasting worldviews, beliefs, and values; tensions, rather than tolerance, are often the result. In his conclusion, Hibbert proposes an ideal "re-conceptualized secularism" that is "tolerant . . . with the commitment to non-discrimination" but also recognizes "secularism's troubled past, particularly in regard to secularity's materialist worldview and the tradition's historical intolerance."[4] It is not just "secularism's troubled past" but also its troubling present that seems to verify the claim of those less optimistic than Hibbert that "secularism in practice has failed to accommodate religion of any sort" and there exists "within the very idea of secularism an inherent hostility toward religion."[5]

Historically speaking, both the practice of separation between church and state and those times when religious institutions have had political powers have proved troubling. At one extreme, when church authorities gained political power, the Gospel message was corrupted and used for purposes contrary to Jesus' vision of the kingdom of God, resulting in injustice. At the other extreme, secular states have suppressed expressions of Christianity

---

1. Hibbert, *Religion, Nationalism*, 100.
2. Hibbert, *Religion, Nationalism*, 101.
3. Hibbert, *Religion, Nationalism*, 101.
4. Hibbert, *Religion, Nationalism*, 116.
5. Hibbert, *Religion, Nationalism*, 101.

through merciless oppression. Even in settings where freedom of thought and expressions of faith are permitted (and even encouraged), tensions and struggle with secularizing trends are inevitable. What should evangelism and mission look like in the context of secularization?

For this volume, secularization will be viewed as the movement of an anthropocentric ideology toward dominance that contrasts or opposes theocentric or religious worldviews. The focus is on a transition away from religious thought or influence and toward humanist or materialist ideals. In contrast, the essence of evangelism (the communication of the Gospel) and mission (the expression and promotion of the kingdom of God in new contexts) is the attempt to influence a society toward a Christ-centered worldview that impacts all levels of life.

What Is the "Secularizing World"?

By "secularizing world," we are not saying that secularization is the only challenge we face or even that it is the dominant phenomenon. The suggestion is that secularization is a significant dynamic that has worldwide implications; thus, it is worthy of consideration in missiology, particularly because it opposes the Gospel mandate. To ignore this influence that shapes worldviews, beliefs, and values in many global settings is to jeopardize our efforts to present a resonating and appropriately contextualized message of the Gospel.

It is probably safe to claim that secularization is a global phenomenon. In fact, the secularization–religion tension has always been present. It is represented in the story of the garden of Eden with the serpent's subversive question, "Has God said?" (Gen 3:1 NLT). The strength of the tension varies in different contexts, but it is always present. This is understandable in light of the human struggle to integrate the "how" with the "why" of the world. In Johannes Sloek's terminology, we deal with the "logos" of life (*how* we live life) while constructing the "mythos" of meaning (*why* life is significant).[6] For some, the "why" is determined by forces—loving or malevolent, personal or impersonal—outside of human control. For others, the predominant narrative is secularizing, proclaiming with the ancient Greek philosopher Protagoras that "humanity is the measure of all things." In contexts where such a worldview has been embraced—and there are few contexts in which this narrative is not felt—there is a call to answer the challenge with robust missiological thinking. At the same time, even while acknowledging a global influence, it is important to keep in mind that this conversation

---

6. Sloek cited in Armstrong, *Battle For God*, xiii.

is of particularly Western concern. As Seiple, Hoover, and Otis point out in the introduction to *The Routledge Handbook of Religion and Security*: "While Western academics have indulged a long, intramural discussion of secularization, most of the rest of the world has demonstrated no interest in secularizing, much less theorizing *ad nauseum* about it."[7]

It is also important to acknowledge works done in the past, such as Niebuhr's classic work in *Christ and Culture*, in which Christ *in, over, against, in paradox*, and *transforming* culture are considered with clarity and depth.[8] This work, as well as the work of those who have evaluated Niebuhr's project, is especially relevant when considering secularizing pressures.

The Canadian Secularizing Context

What this volume contributes is Canadian missiological research and reflection on secularization. The authors recognize their historical and contextual situation in Canada. The dominant narratives have changed rapidly over the past few decades, and churches struggle to maintain their voice and the perceived validity of their biblical orientation. Secular viewpoints are affecting the church from the outside through political pressures. One example is the 2018 Canadian Supreme Court decision on the Trinity Western University community covenant in light of changing views of individual rights with respect to gender and sexuality. The secular narratives are gaining such momentum that the Prime Minister, Justin Trudeau, feels comfortable equating his liberal values to Canadian values and limiting government funding to those charitable agencies that sign a form agreeing with abortion rights.

But secularization is also a significant influence within the church. How does an evangelical church maintain standards that it believes correspond to God's desire for his people and yet respect the Canadian value of individual rights assumed by many of its members? How does a Christian community—without alienating people—address secular societal assumptions that threaten to undermine biblical principles? Christians through the ages and around the world have struggled with the biblical concept of being *in* the world but not being *of* the world (John 17:14–15 NLT). What is the proper orientation that is centered on Christ, brings in the kingdom, maintains integrity with the word of God, and is able to confront the spiritual power of secularism?

---

7. Seiple et al., *Routledge Handbook*, 2.
8. See Niebuhr, *Christ and Culture*.

An Overview of the Contributions

How do the chapters in this volume contribute to the conversation about evangelism and mission in a secularizing world? The first part of the book explores this topic from the perspectives of the agency (parachurches and mission agencies), assembly (local churches), and academy (seminaries and Bible colleges).

Sam Chaise (chapter 1) addresses the role of the agency in his contribution entitled, "Doing Things We Have Never Done Before." He begins by describing the secularizing movement in Canada over the past thirty years and provides seven suggested responses for the church. These responses encourage epistemological humility coupled with a spirituality that functions within the "thought-world" of others, as the church responds to and dialogues with their concerns. This allows believers to be "curious and engaged rather than defensive and fearful." He then addresses the role of the agency directly as mediator between "thought-leaders" of the academy and practitioners in the local church. The agency facilitates the reflection of the academy into creative initiatives that stimulate the health and multiplication of the church. The agency functions as the "research and development department," helping the church navigate the secularizing influences of their context.

In responding to this chapter, Minho Song affirms the key points that Chaise makes. He also adds to the discussion, however, by noting that first-generation immigrants connect more with modernity, while the next generation, influenced by postmodernity, are more likely to question the exclusive Christian narrative. Each orientation requires its distinct approach.

Connie denBok (chapter 2) makes observations on secularization in Canadian churches as an insider of the United Church of Canada. She addresses "the deterioration of confidence that the twenty-first-century Church has in its own institutions, its message and doctrines, and its ability to transform and be transformed" and describes eight possible responses to such a shift. These responses demonstrate different approaches in the search for an effective way to uphold the message of the Gospel so that a response can be given to the observed secularizing trend. Each response includes insightful critiques that highlight possible negative consequences. In advocating the latter two strategic approaches, denBok suggests that the church in Canada is "at a crossroads where we will be converted more wholly to Christ or we will be converted to the Spirit of this age."

Michael Krause responds to denBok by proposing a metaphor as a way to envision her approaches to the secularization process. He suggests that the "tapestry" of Christendom has been "unravelled" by secularism so that the "metanarrative" of the Christian story is lost. He then captures each of denBok's reactions to secularism as a response dependent on different stages of the unravelling process. He concludes that clarity in "discerning our location" in this unravelling will help determine the appropriate response.

Ed Smither (chapter 3), the current president of the Evangelical Missiological Society, provides a perspective from the academy on engaging secular Muslims through a reflection on art and history. "Augustine: Son of Her Tears" is a movie made by North Africans about the faith journey of Augustine of Hippo, a major figure in their history. Smither suggests that the film speaks to secular, North African Muslims "who are indifferent to or even fed up with modern Islam." Many of the personal struggles as well as the spiritual and intellectual questions engaged by Augustine in the movie resonate with North African Muslims today. Smither suggests two universal lessons from this reflection that can help engage a secularizing world—historical reflections, which often challenge current ideologies, and the power of story as an important vehicle to express faith.

John Franklin has a few "quibbles" with Smither's chapter. He points out that the phrase "secular Muslim," which sounds like "an oxymoron," has not been defined, and he wonders why the film would not interest "devoted" Muslims. He also provides a summary of Charles Taylor's delineation of the concept of the "secular," wondering which definition best fits in the North African context that Smither is describing. Along with engaging some of the themes of the film that Smither specifically deals with, Franklin notes that the film is "a soft apologetic" and, while hoping for a fruitful reception, wonders if it truly can provide a gospel impact or if it may prove to be "just more information devoid of any personal engagement at all." He concludes by addressing Smither's "missiological lessons" concerning mission and the arts and suggests with approval that the arts do create "space for conversation," and mission leads toward "ongoing transformative experience."

The second part of this volume, *Mission to the New Generation*, addresses the impact of secularization on the generation whose values and beliefs are still being shaped, as they explore their place in this world. From the perspective of a university chaplain, Johnson Hsu (chapter 4) provides a description of the "interplay" when international students of faith confront secular ideologies at the University of Toronto–Scarborough. He first notes the secular influence of relegating religion to the private sphere among students, staff, and administrators, so that their "public faces" are devoid of any religious expression. Private conversations, however, often indicate a Christian identity, if not a living faith. He wonders if "the perception of the university as a secular space caused a hiding of religious identities." He also notes that the secular environment often serves to strengthen people's faith, as they find strength from other believers to confront secular ideologies. Finally, he notes that the "twin currents of Progressivism: secularism and multiculturalism" conflict when the need for increased expressions of faith are perceived and accommodated; thus, pushing back against the marginalization of religion.

David Cheung (chapter 5) provides a statistical analysis of Generation X and Millennials with respect to religious trends. He demonstrates the growth of secularism and the decline in religious faith statistically over the past forty years and, by citing current examples, concludes that the trend is continuing. In his conclusion, Cheung urges the church to empower believers to engage in "incremental evangelism," so that many people can be exposed to the Gospel message over a long period of time.

Matthew Friedman (chapter 6) reflects on the impact of Western secularization on second generation Muslims in North America. Many young people from a Christian background have abandoned their parent's faith because of secular narratives, and this is also true of many Muslim young people born in North America. Friedmann proposes that this common concern for the impact of secularization can be a helpful point of contact for dialogue with Muslims. He further describes and promotes early Spanish missionary Ramon Llull's strategy of irenic dialogue as the path to present the truth of the Christian faith.

The third part of this book, *Mission in Global Christianity*, considers intercultural issues as they relate to secularization. Glenn Martin (chapter 7) explores the lack of influence that secularization has had in Africa in his contribution, "How Africa Might Save Global Christianity." Citing Cahill's work in 2010—*How the Irish Saved Civilization*—about the church in the Middle Ages, Martin suggests that Africa may play a similar role against the onslaught of secularization. Noting a number of distinctives in African Christianity, including decentralization, preference for orality, holistic approach, and supernaturalist outlook, he observes with others that the hope for Christianity in the West may lie with African immigrants who bring a fresh movement of the Christian faith.

Facing current narratives emerging from the Residential Schools legacy in Canada, Joanne Pepper (chapter 8) considers the question, "Do Missionaries Destroy Culture?" She considers the assumptions behind that question and proposes a "more fundamental query. . . . Does the change brought about by the Gospel—the message proclaimed by the missionary—bring positive or negative transformation to cultures?" She suggests that a negative impact occurs when a confusion of Gospel and culture leads the missionary to impose their culturally shaped conscience upon their audience. This danger, however, should only cause the missionary to proceed with caution but not abandon the task. When change toward the Gospel and all its implications are self-initiated and not imposed, then the Gospel "strengthens, enriches, and uplifts global cultures."

The fourth and last part of the book, *Mission and Strategy for a Changing Context*, considers philosophical and practical approaches to address secularization from a Christian orientation. James Watson and Narry Santos (chapter 9) explore how Christians can facilitate mission within a secularizing context through an application of the Acts 18 description of "tentmaking." Building on this image, "Tentmaking: Creative Mission Opportunities within a Secularizing Canadian Society" suggests that a bivocational or "business as mission" approach in the Canadian setting can be an effective way to bridge the sacred–secular divide and make a Gospel impact. The authors consider three models that are currently being used by both established churches and missionaries to Canada so that they can connect with religious "nones" (who decline to be affiliated with any religious entity): missional groups; small church plants; and larger church initiatives. A key principle in these models is empowering staff and volunteer leaders to engage "nones," as the former seek—through both reflection and action—creative ways to merge work and mission.

In "Technology as Loose Cannon on the Deck of Secularization's Ship," Glenn Martin (chapter 10) challenges Christians to view technology as a "friend" to confront secularizing trends. While noting the importance of technological advances in all eras of Christian mission, the author considers the downsides of technology to Christian mission and suggests that the response is to be "proactive." In light of secularizing influences of technology, he concludes that, for the Christian practitioner, technology "is a handmaid of missions only inasmuch as it serves as a bridge to individuals and communities and ethnicities and their mediums of language and communication."

In the final contribution, Steven Shetterly and Rhonda McEwen (chapter 11) point out some epistemological fallacies as an Achilles's heel for secular ideologies in "Their Eyes Were Opened: A Holistic Epistemology for Missional Discipleship." They challenge Christians to recognize and embrace the reality that knowing is "an integrative, intuitive, and subjective process." The authors promote a holistic, rather than strictly rationalist, approach to gaining faith with important implications for discipleship. "Leaps of faith" are an integral part of the human experience to discover knowledge, both for believers and those with a secular mindset. One key application for discipleship from these insights is "helping people tell their story in light of God's story," with the conviction that a person's faith journey is one of practice that leads to belief.

Narry F. Santos provides a fitting conclusion, calling for "next steps" and drawing appropriate suggestions for a sound, missiological, and Canadian response from each of the contributions.

Serving in Hope

One final thought on the spirit of hope that runs through these contributions as you, the reader, begin to engage these authors. It is easy to feel overwhelmed by the secularizing trend in Canada and other parts of the world as a dominating force thwarting our efforts to introduce the transforming message of the Gospel. Exiled to the Isle of Patmos, the apostle John had even more reason to fear. The threat of Rome and the Jewish authorities loomed like a massive wave to sweep away the early church. The fragile new order of the kingdom was in danger of disappearing before it had time to grow. At this moment, John is ushered into the throne room of God, where, before the throne, he sees the sea "as still as glass" (Rev 4:6). The sea represents chaos, while the stillness of the sea communicates God's supremacy over all creation and spiritual powers. What seemed a threat to John on earth was immobilized in the presence of God. Similarly, we do not face a battle in which the outcome is in doubt. We are victors in Christ, called to live out the faith, hope, and love that Jesus accomplished through his death and resurrection. It is the redemption of all creation that is at the heart of God's mission, and the future is full of light. We serve with hope and joy, not desperation. While secularization is currently a dominant trend in our experience, it cannot last. God's mission has been accomplished, is being accomplished, and will be accomplished. *Soli Deo gloria.*

Bibliography

Armstrong, Karen. *The Battle for God: Fundamentalism in Judaism, Christianity and Islam.* London: Harper Collins, 2000.
Hibbard, Scott. "Religion, Nationalism, and the Politics of Secularism." In *The Oxford Handbook of Religion, Conflict, and Peacebuilding*, edited by R. Appleby, 100–123. Oxford: Oxford University Press, 2015.
Niebuhr, H. Richard. *Christ and Culture.* New York: Harper & Row, 1951.
Seiple, Chris, et al., eds. *The Routledge Handbook of Religion and Security.* New York: Routledge, 2013.

Part 1

Mission Perspectives from the Agency, Assembly, and Academy

I

Doing Things We Have Never Done Before

SAM CHAISE

WE HAVE NEVER BEEN here before. The Canada in which we live has not existed until now. This means that we will need to try things we have never tried, think thoughts we have not had to think, imagine futures we have not yet seen, and act in patterns we have not yet experienced—if we want to see outcomes different from what we are seeing today. This assumption underlies everything that is in this chapter. This also means that, if we are honest about it, none of us can be *certain* about what we are to do. But we know that, if we keep doing what we are already doing, we will continue to see what we already see. If we want to see different outcomes, we will have to not just do things differently but rather do *entirely different things*.

My Context

Context matters, of course, and I speak out of a particular context. I am male, born in London, England, to parents who had emigrated from South India, and have lived almost all of my life in Canada. My parents were Christians, so I grew up in the Church. Most of my adult life, I have earned a salary from churches or Christian organizations, so I am the definition of an insider. In other words, the current system of churches and Christian agencies has "worked" for me, so perhaps I am exactly the wrong sort of person to be writing this chapter. Perhaps this chapter should be a panel discussion with people who are not a part of the Church and who have mixed feelings about Christianity.

I am fifty-five years old; that makes me a young Baby Boomer, which means, I have never known a time when Christianity was dominant in my culture. This means that I do not long for the "good old days," because I have never known them. (As a side-bar, I would question whether they really were all that good for all peoples in Canada.) I spent many of my early years in ministry, church, and congregational planting, which means that for twenty-nine years, I have been thinking about how Gospel and culture intersect and interplay.

Canadian Context

As we begin to think about the Canadian context, we realize that there are many contexts, not just one—urban Toronto is not the same as rural Saskatchewan. At the same time, in our era of hyper-connectivity, which includes the rapid sharing of information, stories, and opinions through digital networks, these various contexts are more alike than ever before.

Something is very different in the current Canadian *zeitgeist*, compared to the one thirty years ago. We observe it numerically, as we measure things we think might be important, such as people in seats on a Sunday morning and dollars in offering plates. We see it in public and cultural discourses, as attitudes toward Christianity in particular and religious belief systems in general grow more negative. We participate in it relationally, as the life patterns of our friends and families (and perhaps ourselves) embody practices and values that are less expressive of God's shalom and more expressive of non-shalom than they might have been a few decades ago.

We can see this change through different lenses: postmodernity, post-Christendom, neo-liberalism, or the triumph of subjectivist-expressivist attitudes. These and other influences have interplayed, leading to the new Canada that we face. How might we describe the salient features of this new reality? While we might debate specifics, I think we can agree that:

1. There is no belief in a single conceptual, ontological Truth that lies outside our experience and to which we aspire. We have multi-truths: your truth and my truth.

2. There is a growing rejection of Christianity. Christianity is not seen as having a positive influence in the Canadian mosaic. The question being asked today is not whether Christianity is *true*, but whether it is *good* for Canada and for being human. Increasingly, the answer is "no."

3. There is a growing rejection of religion (of any sort) as a shaper of culture and values. We are moving past ambivalence toward religion and moving fast toward antipathy, especially when religion is seen to hinder personal freedom. Rather than desiring a secular space that values all religions and non-religion, Canada is shifting toward

privileging non-religion over religion in the public square and in cultural discourse.

4. Spirituality is valued as an individualistic, private experience, but it is seen as over-reaching if it impinges on the freedoms of others.

5. "Jesus" is a positive brand, but "Christianity" is not.

Meanwhile, in the Church, we might note that evangelicalism has fragmented. The relatively recent big-tent coalition, with its iconic figures of Billy Graham and John Stott, has fragmented into multiple camps with varying labels, each seeking to be a reformation or rejection of the evangelical movement. For the most part, these fragments are not in dialogue with one another but rather in competition for attention, influence, and dollars.

How Might We Respond?

In listing some of the things that are different now than they were thirty years ago, I am not saying that these are necessarily completely bad changes. A lot of violence has been perpetrated in human history by people who believed they had found ontological truth, so maybe a little epistemological humility is good for us as a species. And while I love Jesus, I do not love everything about Christianity, so I feel little need to defend it. Maybe the fact that people like Jesus but not Christianity is not all bad. Maybe it is time for us to stop seeing the current situation as a problem but instead discern the opportunities the Spirit has put in front of us. It *is* different than it used to be (so that part is hard), but that does not mean that there are no positives in our environment.

How might we respond? Let me offer some thoughts. These are not everything that could be said. They are not linear nor do they build on each other. Think of them as pieces of a larger mosaic.

1. We need to acknowledge that we do not know, for sure, what to do.

We cannot be certain. We do not know where this cultural shift will end up, and it may last longer than some of our lifetimes. This means that we do not know all the steps we will have to take because the ground is going to keep shifting on us. Our journey will be more akin to an improvisational dance than a straightforward walk.

We are in a time of massive multi-polar and multi-valent change, and our job is to navigate as well as we can. This need not discourage us; the Church has been here before in the last 2,000 years. This means, though, that we need to learn how to lead when we are not certain where we are going and we need to learn how to dance steps we have never danced before.

2. We need to shift from framing evangelism as "agreeing with these ideas" to evangelism as "tour guides on an interior journey."

Our culture does not mind conversations about spirituality, but it detests having religion or epistemic certainty marketed to it. To be a tour guide is to help others journey by responding to their questions, noting and suggesting that attention might be paid to certain things. We share our own travel experiences and suggest practices that facilitate the journey.

We need to stop insisting that others use our vocabulary or enter our language world; instead, we need to learn how to be missionaries into their language world. Rather than insisting that people enter our thought world, let us learn how to enter theirs. After all, is not God larger than our linguistic attempts at articulating him? Might we even be playfully adventurous in our tone, curious and engaged rather than defensive and fearful?

3. Let us shift from "certainty" to "confidence."

Certainty is a product of modernity, not a product of the Spirit; certainty is usually about a body of knowledge that is "out there" that we think we can know objectively. Confidence, on the other hand, is about trusting something—trusting Someone—and trusting the story that that Someone is writing. The early Church did not try to convince people of its understanding of an ontological category called "god"; rather, this Church era declared and demonstrated that Jesus had risen from the dead and had reordered all of life into a new pattern that was observable by the people around them.

4. Let us value people's freedom as much as God values theirs.

Jesus let people walk away from him when they disagreed. Do we do that? Or do we get mad, shaken in our confidence? We should be fans of a multi-religious, pluralist society because in that sort of society, religion is a valid topic for private and public discourse. In that sort of context, the Spirit can be in the conversation. What we should guard against is society sliding into an ideological secularism where religion as a category is privatized into the non-tangible and non-public spheres of life. We do not need a privileged place in society as Christians—after all, we worship a Savior who gave up his privilege—but we do want to co-labor with other faith groups to ensure that all faiths are at the table.

5. Let us return to an embodied apologetic, instead of keeping an apologetic that is trapped in words.

This is how the Church began. People saw something at Pentecost and wondered what was going on, so Peter told them. Or people saw the way those early Christians loved each other, so they became intrigued and decided to find out more.

A few years ago, I visited a food security project in South India and was shown its "Demonstration Farm," where they grew small sections of various crops and showed local farmers what they were doing. In my naivety, I asked why they went to all that trouble. After all, would it not be faster and more efficient to save a step by training the farmers with the better crop-growing techniques? Our project coordinator looked me in the eye and said these simple words, "We do this because 'seeing is believing.' When they see the crops we are growing here, they will want to know how we do it." In the Kingdom of God, the Church is the demonstration farm of the Kingdom because seeing is believing. When people see the Gospel, they may want to hear the Gospel. Let us learn how to be artisans of the common good,[1] who are people and communities that cultivate grace and irrigate soil for the Kingdom to be planted.

6. Let us become local gardening experts.

We are not looking for a "silver bullet" (one expression of the Gospel that will work everywhere). We are not franchisors of a salvation product; we are gardeners of the kingdom. The global Church is not a factory with an assembly line, churning out clones of salvation; the global Church is a network of community gardens, learning from one another but not trying to clone one another. Gardens are all recognizable as gardens, but no two are exactly alike.

1. Allen, "On New Year's Eve."

Imagine if every local church was *the* expert on their particular context and became experts at embodying and articulating the Gospel in their setting. The local church is where the rubber hits the road: it is where the Gospel is seen and then heard. It is where, in micro-ecosystems of relationships, the people of Jesus learn to be tour guides of the Kingdom and gardeners of their local demonstration farm.

7. Let us experiment and be playful about it.

If we have never been here before and cannot be sure where we are going, then we might as well enjoy the ride. Genuine creativity comes when the mind is relaxed, as any musician or painter knows. Anxiety and anger are not the seedbed for innovation. Might it be time to recover the fruit of the Spirit that we call "joy"? And then, out of that joy, with curiosity and eagerness, might we discover how the Spirit wants us to be gardeners of the Kingdom in our context? We would not always get it right; in fact, for a while, we may mostly get it wrong. That is okay. If we rarely fail, it means we are not trying hard enough. Think about how many experiments "fail" before a new product is invented.

When we are obsessed with short-term numerical success, we are like the CEO of a business that focuses on quarterly profits to the detriment of the long-term health of the corporation. If we are to genuinely engage the mission field that is Canada, then *we have not even come close* to the level of innovation that is needed. Most churches and organizations speak the language of mission but operate the apparatus of Christendom. Most churches still have a Worship Service as the central and primary program. Nearly all of us, from Catholic to Baptist to Pentecostal, are running the same model of Church, just with different graphics, fonts, and styles. It is time to run many different experiments with many different models because we do not yet know what patterns will most effectively embody faith in the cultural shifts of today and tomorrow. We need to develop Research and Development (R&D) departments.

Role of the Agency

This chapter is meant to specifically address the role of the "agency" in the task of mission and evangelism in a secularizing Canada, so let us turn to that specific topic.

The "agency"—whether it is a denomination, a network of churches, a parachurch organization, an affinity of pastors, or something else—is in the middle, between the "academy" and the "assembly," playing a mediating type of role. The academy is, at its best, the cutting-edge of thinking: they are the thought-leaders that help the people of God think in new paradigms. The local church is where the action is: it is the cutting-edge of mission, where actual engagement takes place. The agency is in the middle, mediating the theoretical into the concrete. It offers tangible patterns, practices, and paradigms to local churches as tools for the gardening work for the Kingdom.

Given my thesis that we need to try things we have never tried before, the agency has a more important role than ever before.

1. It can act as a curator of the knowledge base that is being created in the academy.

A huge amount of thinking, research, and theorizing takes place in the academy, and the typical local church does not have the time or capacity to sort through all of it. The agency can sift, sort, and offer it to local churches in accessible patterns and chunks. In the old days, agencies were the holders of information, but ever since Google became a reality, the problem is not a *lack* of information but rather *too much* information, with no one to wisely sort it for us. Most of the art in a typical art museum is in storage; curators choose what to display. Perhaps an agency can curate knowledge for its network of people and churches.

One area needing curation is what we have learned from our global mission efforts over the past couple of centuries. There is a significant knowledge base in the mission agencies that specialized in pioneer mission and evangelism, and that needs to be curated and re-contextualized for the Canadian landscape.

2. The agency can cultivate an environment that generates new Church expressions, along with the infrastructure and patterns that can sustain those new expressions.

This is a different task than helping existing models get better than what they are already doing. We need to do that, of course, but we have spent the last thirty years doing that, so maybe we need to do something else as well. The agency can be the R&D department, with local churches running (or being) the experiments. What might this look like?

Here are three ideas. First, given current trends, it is inevitable that bivocational ministry is going to be the norm, which should be celebrated. Part of the reason our innovation is stunted is because the pay checks of clergy and denominational executives are tied to getting enough of a crowd together in seats on a Sunday morning so they can pay us. (This has been true of me for most of my life.)

If we did not need to make money at this, we would be more innovative. The agency can develop ways of affirming bivocational ministry—to ensure that it is not seen as second class—and also provide continuing education opportunities to bivocational ministers in a similar way to monovocational ministers. I can imagine a day when "fulltime" and "bivocational" cease to be categories of significance, which is now true in many parts of the world.

Second, the agency can help churches develop multiple metrics that are contextual to its reality in order to help them understand what "success" looks like in a post-Christendom reality. Third, the agency can help churches figure out how to assess outcomes for its initiatives (instead of managing processes) and how to get timely feedback so that the initiative can be adjusted in real time. In other words, if we are going to be more innovative, we need to exert less control on processes and operational decisions and exert stronger attentiveness on desired outcomes.

3. The agency can act as an aggregator of knowledge from the local churches in its network.

As mentioned earlier, local churches need to be experts on their own context. However, every local context inhabits a non-local context of discourse and influence, such as pop culture and social media. Every micro-context inhabits a macro-context. While face-to-face local relationships are influential, the non-local meta-conversations and influences that take place—through traditional and new media—are significant in shaping our culture. People are watching the latest Netflix show whether they are in Weyburn, Saskatchewan, or downtown Toronto.

This means that even though churches are not trying to mimic each other, they can learn from each other. If we are all experimenting, let us learn from one another's experiments. The agency is in a unique position to aggregate learnings and share them across its network. This is more than just sharing stories—what the stories *mean* and what they might *imply* for other contexts also needs to be shared. In this way, the system learns faster than if every local context did not share its learnings.

4. The agency can act as a pooler and sharer of risk.

This is a critical role, and it is not one that has been discussed adequately. If we are going to enter an era of adventurous innovation, some churches will need to experiment with higher risk innovation. Right now, this is not happening because we are asking each local church and each local leader to bear all the risk of that innovation. Might there be a way to pool the risk of innovation? This is exactly what insurance companies do: they pool risk. They do not reduce the total costs to the group of clients; rather, each client pays more in premiums than if they did not have insurance in order to avoid the risk of being the unlucky client who experiences a catastrophic event that also decimates their finances. Might we figure out how to pool risk when it comes to ministry innovation?

There are two different types of risk to pool—reputational and financial. We need to pool *reputational risk*. Right now, pastors and other leaders develop a reputation fairly early. If their first ministry setting produces "success," then they have a good reputation; if not, they do not. Our current system is designed to avoid innovation and to perpetuate the existing set of models. If we are going to radically innovate, we need to build a system where failure is not fatal to one's ministry career or salary. At the very least, the agency can provide the relational support that is critical for people who are innovating, so that they do not feel all alone. As we experience the inevitable fear that accompanies risk-taking, spiritual formation in supportive relationships will keep us centered.

We also need to pool *financial risk*. Engaging in experimental forms of ministry may mean that the people we reach are not the ones who are going to fund the ministry we are doing. How can we pool that financial risk? This is a critical need and one that I have not seen discussed. If we are honest, we would admit that the avoidance of financial catastrophe is a bigger driver of ministry decisions than we would like to think.

To summarize, the critical role for the agency is that it should be the R&D department for the church. It can cultivate innovation and experimentation but in a disciplined and thoughtful way. It can put together relationships in ways that generate new things. It can offer support when things fail, as they often will, and can treat failure as an opportunity to learn. This is exactly what businesses do. This is how innovative companies work. They do not throw a bunch of information at individuals and hope that they can figure it out on their own. The R&D department is a team with rapid learning, rapid adjustment, and disciplined movement toward new possibilities.

Challenges

The future is full of possibilities, if we are willing to face it with a spirit of expectation and with the courage to make the changes we need to make. However, we face two immense challenges.

First, our entire ecosystem—from schools to agencies to churches—was designed and created in the era of Christendom and is optimized to produce our current results. Pastors get paid for certain things; ministries get donations for certain things. Very few congregants and very few donors are willing to invest in the unknown and experimental. There are some promising experiments taking place at the level of the local church, but if we want to accelerate the innovation, we will have to innovate new sorts of agencies so that various types of innovation are diffused more quickly throughout the ecosystem.

Second, not that long ago, when I was in graduate school, I wrote my papers on a typewriter. Remember those? Now, we are almost past the era of computer keyboards; we are in the era of voice recognition. Artificial intelligence is just around the corner. Most of the agencies that I know of started in the typewriter era. *What we need today is not a better typewriter.*

What encourages me in all of this is that God is not surprised or overwhelmed. He is not wondering what to do. As always, God is just looking for people who are willing and choosing to go on the adventure. So, the question we need to answer is this: "Will we choose to go?"

Bibliography

Allen, John L., Jr. "On New Year's Eve, Pope Francis Delivers His 'Silent Majority' Speech." *Crux*, December 31, 2017. https://cruxnow.com/vatican/2017/12/31/new-years-eve-pope-francis-delivers-silent-majority-speech.

Response to "Doing Things We Have Never Done Before"

Minho Song

Sam Chaise and I spent our formative years in theological training together in Vancouver back in the 1980s. When I started, I was completing assignments on a typewriter; but by the time I graduated, I remember owning a personal computer and a dot printer. It sure made student life much easier. Here we are now, over thirty years later, discussing evangelism in an ever more secular and pluralistic world. The playing field has certainly changed, and if we are going to remain relevant, we must find new ways to communicate the Gospel to the people of the twenty-first century.

Chaise's chapter "Doing Things We Have Never Done Before" has many insightful ideas that we cannot afford to ignore. There are three important points that I take away from the chapter.

"I have never known a time when Christianity was dominant in my culture . . ."

This is a very helpful observation. While we bemoan the demise of Christendom and how the ways of expressing faith are no longer making significant impact, we need to realize that the younger generations we are trying to reach (that is, those younger than the Baby Boomers) do not even know the issue at hand. For them, the loss of Christendom is a moot point. Frankly speaking, many could not care less.

Since we are dealing with a new generation, who cannot relate to the term Christendom, our attempt to bring the Gospel to them should not be something that is reactive but rather proactive. Our approach should not be in response to what happened to the Church—the fall from its glory days—but simply seeing this generation in its own context, having been powerfully formed by the current forces of postmodernity. Though it is a product of the past, the new generation defines truth and goodness in new ways, unrelated to Christendom. This calls for a radical departure from the way we have done Church. Chaise is absolutely right in that we are in uncharted waters.

"We should be a tour guide . . ."

This can be a useful metaphor in engaging with secular minds. But we should also be aware of its limits. As Chaise points out, we need to think differently about the process of evangelism—not so much as "agreeing with these ideas" but as "tour guides on an interior journey." I agree. People are looking for something that is good for them, not necessarily something that is true. They would welcome someone who comes along rather gently and shows them the way like a tour guide. I understand that. But I wonder if, by doing so, we are doing justice to the biblical notion of being a witness. There is much difference in tone between being a tour guide and a witness. A tour guide caters to the wishes of a tourist whereas a witness has a keen responsibility to relay what he or she has experienced.

The challenge for us is to behave like tour guides while having the heart of a witness. It is a tall order, requiring maturity and integrity. For this, we will need fresh lessons from the Holy Spirit.

"Let us return to an embodied apologetic. . ."

I could not agree with Chaise more. We are living in a world where people want to see ideas as more than ideas; they want to know whether ideas can be realized, whether they can become a way of life. Nothing can be hidden or manipulated. All is out in the open for everyone to see.

People want to come and be part of a fellowship where sharing and caring are more than words but rather a way of life. In order to demonstrate how ideas such as love and forgiveness are actually incarnated, the Church needs to move its focus from Sunday morning worship to wherever God's people are during the week. This calls for innovative and courageous ways to communicate the Gospel.

Chaise has many great ideas that he will develop into action plans in due time. In this chapter, he has articulated a refreshing way of examining the postmodern context for evangelism. We have been encouraged to take more steps to be innovative in order to communicate the gospel to the next generation.

One area I want to encourage the author to consider carefully is the multicultural context of major Canadian cities. This is important for someone coming from the perspective of an agency (having a wider perspective than that of an assembly or academic institution). In the Greater Toronto Area, for example, more than half of its six million inhabitants speak languages other than English as their mother tongue. They are first-generation immigrants who now call Canada their home. Other urban centers such as Vancouver and Montreal are similar in this regard.

When it comes to sharing the Gospel, first-generation immigrants need to be treated differently from more established or mainstream Canadians. First-generation immigrants may not reflect the values held by younger postmodern Canadians. It is more likely that first-generation immigrants are products of modernity rather than postmodernity.

"A growing rejection of Christianity" is a concern not so much for first-generation immigrants but more so for the next generation of people in postmodernity. The issue with the former is the lack of opportunities to see the Gospel embodied with meaningfulness. For them, the issue is not so much the preference of confidence over certainty; instead, they are waiting for the Gospel to be told in meaningful relationships.

2

Returning to Ancient Paths

Connie denBok

Introduction

For some of us, there is a pang of loneliness in the world of evangelical mission. The Canadian Church is an ecosystem, a deeply inter-related web, of not only Evangelicals and Pentecostals but also Roman Catholics, Anglican, United, and influential mega-churches and network churches.

There is a Canadian narrative, which echoes the prophet Elijah—that he was the only one of his kind left in Israel, that he was harassed and alone, and that other gods and other political systems had superseded the God of his ancestors. Of course, we know that there were others like him. But in the days of Elijah, there was reason to suspect that kings, queens, and other gods had usurped the Lord God, and that the hearts of these people could not be turned to God—not in that time and place. In this time and place, we might also wonder if the Kingdom of God is under siege by the prophets of Baal or secularism. I thank the Evangelical Missiological Society for its faithfulness, its conviction, its encouragement, and its love for the world that God has always loved through Jesus Christ.

I would like to address the issue of evangelization in a secular society confessionally, in both senses of the word: confession in anticipation of a day when every knee will bow and tongue confess that Jesus Christ is Lord and confession as part of a generation and movement within the ecosystem of the Canadian Church. In an ecosystem, seemingly unrelated organisms have a profound effect on one another. My vantage is specifically that of a baby boomer who was baptized into the largest and fastest growing denomination in Canada and will retire some time in the next decade as an ordained minister of one of the most rapidly declining.

Canadian Church Ecosystem

The United Church of Canada lived its first forty years on the vanguard of the largest evangelistic church planting movement this country has seen and, as you know, has spent the last forty years swinging with the Canadian pendulum toward a fragmented assortment of beliefs, some of which are not recognizably aligned with the small "c" catholic tradition that the Christian Church of all times and ages holds in common.

I say this at the outset because when we consider the secularism of our Canadian context and the challenge of evangelism, we must name the deterioration of confidence that the twenty-first-century Church has in its own institutions, its message and doctrines, and its ability to transform and be transformed. We are tempted to shame ourselves and distance ourselves from each other when someone speaks "as a Christian" with naivety, racism, homophobia, or blatant self-promotion.

As our culture becomes more secular, it has also become more polarized and harshly judgmental. Peace-loving believers are easily divided or turned against each other under criticism, eager to demonstrate that *we* are not *that* kind of Christian—not like Americans, the elite, fundamentalists, or those heretics who ordain atheists and call themselves a church. If I may tell a story as to how that unfortunate tendency emerged in the mainline churches of Canada, perhaps it will offer some insight as to how the collapse of one part of an ecosystem places new pressures on the whole. There are pressures felt within the broader Evangelical community, and it seems to me that Canadian Evangelicals are as divided by good intentions as the United Church was when it diverged from its initial mission of evangelism and Christian unity.

Through an act of Parliament, the United Church of Canada was formed in 1925, a union of the large Methodist Church, the much smaller Congregationalist Church, and the majority of Presbyterians. The venture was pragmatic. Towns and villages were being built along rapidly expanding railway lines in western Canada. The new communities needed churches. If Protestant denominations of similar outlook cooperated, they could avoid duplication and create a presence in more towns and villages. The centerfold of the first edition of the United Church Observer was a banner with the words, "Canada for Christ." Then, at the end of the Second World War, suburban Canada exploded with a postwar housing and baby boom. New churches were built in every neighborhood. Until the mid-1960s, the United and Anglican Churches opened a church a week across this country, often in the wake of evangelistic crusades by Charles Templeton and even Billy Graham.

Between 1962 and 1965, the Roman Catholic Church reinvented itself for the modern world with Vatican II. The Anglican Church of Canada did not want to be outdone by the Catholics and invited Pierre Berton, a Canadian media celebrity, to critique Canadian Christianity, although he did not pretend to be either a theologian or Christian. His work was published as a book, *The Comfortable Pew*. It was a scathing condemnation of Protestantism in Canada as smug, insular, and disengaged from society, and it became an immediate bestseller.

The Board of Evangelism and Social Service of the United Church of Canada did not want to be outdone by the Anglicans, so it commissioned Pierre Berton and other writers to critique the United Church and received a document called "Why the Sea Is Boiling Hot." The irony is that these Canadian churches had been deeply engaged with Canadian society, particularly with the poor. In Toronto, for instance, Scott Mission, Fred Victor Mission, and many other missions—for the poor, the addicted, single mothers, immigrants, the sick, and prisoners—were created and supported by local churches and denominations before government gave social aid a thought. Hundreds of city missionaries acted as social workers on behalf of the same churches accused of disengagement. If the churches of Canada did satisfy the Canadian media, they served the poor, the immigrant, the prisoner, and the orphan at a time when no one else saw the need.

In the face of public criticism, two things happened. The first is that these dominant Canadian Protestant Churches were eager to deflect criticism and to demonstrate that they were not *that* kind of Christian. Prior to the mid-1960s, the United Church had an evangelical pietist bent with roots in holiness Methodism. The Church also had an affinity for the scholarly academy, championed by former Presbyterians. There was also a minority that embraced socialism, advocating Marxism as the modern expression of biblical justice. When Dr. Robert McClure, a United Church medical missionary doctor in China, supported the Communist Revolution in 1949, he was reviled in Canada, but he was elected Moderator of the United Church for the 1968–1970 term. I remember bringing home a large poster of Mao Zedong from my United Church Sunday School middle-school age class during his tenure.

Until the 1950s, the United Church of Canada was a booster of Evangelistic Crusades, endorsing Billy Graham and Charles Templeton. In the early 1960s, a fictional movie about an immoral huckster named Elmer Gantry became synonymous with revival evangelism in the popular imagination. In the face of public ridicule, the Board of Evangelism and Social Service was embarrassed to be associated with evangelistic crusades. Seminary professors, denominational executives, and ordained ministers of large urban churches eagerly distanced themselves from that portion of their shared history. German biblical critical theory was adopted in seminaries and prestigious pulpits as a definitive scientific methodology for interpreting scripture. Personal piety and bible reading were mocked in our seminaries in a demonstration that our scholars were modern, socially relevant, and not *that* kind of Christian. The United Church department of Social Services, which had supported direct services through local missions, exchanged these for social activism, lobbying governments to provide comprehensive services on our behalf. Free of former restraints, some in the church eagerly joined the sexual revolution.

In isolated pockets of the denomination, extreme views were normalized. In the spring of 1988, I was a member of Saskatoon Presbytery at a meeting where candidates were presented before ordination. One young man stood and confessed that he had entered seminary naively believing in prayer and that the bible was the word of God, but since then, he had overcome those naïve beliefs and no longer believed in God. The principal of the seminary stood and began to applaud, followed by other professors and former graduates of that college, followed by other ministers of his theological persuasion, followed by the lay representatives of their churches, followed by those who did not want to stand out by not standing—leaving very few of us in our seats, feeling awkward that we did not join the joyful standing ovation. In 1993 Moderator Bill Phipps made headlines, declaring that he did not believe Jesus was raised from the dead. In 2015 an ordained minister of the United Church all but demanded she be tried and vindicated as a non-theist—that is, one who did not believe in a supernatural God. She almost succeeded, but her hearing was cancelled indefinitely.[1]

No one wants to be marginalized by the cool kids in class. However, an institution that has lost confidence in its own message cannot evangelize its own message. I would like to suggest that the lack of confidence in my corner of the Canadian Church ecosystem has sent tendrils into the rest of the Canadian Church, and both Evangelicals and the other churches descended from the Reformation have been affected. Our social issues have become your social issues, and the contagion has been intentional.

If we, the Christian Church, do not believe that life, death, eternity, our children's future, our neighbor's future, and the future of the planet are directly linked to faithfulness and faith in Jesus Christ and that God has a past, a present, and a future, then we, the Church, will still proclaim, but we will evangelize another message, perhaps social progressivism.

---

1. See Perkel, *United Church Postpones Hearing*.

For the past three decades, we in the United Church have sent emissaries throughout Canada and to the United States, to denominational leaders among the Anglicans, the Mennonites, and to the TIM Centre, most often for advocacy on progressive-leaning social issues. Given that the Church in Canada is united neither in mission nor evangelism, I would like to explore eight responses by the Canadian Church as it searches its way into the coming decades.

Eight Responses to Secularism by the Canadian Church

The first is nostalgia for a golden age of the past. "If Christians would just get back to the bible or rent a tent and bring in an evangelist, things would be well again." We know it used to work. Many things were easier for the Church in a traditional society—when one parent worked full-time, five days a week, and the other cared for house, children, laundry, and shopping. One salary bought a little house in the suburbs, where everyone could walk to church on Sundays. The wish is, "If only we could go back to the good old days, when women could just stay home and raise godly children, then we could get some of that old-time religion, and everything would go back to normal"—meaning 1955, I think. I do not wish to argue the goodness or the badness of that dream. But if discipleship had been happening in those good old churches, perhaps the children of those churches would be following Jesus today.

A second response might be "if you can't beat them, join them." This is hugely attractive, I think, because we have adopted the secular viewpoint that secularism is a neutral response to a multicultural and interfaith society. While secularism presents itself as an objective equalizer, inclusive of all peoples and beliefs, Tim Keller reminds us that secularism is anything but neutral: "To move from religion to secularism is not so much a loss of faith as a shift into a new set of beliefs and into a new community of faith, one that draws the lines between orthodoxy and heresy in different places."[2] Secularism has all the characteristics of a religion: it claims to explain the origin and meaning of life; it has internal systems of morality that, it asserts, apply to all enlightened people; and it claims absolute truth apart from empirical evidence, including the belief that no absolute truth can be known through one belief system over another—with the exception of itself.[3] For example, anyone applying for a government grant from the Canadian government to hire a student must understand that they do so in a changed ideological and

---

2. Keller, *Making Sense of God*, 31.
3. Keller, *Reason for God*, 16.

religious climate. Every rational, educated, and caring Canadian is expected to check a box complying with this government's definition of reproductive freedom.

If secularism is one religion among the many religions of Canada, it must be understood as an aggressively proselytizing faith, insisting that its truths supersede the Jewish and Christian claim to Sabbath, the Catholic medical practitioner's abhorrence of ending fetal life, a Christian College's ability to regulate the moral life of its student body, and ancient understandings of humanity as male and female in the image of a Creator. Children are evangelized in secularism through primary school, entertainment media, and social media. Like other Empire religions—the Hellenists, who tolerated religions that adopted Greek culture, or the Romans, who embraced all faith systems that acknowledged the supremacy of Caesar—secularism embraces the private practice of personal faith, but it is intolerant of competitors to its right as supreme arbiter of moral choices. Unlike other Empires that have conquered by force, secularism has emerged from within our own ranks—speaking of the United Church, for instance—but emerges wherever leaders have had a liberal arts education from universities, where they or their teachers were also proselytized. If the Church assumes that secularism is an ideologically neutral system which guarantees that one religion must not claim truth over another, Christian evangelism must have lowest priority—even within the Church. No system other than secularism has the right to impose its beliefs on others, including one's own children.

The third response to secular society is the use of contemporary communication, mass advertising, literature distribution, social media, back-to-church Sundays, and more. Some of us remember the "I found it" billboard campaign of the 1970s, the March for Jesus Movement of the 1990s, and other attempts to bring our message into interface with popular culture. We invested good people, good dollars, and good intention; but here, in Canada, the recipients were already in church. They were very good campaigns, but the fruit was limited. For the generation of churches that marketed themselves as "Church for people not into Church," we thank God that they kept some of the next generation church young adults, but their impact on those who have been dechurched and secularized for generations is negligible. I do not criticize creative use of media. Reliable, firsthand sources tell me that thousands of young people a day are turning to Christ in countries resistant to Christian missionizing in response to bibles and discipling materials shared electronically by colleagues. But that is not happening in Canada at this time.

The fourth response to Canadian secularism is more obvious to us in its American expression than our own—that is, using the influence of religious groups to align the courts and civil governments with Christian-motivated agenda. There are hazards with this strategy.

The most obvious is the corrupting influence of power. In 1981 Billy Graham spoke with discernment regarding the Moral Majority movement, when he said, "It would disturb me if there was a wedding between the religious fundamentalist and the political right. The hard right has no interest in religion except to manipulate it."[4] Canadians in my social circles mock the generation of Graham's son for a dubious relationship between religion and power. But same-sex marriage, policies regarding transgender persons, and one of the legal teams opposing Trinity Western College in the courts have all been funded and supported by activists from the Religious Left in Canada, who have made these their cause and gospel. The Political Right and the Political Left have their own gods whom they serve, and we, the Church, are easily distracted from the good news when we worship at those altars in high places instead of the one that is uniquely ours to share.

A fifth way that we may respond to our culture's resistance to faith in Jesus Christ is the speaking of prophetic truth to power in the tradition of the Old Testament Prophets. An Elijah confronts Ahab, and the people of God must choose whom they will serve. Martin Luther, Dietrich Bonhoeffer, and Martin Luther King Jr. were heroes, willing to become martyrs of the faith—each controversial in his own time, and each vindicated by history. The challenge is that it is very difficult to know in real time who has been a genuine prophet of God, who was mistaken, and who was simply a crackpot with anger management issues. Prophets emerge in every age, but prophetic authenticity is often discerned and verified by history, well after the fact. Should the Christian Church have recognized Brigham Young as a prophet because the movement he helped found grew large and successful? Or Fred Phelps of Westboro Baptist Church because he was the unpopular voice against the status quo? Like the politics of power, prophetic ministry has a genuine origin in God, but it is easily confused with other motivations. The voice that speaks truth from a place of anger and that desires to dominate through force of strength may resonate in times of need, but it is not God's.

A sixth response to secular society is sometimes called the Benedict Option, popularized by a book of the same name. It is a withdrawal of believers and their children from the public forum. When the Roman Empire collapsed in the fourth century, civil order collapsed—the government, the military, the justice system, and religious institutions. When the social order was in free fall, Benedict of Nursia, a sixth-century monk, regularized a

---

4. Michaels, "Billy Graham," 114.

pattern of life for distinctly Christian communities that withdrew from the chaos and laid the foundation for better times to come.

A woman in my church was a child in Cuba in the years following Castro's Revolution. Her father, Armando A. Rodriguez Borges, was a Methodist pastor in Holguin and district superintendent for the Eastern province (Oriente), and in 1968, he became bishop of the newly nationalized Methodist Church. At the end of 1961, Castro declared that communism would be Cuba's sole national ideology.

The new requirement of adherence to communist principles led to a mass exodus of the country's missionaries and pastors in 1962, leaving many congregations without a pastor. Rodriguez Borges remained and led a group of approximately sixty young people, who became lay preachers in the mountains and countryside in Oriente. He simply placed them where there were no pastors. Then, he created what was not a seminary but rather a training center for young people who would be lay ministers in charge of the congregations without pastors. Twenty-seven young people trained in Holguin for a month and then were sent to the different pastoral charges. Every couple of months, they came back to Holguin for training, one week at a time. Most of those young people eventually fulfilled their requirements for seminary and became ordained ministers, superintendents, and church leaders across the country.

While Christians were not openly persecuted in Cuba, they were isolated, mocked, and restricted in their choice of professions, forced to associate mainly with one another. Preaching and the gathering of Christians outside government-sanctioned churches were prohibited. As in other communist countries, these isolated pockets of underground and semi-underground churches became the rootstock of a vibrant religious revival as soon as restrictions were lifted. If the Christian Church in Canada was a stock portfolio, I would invest in leaders and communities that have the courage and pain tolerance to stand in contrast to the *zeitgeist* of their times.

My father and seven of his eight brothers and sisters immigrated to Canada from Holland. Some sent their children to Christian schools and retained a strong identity in the Reformed community; others did not. Those families who kept their children somewhat separate, in Christian Schools and friendship networks, were five times as likely to have grandchildren who profess Christian faith. Those of us who are parents need to consider the powerful forces of secularism that proselytize our children, to what extent we ought to consider withdrawing them from that world while they are most vulnerable, and to how we are to prepare them for re-entry. Christians must be salt and light in the world.

A seventh strategy is foundational. In his book, *The Patient Ferment of the Early Church: The Improbable Rise of Christianity in the Roman Empire*, Alan Kreider argues that the early church grew at an average rate of 40 percent per decade, mostly through conversion.[5] For most of that time, Christianity was socially unattractive, technically illegal, and likely to increase one's risk of losing property and even life. The distinctive strength of Christians was not their gathering for worship—the worship gatherings were seeker unfriendly. The only celebrity endorsements came from those who had already lost their lives for the sake of Christ. Kreider notes:

> The Christians' lifestyle embodies their habitus, the reflexes that reveal the inner character that resulted from their conversion. And their character manifests the distinctiveness of their theology . . . the early Christians developed a theology of patience rooted in their understanding of God's character and the life and teaching of Jesus Christ. Their theology led them to espouse ways of doing things that were patient. These were distinctive, challenging conventional values, and resulted in a distinctive habitus that had to be taught and modeled in many areas of life. This habitus, they believed, attracted people to faith in Christ and to membership in the Christian communities.[6]

Kreider cites the deep catechism of believers into a life of humility, patient perseverance, extravagant generosity, and selfless love. These qualities are sometimes called Fruit of the Holy Spirit, Righteousness, Holiness, or Character. They generated admiration and credibility for despised Christian communities that remained faithful, loving, and generous in contrast to the surrounding culture. While the preaching zeal of twenty-first-century Christian leaders for sexual purity, financial transparency, and accountability of power is well-known, the long patient development of personal and community character is a more likely road to its fulfillment than pulpit preaching and blanket apologies for moral failures and more compelling than denials and cover-ups.

I recently had the opportunity to hear a man who was a leader of the underground house movement in China during the 1980s and 1990s. Brother Yun was jailed four times, tortured, and had both shins smashed with sledge hammers so that he would never walk again. Listening to him, I hear the stories of miracles and deliverance as possible, but my faith is kindled by his obvious love, his humor, his humility, his confidence in Christ, his patience and resilience in the light of his trials, and that it had

---

5. Kreider, "Patient Ferment," 99–100.
6. Kreider, "Patient Ferment," 7–8.

amplified his love for Jesus and desire to proclaim him. Nothing speaks to the supernatural power of God, the depth of Christ's love, and the cost of discipleship more eloquently than the person who will pay a high price. Character development, listening prayer, humility and confession of sin, and the ability to submit one's will for the sake of Jesus—no matter what the consequences and cost—are the fruit of intentional discipleship. There are movements emerging in Canada equipping believers for such a lifestyle. Church Renewal out of Steinbach in Manitoba is having a significant impact on Canadian church leaders. Without this keystone, other evangelistic strategies are ineffective.

A final strategy is linked to the one above. It is the witness of a believer who can maintain confident integrity in order to be a blessing in a hostile environment. I think of Joseph in the service of Pharaoh, Daniel in the government of Babylon, and Esther in the palace of Ahasuerus. I also think of the Dutch and French resistance in Europe, ordinary citizens who continued to live and work for righteousness in a place and time that demanded unrighteousness. It is the strategy of the martyrs of the early church, the ones who died and the ones who continued to live faithfully. It is not a tactic that can be self-chosen until the time of sacrifice forces a decision.

Conclusion

If we are to discuss Canadian Mission and Evangelism in a Secular world, we must recognize something more complex than cognitive issues at play. There is something other than methodology, education, or motivated self-preservation. We will need to ponder how this impulse to leave the ancient paths has infected the confidence of the Western Church and where that is taking us. We must at least wonder why so much of the Canadian Church has developed an irresistible attraction toward the very things that other generations have thought unthinkable, including an aversion to evangelism. There is no immunity through isolation. The Church is a body; it is an ecosystem where one has a profound effect on the others. There are forces tugging at our children's hearts like a powerful undertow. The very Canadian impulse to "go along to get along" and to acquiesce for the sake of peace is a symptom, not a cause.

There are no good old days, but there are ancient paths. We are at a crossroads—where we will be either converted more wholly to Christ or converted to the spirit of this age. The Church in Canada will serve one or the other. It cannot serve both and evangelize in Christian mission.

Bibliography

Barkway, Michael, et al. *Why the Sea Is Boiling Hot—A Symposium on the Church and the World*. Toronto: Ryerson University Press, 1965.

Berton, Pierre. *The Comfortable Pew: A Critical Look at Christianity and the Religious Establishment in the New Age*. Philadelphia: JB Lippincott, 1965.

Dreher, Rod. *The Benedict Option: A Strategy for Christians in a Post Christian Nation*. New York: Penguin, 2017.

Keller, Timothy. *Making Sense of God: An Invitation to the Skeptical*. New York: Penguin, 2016.

———. *The Reason for God: Belief in an Age of Skepticism*. New York: Riverhead, 2008.

Kreider, Alan. *The Patient Ferment of the Early Church: The Improbable Rise of Christianity in the Roman Empire*. Ada, MI: Baker, 2016.

Krotz, Larry. "Atheist in the Pulpit." *The Walrus*, November 16, 2016.

Michaels, Margaret. "Billy Graham: America Is Not God's Only Kingdom." *Parade Magazine*, February 1, 1981.

Perkel, Colin. "United Church Postpones Hearing for United Church Minister Indefinitely" *The Toronto Star*, November 14, 2017.

Wingeier-Rayo, Philip. "Methodist Church in Cuba: A Momentous 50th Anniversary. Parts 1–2." *United Methodist Insight*, February 08, 2018.

Response to "Returning to Ancient Paths"

Michael Krause

Thank you, Connie, for your excellent delineation of the responses to secularism in Canada. It resonated with me on a number of levels—perhaps most significantly, the subtle wistfulness about the state of the Church in Canada today. My vantage point is also that of a Baby Boomer, but one with a more eclectic Protestant religious background that includes German Baptist, Charismatic, and Pentecostal elements and a plethora of experience in multi-denominational and multi-faith contexts.

Secularism has, for the most part, succeeded in dethroning Christendom from its place of privilege and power—especially in Canada and Western Europe. By Christendom, I mean the institutional alignment of Christianity with political power and social influence displayed by the Church's historic impact on institutions (government, education, health), legal decisions (laws about marriage and Sunday shopping), and public opinion (shaming people for being divorced, having sex before marriage, or shopping on Sunday). Instead of secularism, however, I believe that the term post-Christendom better describes the deconstruction of societal norms, and once we determine our location in the process of this deconstruction, it will help us better formulate a missional response. To help us do that, I'd like to propose a metaphor to contextualize Connie's responses to the secularization process.

I believe Christendom is actually another way of saying "Western Civilization"—where Christian values, symbols, ethics, and institutions have deeply and profoundly shaped our understanding of law, politics, religion, literature, philosophy, morality, and meaning. It has proscribed many of the Western world's ways of thinking-and-being and is deeply imbedded in civilization's structures and institutions. What secularism is attempting to do is to unlink Christian thought and meaning from the institutions of society and to delegitimize their control over them. As a result, the very threads of the tapestry called Western civilization are being unravelled. Instead of looking at the tapestry prominently hanging on the wall, we see a pile of detached threads on the floor, disconnected from their framework and anchors, with each thread proclaiming its own significance and uniqueness. Christianity was the fundamental framework that gave shape to the construction of that tapestry; the colors of Christianity were the defining elements of the image portrayed on this tapestry. We must also distinguish the difference between the tapestry (Christendom) and the story it tells (Christianity). For most of Western society, the tapestry of Christendom is already "deconstructed," the Christian underpinnings unhinged, the moral framework dismantled, and the memory of its significance forgotten.

To extend the metaphor a bit further, this unraveling or dismantling of the tapestry could be called secularism—the loss of memory about the tapestry, post-Christendom, and postmodernism (or the resulting mess of individual threads competing for attention). The threads have lost the metanarrative that once bound them together.

The missional question is this: "Where are we in this process of deconstruction?" Our location in it will determine our missional response to it. So if we believe we are still on the wall as a recognizable tapestry, then Connie's "revivalism" response and the "I found it" promotional campaign could be seen as appropriate responses from this location. Let us just preach the Gospel and call people back to Church, embrace the certainty of the Christendom mindset, and make sure we do it all with excellence. I don't believe this response, however, will be effective, as the deconstruction process continues.

If we believe we are at the stage where Christendom's underpinnings are being removed and the framework is being dismantled, if we see the powers-that-be with scissors in their hands trying to cut apart the tapestry, then the proper response might be a prophetic one—decrying the injustice and revealing the secret and destructive deeds done in darkness. We would also want to ensure that proper legislation was being enacted to entrench the right of the tapestry to have the prominent position it has always held. Or, at least, we need to make sure that the tapestry is being displayed as prominently as all of the other paintings and portraits of reality in the gallery. While we are still in the twilight of modernism, our macro-response to secularism needs to be that religion still deserves an equal voice at the table and must therefore still be allowed to express its conscience on issues like injustice, abortion, and morality. The main challenges of secularism are at the institutional level because secularism attempts to separate religion from the state and to delegitimize the rights of the Christian institution—attempting to deny its voice and its right to self determination (like maintaining community standards at Christian schools). This is a worthwhile fight, but it may be one that we eventually lose.

If, on the other hand, we believe that this deconstruction is an inevitable process, that the tapestry will be destroyed and our memory of it will fade, then we might respond by capitulating to the pressures of society and accepting the role secularism assigns us—the marginalization and privatization of our faith and the alignment of the Church with the secular humanist metanarrative, baptizing its values as best we can. Alternatively, we may resign ourselves to collecting the few relevant and recognizable threads of the tapestry that remain and hide away in our monasteries, communes, and home school conventions to try and cobble together a faithful life of following Christ as old-order Mennonites.

However, if we believe we are at the stage of finding ourselves on the floor and among the piles of disconnected truth threads, then our missional approach will be different. The characteristics of postmodern society are heterogeneity (everyone and every story is different), fragmentation (things no longer fit together neatly and logically), and pluralism (all stories and traditions have equal value and equal truth claims). Postmodern society has become disenchanted with the demystified world of modernism (and Evangelicalism) and desires mystery, fantasy, and escape (note the rise of vampires, demons, superheroes, the supernatural, and the unexplained in TV, film genres, and the proliferation of alternate reality games). The postmodern mindset has abandoned the security that is based on a single claim of truth. Postmodernism opens up the possibility for faith in Jesus because it casts doubt on the grand narratives of modernism and secularism, questioning the claim of reason as the only route to knowledge. Postmodernism opens up multiple ways of knowing through things like intuition, mystery, liturgy, revelatory experiences, and communal wisdom as possible ways to discover knowledge and to experience truth.

The postmodern mindset is not as much opposed to faith tradition as it is to faith traditions as structures of power. As such, our missional response should be to learn how to be one clear voice in the midst of the cacophony of many equal voices and how this voice can be expressed with the unction of the Holy Spirit from a community of believers living prophetically. We will need to learn how to lead without power. As Christians, our role will be to help interpret the confusing array of options before people, to provide meaning and significance, and to communicate truth relationally. We should learn what it means to embrace the mystical and the experiential more enthusiastically; we may all need to become both more Catholic and more Charismatic.

Location determines response. We are currently in an in-between place of deconstruction, where, at any given time, any of these missional responses might be appropriate. Will we do the hard work of discerning our location, contextualizing our message, responding communally, being authentic, and living out our prophetic mission? We will need to learn what it means to live without guarantees and without certainty, except the certainty that comes from trust in Jesus—faith as the substance of things hoped for and the evidence of things not seen.

3

Connecting with Secular Muslims through History and Film

The Case Study of *Augustine: Son of Her Tears*

EDWARD L. SMITHER

NORTH AFRICA POSSESSES A rich Christian history, including the stories of martyrs such as Perpetua and Felicitas (d. 202) and theologians like Tertullian (ca. 160–ca. 220), Cyprian (195–258), and Augustine (354–430). While many educated North Africans today may know these names, they do not know their faith stories. Is it possible to share the Christian message with a people through their own history? What if a high-quality feature film was developed that captured that story? This is the vision of a group of Middle Eastern and North African Christians who created *Augustine: Son of Her Tears*, which was recently released and is currently premiering at film festivals and special showings around the Arab world. Following a brief background on the making of the film, its synopsis, and its initial distribution, I will discuss why Augustine's story is meaningful to secular North Africans and consider what lessons in cultural engagement might be learned.

The Making of Augustine: Son of Her Tears

During the Third Lausanne Congress on World Evangelization in Cape Town, South Africa, in 2010, a group of Middle Eastern and North African Christians with decades of experience in Christian media began talking about making a film on the faith journey of Augustine of Hippo. Once a North African member of the group drafted the script, they approached acclaimed Tunisian producer Abdel Aziz Ben Mlouka about making the film. In addition to private funding, the group also secured resources from both the Algerian and Tunisian governments. Finally, leading Algerian and

Tunisian actors were cast, including Ahmed Amine Ben Saad who played the role of Augustine and Aicha Ben Ahmed who played Monica. Written, funded, directed, and performed by North Africans—most of whom are not Christians, this film is truly a North African cultural product.

Essence of the Film

This is how the filmmakers described the film:

> When Hedi, a young filmmaker in Paris, is chosen to create a documentary about St. Augustine, he begins his journey to learn about an influential philosopher who shaped the western world. To learn about the North African St. Augustine, Hedi must face his Algerian heritage he left behind years ago. Hedi comes to find that this fourth-century man's life is not so different from his own. Transported into Augustine's world, Hedi's research reveals how Augustine witnessed an undeniable relationship between his mother and God that challenged him to seek the truth for himself.... In turn, Hedi finds parallels in confronting family, love, God, and truth. He is challenged to reevaluate his own priorities and how they will define his life.[1]

Overall, the film faithfully narrates Augustine's *Confessions*, capturing the period of his rebellious and wandering youth, his educational path, and his career teaching rhetoric in Carthage, Thagaste, Rome, and Milan. We meet Ambrose of Milan, the deacon Simplicianus, and, of course, his mother—three key individuals who helped Augustine grasp the Christian faith. The film ends with Augustine believing the Gospel and being baptized by Ambrose in Milan.[2]

Initial Premieres and Showings

At this point, the film has been shown in special premieres and film festivals. Beginning in October 2016, the Tunisian Ministry of Culture showed *Augustine* at a premiere leading up to the fiftieth anniversary of the famed Carthage (Tunisia) Film Festival. In 2017 and 2018, special premieres and showings took place in Alexandria and Cairo (Egypt), Beirut (Lebanon), Oran (Algeria), Rabat (Morocco), as well as at the Vatican. The audiences have included government officials, particularly those connected with the

---

1. "Story."
2. For a scholarly account of this period, see O'Meara, *Augustine*.

ministries of culture, as well as other influential members of society. In countries where there are ancient Christian churches, such as Egypt and Lebanon, leaders of these communities have attended alongside Muslims.

Augustine for Secular North African Muslims

Everyone involved in viewing the *Augustine* premieres—from North African Muslim culture ministers to Coptic priests in Egypt to the North African actors themselves—has a rightful claim to Augustine. As the film continues to circulate in the Mediterranean world, why is it meaningful to secular North African Muslims? What does Augustine mean to educated, cultivated, and (in some cases) financially well-off Muslims, who are indifferent to or even fed up with modern Islam, including its extremist expressions?

Intellectual Biography

First, Augustine connects with secular Muslims because of his intellectual journey. Reared in a fourth-century African Catholic context, Augustine rejected what he perceived was the anti-intellectual posture of the church leadership. Struggling with the crude stories from the Old Testament, he gravitated toward the Manichean sect, a group that offered him space to think and pose questions and packaged their ideas in much eloquence. They also had something to say about the problem of evil. Eventually growing tired of eloquence that lacked substance, Augustine's mind and imagination were captured by Platonic philosophy. During this philosophical journey—and a career path, teaching rhetoric, that led him to Rome and then Milan—Augustine encountered Bishop Ambrose. In Ambrose, Augustine found a man trained in philosophy who could also communicate well, qualities that did not contradict his Christian faith. Ambrose's allegorical approach to Scripture resolved many of the problems Augustine had with Christian ideas. In addition, the Milanese deacon Simplicianus, who spent much more time with Augustine than Ambrose did, answered many of Augustine's questions. Augustine wrestled with many intellectual questions in his faith journey, and this path of reflection connects with thinking North Africans today.

A Spiritual Journey

Second, though Augustine was a deep thinker, it did not mean that his journey was not deeply spiritual. From *Confessions,* his spiritual struggle was probably greater than his intellectual pursuits. Augustine confessed challenges with overeating, overthinking, longing for the praise and acceptance of others, and, of course, sexual temptation. In fact, he described his conversion to faith in terms of freedom from the flesh.[3] This moral and spiritual struggle ought to resonate with many modern secular North Africans.

A Messy Story

Third, Augustine's story is also relevant because it is messy. He grew up in a home with a pagan and sometimes violent father alongside a godly, praying, and sometimes controlling mother. Ironically, in *Confessions,* Augustine is more critical of his Christian mother than his non-believing father. A man of his times, Augustine took a mistress and cohabitated with her for many years. Together, they had a son. Because his mistress was from a different social class, their marriage was not legally permissible. As Monica pushed Augustine to marry, Augustine was forced to send his mistress home to Africa, which he likened to having his own flesh ripped out. Later, Augustine experienced the unthinkable when his son, Adeodatus, died while still in his teens. Augustine's family story is raw, painful, and relevant to many North Africans today.

Faith Stories within a Faith Story

Finally, the shape of the *Augustine* film—in which Hedi's story intersects with Augustine's journey—allows modern viewers to personally enter into Augustine's faith. Within its story structure, the film actually parallels the eighth chapter of Augustine's *Confessions.* In telling his own story, Augustine also narrates the faith stories of four other converts—testimonies that clearly encouraged him in his own journey, which he used, in turn, to influence his readers toward the Gospel.

He remembers how Simplicianus told him the conversion story of the philosopher and rhetor Marius Victorinus. Victorinus, who had been a pagan, became convinced of the truth of the Gospel through reading Scripture. Simplicianus urged Victorinus to forsake his public reputation and

---

3. See further Augustine, *Confessions* 8.30.

declare his faith in the context of the church, which resulted in his conversion.[4] Reflecting on this, Augustine wrote: "I was fired to imitate Victorinus; indeed, it was to this end that your servant Simplicianus had related it."[5] Augustine had much in common with Victorinus: both men were interested in philosophy, were on a similar career path, had concerns about their public reputation, and had an interest in the Bible. Augustine was encouraged to pursue Christian faith because Victorinus had it. In a prayerful commentary intended for his own readers, Augustine adds: "Come, Lord, arouse us and call us back, kindle us and seize us, prove to us how sweet you are in your burning tenderness; let us love you and run to you. Are there not many who return to you from a deeper, blinder pit than did Victorinus, many who draw near to you and are illumined as they become children of God?"[6] Through relating Victorinus's faith story within his own faith story, Augustine seems to have his philosophically-minded, career-oriented readers in mind.

In the very next passage, Augustine tells of a visit from Ponticianus, a Roman functionary, who told Augustine and his friend Alypius about the Egyptian monk Antony. While narrating Antony's call to the ascetic life, Ponticianus also related the story of two Roman officials from Trier, who, after reading the *Life of Antony*, resigned from their posts in order to pursue an ascetic lifestyle. Intrigued by their accounts, Augustine wrote: "Even while he [Ponticianus] spoke, you [God] were wrenching me back toward myself . . . that I might perceive my sin and hate it."[7]

Ponticianus's account connected with Augustine for a number of reasons. First, there was probably a cultural connection because Ponticianus was an African who was telling the faith story of another African (Antony) to two other Africans (Augustine and Alypius) in Milan. Second, Antony's conversion to an ascetic lifestyle—as well as the similar conversion of the officials from Trier—was meaningful for Augustine because one of his biggest obstacles to faith was sexual immorality. In fact, Augustine introduced the entire Ponticianus encounter with this prayerful commentary: "Now I will relate how you set me free from a craving for sexual gratification."[8] Third, Augustine, who had been quite infatuated with career ambitions, identified with the two officials who set aside their careers for the sake of the Gospel. At the conclusion of his conversion account, Augustine testified that he was

---

4. Augustine, *Confessions*, 8.2.3–5.
5. Augustine, *Confessions*, 8.5.10.
6. Augustine, *Confessions*, 8.4.9.
7. Augustine, *Confessions*, 8.7.17.
8. Augustine, *Confessions*, 8.6.13.

"no longer ... entertaining any worldly hope."[9] As a result, he also resigned from his imperial post before moving back to Africa to pursue a monastic lifestyle.[10] Augustine's narrative of Antony and the two officials reached others with the Gospel, including those whose career ambitions were poisoning their spiritual lives or others, like Augustine, who struggled with sexual immorality. Perhaps Augustine's African readers were especially attracted to the African angle of Ponticianus's story.

Augustine's testimony in *Confessions* is one of the most celebrated conversion accounts from the early church. Through narrating faith stories within his own faith story, Augustine does seem to have an evangelistic purpose for his late fourth-century and early fifth-century readers, who could probably identify with at least one of the characters mentioned in Augustine's narrative. It seems that the new *Augustine* film might also engage modern North Africans, who may relate, in some way, to Augustine's story as well.

Lessons in Cultural Engagement

Mission through History

First, since this film is a faithful presentation of the historical Augustine, it shows us that it is possible to evangelize a people—in this case, North African Muslims—through their own history. I found this to be true in my own journey while living, researching, and teaching in North Africa.[11] On several occasions, I had the opportunity to present academic papers and lectures on the early Church in North Africa and on Augustine, who was the subject of my doctoral research.[12] Interestingly, most of these opportunities were encouraged or organized by North African academic colleagues—themselves atheists, secular, or just intellectually curious—who thought it would be good for North African Muslims to know more about the region's Christian past. They saw Augustine as an important figure who was largely unknown, and they wanted to change that.

Once, I had the opportunity to give a two-hour presentation on the history of early North African Christianity to the National History Society. During the question and answer time, a rather frustrated graduate student stood and asked: "We are Muslims; what does this history have to do with

---

9. Augustine, *Confessions*, 8.12.30.
10. Augustine, *Confessions*, 9.2.2.
11. See further Smither, "Remembering the Story," 298–303.
12. See further Smither, *Augustine as Mentor*.

us?" While affirming his good question, I responded that I (a North American) really had no answer. Rather, only he and other North Africans could determine what this period of history and what figures like Augustine meant to them. Most North Africans I met were proud of their history—even their pre-Islamic Christian past that they hardly knew. In my experience, these did turn into encouraging opportunities to share the Gospel through their own history.[13] *Augustine: Son of Her Tears* offers a new and exciting avenue for North Africans to celebrate their past and also ponder its meaning.

Mission through Story

Throughout the Arab-Muslim world, Christian witness, like the ideologies of political movements, has often been regarded as propaganda and has typically been met with resistance. This becomes even more difficult when the evangelists come from the western world. On the contrary, *Augustine* is not propaganda. It's an attractive, winsome, and beautiful story, crafted by veteran filmmakers and interpreted by acclaimed actors. Many missionaries today are rightly focused on letting the biblical narrative speak through storying and through telling their own faith stories as well. This new film on *Augustine* is another storytelling opportunity that can clarify the Gospel story.

Bibliography

Oden, Thomas. *How Africa Shaped the Christian Mind: Rediscovering the African Seedbed of Western Christianity*. Downers Grove, IL: InterVarsity, 2008.
O'Meara, John J. *The Young Augustine*. Rev. ed. New York: Alba, 2010.
Smither, Edward L. *Augustine as Mentor: A Model for Preparing Spiritual Leaders*. Nashville: B&H Academic, 2008.
———. "Remembering the Story: Historical Reflection Leading to Spiritual Dialogue." *Evangelical Missions Quarterly* 45.3 (2009) 298–303.
"Story." *Augustine: Son of Her Tears*. https://www.augustinefilm.com/story-2/.

---

13. See further Oden, *Africa*, 134–42.

Response to "Connecting with Secular Muslims through History and Film"

John Franklin

It is my task to provide a brief response to this interesting chapter by Ed Smither. His focus is on a film depicting a portion of the life of St. Augustine, who lived from 354–430 and is a key figure in the history of Christian theology. Augustine, a North African, tells of his personal spiritual journey in the celebrated, classic work, *Confessions*.

Smither's interest is to discern a way to reach contemporary secular Muslims of North Africa with the Gospel, and he believes he has found a way through a cinematic telling of the early life and conversion of Augustine. I think it is worth noting that the idea for this film was birthed in 2010, at the third Lausanne Congress on World Evangelization in Cape Town, South Africa. This is a good chapter, taking up a case study approach and providing an innovative model for missional engagement. For my response, however, I will note a number of quibbles with the chapter.

My first quibble is with the use of the phrase "secular Muslim." It would be easy to see this phrase as an oxymoron. Surely, if you are a Muslim, you are not secular or, indeed, if you are secular, you are not a Muslim. But, of course, things are often more complex than they at first appear. Smither has not told us what he means by "secular Muslim," and what is meant may be obvious to those who are well familiar with the Muslim world. What I think is meant is that the culture in question—North Africa—is religiously Muslim and politically secular. But what it means for the individual remains uncertain. Is this a Muslim who is like a nominal Christian—culturally Muslim but non-practicing? If non-practicing Muslims who live in a Muslim culture are the target audience, what about practicing Muslims? Would this film and the history it recounts not be of interest to both "secular" and devout Muslims? Perhaps there are reasons to target only the "non-committed."

Given that there is reference in this chapter to the "secular" and the theme of the book also includes the term "secularizing," I want to take the liberty to offer a brief footnote on the notion of the secular. I draw from a work by Canadian philosopher Charles Taylor.[1] The first use of secular is the traditional one, which views secular as having to do with earthly matters and sacred as referring to matters connected with the Church. The second use of secular has a post-enlightenment account, which considers the public square as a place free of religious presence. A secular person is one who affirms no religious affiliation. This is also the view that takes up the secularization thesis that over time, religious influence will continue to diminish and eventually disappear. The third account of secular refers to a social context in which religious belief is simply one option among many and those options may all be contested. It is a context of pluralism. On this view, there is no default position for the culture—just a host of live options among which are religious beliefs. So a secular age may well include plenty of religious belief and widespread religious commitment. It would be interesting to know which of these three meanings of secular would best describe the situation in North Africa.

Smither raises the question of what the story of Augustine would mean to North African Muslims who are educated, cultivated, and, in some cases, financially well-off—Muslims who are indifferent or even fed up with modern Islam, including its extremist expressions. He answers this question by noting four themes that show up in the film.

The first theme is "intellectual biography." Augustine's intellectual engagements were rich and diverse. This does suggest that the target group for the film would be the educated North African. It is hard to tell whether Augustine's encounter with Platonism, Manichean religion, or the Christian instruction of Bishop Ambrose—all part of Augustine's intellectual journey—would appeal to the contemporary secular Muslim. However, it is true that the questions that Augustine was asking 1600 years ago are still being asked today: questions about religious authority or scripture, the problem of evil, God, and how we are to live and make our moral choices. What is manifest in this story is the important role played by serious thought in Augustine's path toward Christian commitment.

This leads me to the second theme of "a spiritual journey." The opening statement in this section gave me pause. Smither writes, "Just because Augustine was a deep thinker did not mean that his journey was not a deeply spiritual one." It seems to me that the underlying assumption of this statement is that there is a certain incompatibility between deep thinking and deep spirituality. Put another way, it suggests a tension between faith and reason. Augustine is a figure who shows that such a tension is not at all

---

1. Taylor, *Secular Age*, 2–3.

necessary but rather that deep thinking and devout believing can coalesce in full harmony. I think Smither is right to note that Augustine's spiritual struggles may well have been a greater challenge than his intellectual struggles. It would have been good to hear a bit more about how those moral and spiritual struggles resonate with modern secular North Africans.

The third theme is "messy story." It is certainly true that the life of Augustine as depicted in *Confessions* is not idealized, and this is a good thing in our contemporary world. The story as recounted in the film makes clear that his life contains the all too familiar elements of difficult family situation, sexual impropriety, grief from loss and death, and the disrupting experience of wrestling with deep and difficult intellectual and spiritual issues. There is integrity to this story, a tell-it-like-it-is quality that may well have appeal in our contemporary context. We are all too quick to cover up the truth about our humanity—not so with Augustine.

The final theme is that of "faith stories within a faith story." This is the structure of the film, and it also shows up in the eighth chapter of *Confessions*. As Augustine tells his own story, he narrates the stories of others who have come to faith and have, in one way or another, influenced him in his own faith journey. Two figures stand out. One is Victorinus, who left his pagan beliefs and, by reading scripture, was gripped by its truth and became a Christian. Augustine identified with Victorinus through a common interest in philosophy, similar career ambitions, and an interest in the Bible. The second figure was the monk Anthony. On hearing the story of Anthony, Augustine was deeply moved, eventually resigned his post abroad, and moved back to Africa to pursue a monastic lifestyle.

I want to note here that the life of Anthony (251–356) was a narrative that had a profound, widespread influence in the early Church. The biography of Anthony, written in Latin by Athanasius, influenced Augustine's conversion, but well beyond that, it also influenced the spread of monasticism in Europe and the devout life that characterized the monastics. My sense is that Smither hopes that the modern rendering of the biography of Augustine in film would carry an influence not unlike his early counterpart, St. Anthony.

Smither thinks that Augustine may well have had an evangelistic purpose in rehearsing the stories of these converts to faith. We might call Augustine's effort a soft apologetic, hoping to nudge his readers toward an embrace of the Gospel.

The last section of Smither's paper offers very brief comments on four missiological lessons from the making and showing of *Augustine: Son of Her Tears*. The first lesson is "mission through history." The film draws on a small piece of the history of North Africa to speak to contemporary members of that community. Though it is true that the Gospel is woven into the fabric of the story—specifically Augustine's conversion—it is not at all clear how this will be received by those who view the film. What I have in mind here is how an effective rendering of the Gospel requires a receptive posture from those who are exposed to it. The story and the history can be received as just more information devoid of any personal engagement at all. What can be acknowledged, though, is that the narrative and artistic means of presentation found in the film opens a possibility for fruitful reception of the story, including its Gospel component.

The second lesson for the missiologist is "mission through story." In this section, Smither raises the question of propaganda and how the presentation of the Gospel is often seen as propaganda. However, he leaves us in the dark as to what he means by propaganda. When he concludes this brief section by saying that "the new film on Augustine is another storytelling opportunity that can clarify the Gospel story," it seems reasonable to ask whether this is a case of propaganda and, if it is, whether that is a bad thing or a good thing. One gets the sense that the story of Augustine is secondary to the more fundamental purpose of clarifying the Gospel.

I want to make two concluding observations. First, my observation related to missiological lesson three—"mission through making culture." Here, Smither references Andy Crouch's book, *Making Culture*, which suggests that the redeeming of culture is best achieved by the effort to make culture. This is precisely what the filmmakers have done. This project is a case of engaging what we call the cultural mandate through the means used to tell the story. At this point, I would like to comment on the value of the arts for the missional task. Western Christianity has been characterized by its bent toward theology and a conceptual account of belief. Presentations of the Gospel are often geared to changing how we think and what we believe. They are not unimportant. However, the arts provide an alternative to this approach by speaking to and through human imagination and opening us to vistas not available to merely didactic accounts of our faith. Film is one genre of art that engages human imagination and helps us get at the truth of things. In addition, other art forms—like poetry, story, visual art, drama, dance, and music—can accomplish the same. Those engaged in mission would do well to be more intentional in drawing on the rich and effective resources of the arts. Art is valuable not so much to hammer home a point but rather to open an unthreatening space for conversation that provides a means through which people gain some fresh perspective, discovering something new and perhaps even something transforming.

My final point has to do with the understanding of mission. The film details the life of Augustine with particular attention to his conversion. In his fourth missiological lens ("a new narrative of conversion"), Smither notes: "After all other paths leave him unsatisfied, Augustine makes a life-changing decision in pursuit of authentic faith." The focus of the film appears to be on "conversion." What I want to note is that mission has a breadth well beyond the important matter of conversion. At least on the surface of things, this seems to be a step away from what has come to be known as "integral" mission. Though both the story and the genre in which it is told have the capacity to set a viewer on a new road, where they may embrace an alternate worldview as found in the Gospel, they also have the capacity for ongoing transformative experience—like Augustine had—in which a restless heart is exchanged for a heart at peace through a knowledge of God.

Bibliography

Taylor, Charles. *A Secular Age*. Cambridge, MA: Harvard University Press, 2007.

Part 2

Mission to the Next Generation

4

Infidels in the Temple of Secularism

Johnson Hsu

The Old Faith in a New Setting

As CHRISTIANITY SEEKS TO redefine its place in increasingly secular and multicultural societies, what might this look like?

Toronto has long been recognized as one of the most multicultural cities in the world, so it offers an ideal setting to investigate this question. Within the Greater Toronto Area (GTA), the Scarborough region is often touted as one of the most multicultural settings. Reflecting this diversity, US economist Tyler Cowen recently wrote, "Scarborough is the best ethnic food suburb I have seen in my life, ever, and by an order of magnitude."[1]

Many immigrants to Toronto come from highly-religious cultural backgrounds and from countries where religion and politics are often heavily intertwined. Catholics from the Philippines, Buddhists from Sri Lanka, and Muslims from Pakistan all intermix within the Scarborough milieu. Yet this multiculturalism is within the framework of one of the most secular nations in the world. In this context, by "secular" I mean the separation of church and state exemplified by Western liberal democracies in the English tradition. Toronto lies within the province of Ontario, which is arguably the most secular and inclusive province in Canada, having recently been led by an openly lesbian Progressive Premier.

What impact might large numbers of religious migrants have upon a largely secularized society?

I will be examining that question from a first-hand perspective as a Chaplain at UTSC (University of Toronto at Scarborough). A bastion of

---

1. Pelley, "Ethnic Food," lines 7–12.

GTA secularism is the public university, and the University of Toronto is the largest of these within the GTA. Looking at specific incidents at UTSC, I will analyze several recent events through the lens of culture and religion intersecting with secularism. The push back against secularism may be starting in the most unexpected of places: among the children of recent immigrants at secular universities.

An Overview

While it is open to question whether higher education actually leads to a decline in faith,[2] it is clear that many people of faith believe that there is a challenge from higher education and the secular viewpoint it is seen to represent. Higher education is perceived as one of—if not the greatest—reasons for the decline of religion in the West.[3] 50 percent of freshmen at US evangelical Christian colleges and universities stated that they chose this route influenced by the concern that "my faith might have been threatened at a secular school."[4] In a 2011 Pew survey, the biggest threat perceived by evangelical leaders worldwide remained to be secularism.

Neither is this concern isolated to Christians. Shayk Hamza Yusuf, co-founder of Zaytuna College, has been referred to as "perhaps the most influential Islamic scholar in the Western world."[5] Around 2008, he delivered a lecture entitled, "Secularism: The Greatest Danger Facing Islam." The form of secularism threatening Islam is a question,[6] just as the very origin of Western secularism being "directly linked with Christianity, and especially Protestantism"[7] affects what is meant by this term.

Within Canada, the ideals of multiculturalism and progressivism are interwoven with this idea of secularism. When speaking of secularism, Charles Taylor discussed "manag(ing) the religious and metaphysical-philosophical diversity of views (including non- and anti-religious views) fairly and democratically."[8] Education can be seen as the crucial apex of this secularized modernity.[9]

---

2. Bertrand, "Limits," 1–3.
3. Schwadel, "Education," 162.
4. Hammond and Hunter, "Maintaining Plausibility," 233.
5. Romig, "Islam," lines 11–12.
6. Iqtidar, "Secularism," 51–54.
7. Topal, "Everybody Wants Secularism," 3.
8. Taylor, "Multiculturalism," 78.
9. Oliverio, "Democratic Public," 15.

I will be exploring some of the interplay when people from actively religious cultures intersect with the secular university in a Canadian milieu, which embraces both secularism and multiculturalism. Furthermore, I explore it from the perspective of a follower of Jesus the Christ and as a chaplain at the University of Toronto. Beginning with a short survey of the terms and physical location, we will look at this interplay from several different perspectives within the University of Toronto Scarborough campus.

Secularism Defined?

It would generally be accepted that secularism is related to a "reduction" in the "influence" of "religion," yet the ambiguity of these three terms related to secularism has also invited wide-ranging definitions. By "reduction," do we mean in the number of adherents, in the strength of convictions, or in religious authority? Is "reduction" moving toward a reduced influence or the complete removal of religious influence? Is this "reduction" linear or not, and is it reversible? By "influence," do we refer to individuals or the public sphere? What do we mean by "religion"? In other words, is this secularism synonymous with modernization and rationality or is it simply one of many paths towards modernization?

Religion itself has different meanings in different cultural contexts,[10] and our Western understanding of religion is rooted in European Judeo-Christianity.[11] The very idea that there is a divide between the secular and the sacred can perhaps be seen as a Western theoretical construct, grown out of Christianity,[12] as can be seen by the Western focus on belief being opposed to practice (i.e., orthodoxy versus orthopraxy).[13] At the least, definitions of religion would likely differ when formulated by believers in deity or deities and by those who believe that nothing supernatural exists.

This definition of religion is crucial, since secularism is seen as a negation or opposite to it. In this sense, it lends itself to a very Hegelian dialectic the nature of the *thesis* (religion) would affect the nature of the *antithesis* (secularism). This failure to adequately define "religion" remains a stumbling block to traditional understandings of secularism.[14] Some would even consider secularism itself a "religion," as demonstrated by Justice Hugo

---

10. Hanson, *Religion*, 70. See also Bronk, "Secular," 579–82.

11. Clammer, "Religious Change," 54–56. See also Taylor *Secular Age*, 15; Iqtidar, "Secularism," 51; and Bronk, "Secular," 579.

12. See Iqtidar, "Secularism," 51, and Bronk, "Secular," 579–82.

13. Clammer, "Religious Change," 55–56.

14. Chaves, "Religious Authority," 749–50.

Black in Torcasso vs Watkins 1961, where he referred to secular humanism as a "religion in this country which does not teach what is generally considered belief in God."[15] This ambiguity of terms—including religion—results naturally in an ambiguity of definitions for secularism.

Charles Taylor offers three definitions (or families of definition) of secularism:

1. As separation of religious structures from political structures and the privatization of religion;
2. As falling away from religious belief and practice; a turning away from God; and
3. As movement from a society where belief in God is unchallenged to one where it is one option among others.[16]

Presenting from a Muslim perspective, Humeira Iqtidar echoes Taylor in some ways yet also offers expanded definitions of secularism as management of religion by the state, as "primarily privatization of religious belief and practice" and as a "change in the texture and fabric of religious thought and practice."[17] If secularism arose from Christian soil, then we would certainly expect other soils to produce different definitions of the secular.

In his biography *The Atheist Muslim: A Journey from Religion to Reason*, Ali Rizvi notes that within some Muslim nations, the mosque is the only place where criticism can be voiced: "All of the frustrations, grievances, and problems of the people—political, economic, and social—get packaged up and channelled through a single medium, neatly wrapped up in *Allahu Akbar*."[18] Ironically, this may mean that even secularist movements within Islam are carried out under the auspices of religion.

This may also explain statements such as that by Malaysian Muslim philosopher Syed Al-Attas that "Islam totally rejects any application to itself of the concepts of secular, secularization, or secularism"[19]—or, at least, to a Western understanding of those terms. Similarly, Richard Madson tries to define secularism from Asian perspectives (specifically from China, Indonesia, and Taiwan), while Peter van der Veer addresses secularism from Indo-Chinese understandings that are not simply antireligious but also

---

15. Gottfried, "Thinking About Secularisms," 323.
16. Taylor, *Secular Age*, 1–4.
17. Iqtidar, "Secularism," 53–54.
18. Rizvi, *Atheist Muslim*, 27.
19. Clammer, "Religious Change," 55.

"simultaneously attempts to transform religions into moral sources of citizenship and national belonging."[20]

Clearly, there is no single, absolute definition of secularism but rather variations of secularism arising from the religious soil that incubates its meaning.

Coming to a single operant definition of either secularism or religion is beyond the scope of this short paper, but the key point is that different groups and cultures may all be using the same terms while speaking about very different goals and objectives. Secularism may be seen as a challenge to be faced by many different religious worldviews, but their definitions and end goals of secularism may differ. As Andrzej Bronk summarizes: "There is no single secularism but rather a cluster of related terms and multiple competing secularisms, as there are multiple and diverse forms of religion."[21]

Canada

Few countries in the world are truly multicultural. All countries have had foreigners, traders, and outsiders living within them to some degree or another, but this does not evoke the idea of pan-cultural welcome, integration, and belonging that is attached to multiculturalism.

Countries created by colonialism, incorporating varied tribes and cultures, can also lay claim to a forced multiculturalism. However, in a 2013 study of cultural diversity, Canada was the only Western country to rank in the top thirty amidst these countries.[22] This may not be a positive statistic though, as Gören argues: "Culturally homogeneous countries gain a strategic advantage over their culturally diverse neighbours."[23] In the recent European pull back from multiculturalism, Taylor comments, "Canada is often pilloried as the source of this dangerous and destructive doctrine."[24]

Beginning with its 1967 adoption of a points-based immigration system, continuing through the Trudeau commitment to multicultural policy in 1971, and culminating in the Mulroney passage of the Canadian Multiculturalism Act in 1988, Canada can lay claim to being the most multicultural nation on earth by choice.

---

20. Bronk, "Secular," 582.
21. Bronk, "Secular," 583.
22. Gören, "Economic Effects," 23.
23. Gören, "Economic Effects," 1.
24. Taylor, "Multiculturalism," 96. Taylor notes that the European understanding of multiculturalism differs markedly from that of Canada.

Toronto

Traditionally, immigration to Canada has congregated in Montreal, Toronto, or Vancouver. The BBC program *More or Less* crunched the numbers and declared Toronto the world's most multicultural metropolis—not just in this national trio but also globally.[25] 51 percent of Toronto's population is foreign born, and some 230 different ethnicities call the city home.[26]

From the standpoint of higher education and secularism, Toronto must also be seen as a national if not global leader. Toronto proper is home to nine different colleges and universities, represented at twenty-seven different geographic locations. Given that this ideal of inclusive multiculturalism is likely a modern construct and that not all districts in Toronto are equally diverse, it can be argued that Toronto represents the most multicultural city in recorded human history.

Scarborough

Scarborough was one of the six municipalities amalgamated together in 1998 to form the current city of Toronto. This may be one explanation for the rapper Drake's reference to Toronto as "the six." Scarborough lies at the easternmost of these six municipalities and was once nicknamed "Scarberia," in light of its perceived distance and remoteness. It is surrounded by Victoria Park Avenue in the west, Steeles Avenue in the north, the Rouge River in the east, and Lake Ontario in the south.

As of 2016, Scarborough contained 23 percent of Toronto's population, with a disproportionate amount of visible minorities.[27] 47 percent of Toronto's 338,965 South Asian population resides in Scarborough, alongside 39 percent of its 299,465 Chinese, 28 percent of its Black, and 34 percent of its Filipino populations. These are the four largest visible minority groups in Toronto, and they all reside disproportionately in Scarborough.

For years, the area now encompassed by the Agincourt South-Malvern West riding has been known colloquially as "Asiancourt" due to its large, visible Chinese population. The FourSquare Church network in the US has been sending summer mission teams to Toronto precisely because unreached communities have been brought here from all corners of the earth. Scarborough can reasonably lay claim to being the most multicultural area

---

25. Gray and Davey, "More or Less."
26. Gray and Davey, "More or Less."
27. City of Toronto, "Neighbourhood Profiles."

within this most multicultural city within this most multicultural country; ironic for a place once nicknamed Scarberia.

Within this multicultural milieu are people from countries of origin where the practice of religion is virtually inseparable from national identity, such as Pakistan, the Philippines, and many other countries where the idea of the separation of religion from public life would be entirely foreign. Scarborough contains roughly one-third of both Toronto's Pakistani and Filipino populations, along with significant populations of Syrians and other Muslim peoples. Ishtiaq Ahmed notes: "Since Pakistan had been created in the name of Muslim nationalism, its national identity was inextricably bound to that cultural factor."[28] This intertwining of religion with ethnicity seems common to most Muslim nations, and even for relatively secular Muslim nations like Turkey. As Madokela and Seggie state: "Turkish ethnic identity cannot be separated from its Islamic identity."[29] In a similar sense, a uniquely Filipino Roman Catholicism is intertwined with Filipino culture. Mulder observes: "God is invoked at the beginning of almost every type of endeavor, whether the opening of a session of the Senate, a departure on a sea journey, the inauguration of a snack-bar, or a social at the tennis club."[30]

Thus, a sizable number of immigrant cultures brought into Scarborough epitomizes the intertwining of religious identity with ethnic identity.

UTSC

Scarborough is the location of the University of Toronto Scarborough (UTSC). This campus is primarily a commuter campus, made up of students residing locally. The University of Toronto (U of T) is one of Canada's highest ranked universities. In the Times Higher Education World University Rankings 2018, they are the highest-ranking Canadian university, at twenty-second place.[31] US News & World Report similarly ranks them first in Canada and twentieth in the world for 2018.[32]

Such international rankings play a great part in attracting international students, and the UTSC campus reflects this, with 2,048 of their 12,693 undergraduate students being international.[33] Perched atop a ridgeline, UTSC is the easternmost of U of T's three campuses, and it is flanked to the south

28. Ahmed, "National Identity," 57.
29. Mabokela and Seggie, "Headscarves," 157.
30. Mulder, "Philippine Catholicism," 249–50.
31. Times Higher Education, "World University Rankings."
32. US News & World Report, "Best Global Universities in Canada."
33. UTSC, "Numbers," 7, 17.

and west by the extensive woodlands around Highland Creek. To the north and east, the campus is surrounded by largely residential housing, with an admixture of old cottages and newer suburban builds.

Combined with their high intake from the diverse local community (as demonstrated by the provision of housing for only 765 students), this campus creates a highly multicultural and international student body. As their brochure states, "U of T Scarborough continues to be a popular first choice for students from the eastern Greater Toronto Area and around the world."[34] Established in 1964, UTSC today represents the meeting place between heavily multiethnic Scarborough and students from 86 nations.

Education, especially higher education and science, has long been held to be the vanguard of secularism. While this view is increasingly being questioned and challenged by empirical research,[35] it remains the paradigm for most people.

As early as Auguste Comte (1798–1857), theorists have advocated for education as a means to end the rule of religion.[36] Comte deeply influenced Marx, Spencer, and through them, Durkheim. Virtually all modern secular theorists continue to espouse this dialectic: that education—and specifically, science—will cause the death of religion. In his survey of secularization theories, Tschannen identifies rationalization as the second core exemplar of all modern secular theories, with education being clearly integral to this process.[37]

From the inception of the secularist ideal, there has been a tension between the academy and religion, despite the fact that almost all early universities were connected to religious endeavors. Princeton University, which was founded by New Light Presbyterians, specifically mentions in its Royal Charter "the earnest desire that those of every Religious Denomination may have free and Equal Liberty and Advantages of Education."[38] Harvard's origins lie heavily connected to Unitarianism and liberal Christianity.[39]

The University of Toronto follows that pattern, being established by Royal Charter in 1827 at the urgings of John Strachan, Archdeacon of York, and initially being under the supervision of the Church of England. Its

---

34. UTSC, "Numbers," 18.
35. Bertrand, "Limits," 2.
36. Bertrand, "Limits," 1.
37. Tschannen, "Paradigm," 400–6.
38. Princeton University, *Minutes*, 1:1.
39. Story, "Boston Brahmins," 99–100.

charter purpose begins with this call: "For the Education of Youth, in the Principles of the Christian Religion."[40]

UTSC Case 1: Beneath the Surface

Look beneath the surface so you can judge correctly (John 7:24 NLT).

When I first began at the university, I spoke with many university staff and administrators as I jumped through the various hoops to accreditation as a chaplain. After the formal aspects of the meetings were done, I usually took time to chat and get to know the individuals better.

Time after time, these chats would go to their experiences of faith and reveal religious underpinnings. For these initial meetings, all but one of the contacts I had were with individuals who grew up in various Christian backgrounds. Some grew up in religious homes, and had drifted away from observance, usually in their late teens to early twenties. Others spoke of feeling judged by the church, sometimes around sexual issues that they felt were outdated, yet they continued to identify with faith. Still others expressed that they considered themselves Christian, and we then discussed aspects of what this meant.

These interactions echoed Barna findings, indicating that when movements away from Christian faith occur, they most often occur between the ages of 18 and 29. The Pew research saw this movement occurring before age 24.[41] These interactions also emphasized one of the definitions of secularism—the relegation of religion to the private sphere.[42] In their public faces, these individuals represented themselves as "a-religious" (i.e., with no indication of underlying faith or religion). The sole individual of non-Christian faith from these early encounters was a Muslim. While expressing strong religious faith, the others had not chosen to externally indicate that faith, whether by dress, beard length, or other manifestations of the *sunnah* of Mohammad. As with their Christian counterparts in a secular public university, they had relegated their faith out of the public sphere. Their public face was differentiated from their private faith. Yet in their private conversations afterwards, these individuals all demonstrated an oft-persistent engagement with religion or openness to a re-engagement with the religion of their youth.

40. University of King's College, *Charter*, 3.
41. Kinnaman, *You Lost Me*, 32.
42. See Taylor, *Secular Age*, 4, and Iqtidar, "Secularism," 52.

In categorizing the university as a secular space, we may have labelled a system but perhaps have forgotten that the constituent parts of every human system are human beings, and these human beings are often still immersed in faith, even if it is a lapsed faith. 60 percent of evangelical university students in the US believed that "the major universities in our country today are controlled by secular humanists."[43] What if that narrative is not entirely correct?

Has secularism really separated church from the public sphere or has it forced a thin veneer over the surface of faith—a veneer of dispassionate modernity and secularism? This secular veneer most often hides a Christian rootedness, which reflects its historical cultural roots. It also reveals the nature of secularism as a rooted reaction to Christianity.[44]

When I first began at UTSC, I repeatedly heard that Islam was the dominant religious group among the students. This is outwardly apparent in the large numbers of visible Muslims one sees on campus and in the well organized and funded Muslim Student Association. Christians were not mentioned, yet a strange thing happened. As I began interacting with students at public events, a vast majority self-identified as Christian. Encounters were at public university events, specifically at "tabling" and Treat Tuesdays. In both these activities, I was present under the banner of the Department of Student Life, which oversees chaplaincy at UTSC.

"Tabling" refers to one of the events where student clubs and groups present themselves in public areas of the school. These groups were assigned their own table, thus the name "tabling." Each student club or university group seeks to promote or advertise its services or community in these settings—in a vast marketplace of groups or a social networking flea market. Student Life was there among other campus groups, creating awareness of faith-based chaplaincy on campus.

Treat Tuesday (aka Waffle Wednesday) was a similar event. Set up in one of the university's main thoroughfares, this was a table where the Department of Student Life offered an edible "treat" at lunch hour on Tuesday to encourage students to engage with an existential question. Typical questions would be, "Are people really 'good'?" and "What happens after a person dies?" The intent, once again, was to promote the existence of faith-based chaplaincy services on campus. The "treat" at this time was a halal cupcake.

Students would either approach the tables or be approached as they pass by the tables. I would estimate that I engaged with at least 200 students through these events. I would also estimate that about eight out of ten of

---

43. Hammond and Hunter, "Maintaining Plausibility," 226.
44. Topal, "Everybody Wants Secularism," 2–3.

the non-visibly Muslim students would self-identify as Christian. The typical encounter would be for me to approach the students and engage them, whether about the Treat Tuesday question or around Student Life initiatives. Only a very small percentage (about 10 percent) would mention church or other expressions of religion in their responses. I once introduced myself as one of the Christian Chaplains on campus, implying that it was safe to discuss faith with me. After I would make my introductions, roughly eight out of ten from the non-visibly Muslim students would say, "Oh, I'm also a Christian."

Has the perception of the university as a secular space caused a hiding of religious identities? If students are reticent to openly acknowledge their faith, even in answering existential questions that naturally lend themselves to such expressions, but are overwhelmingly willing to do so when the other person in the conversation opens up about faith, then this seems to indicate a campus culture that discourages public religious expression.

U of T strives to be a place of inclusion and diversity. Here is a key questions to ask: "Have people of faith been made to feel marginalized in this secular inclusive environment, as if secularism meant opposition to people holding religious beliefs? Especially on multicultural campuses, such as UTSC, are our universities the home of hidden bodies of students, staff, and faculty of faith?

UTSC Case 2: Enduring in the Lion's Den

> *So the king gave the order, and they brought Daniel and threw him into the lions' den.*
> *The king said to Daniel, "May your God, whom you serve continually, rescue you!"* (Dan 16:6 NIV)

I will refer to this student as *Enduring* for the sake of anonymity. *Enduring* is a conservative evangelical Christian, who comes from a prosperous and developed European nation. He had high grades that would have gained him entry into the top range of his domestic higher educational options; he came from a country with free and high quality public universities. In other words, there was no reason for *Enduring* to come to UTSC in Toronto.

Yet he chose to come here, both from a sense of God's calling and a desire to study in a highly secular environment, which would allow him to engage and challenge that worldview. Essentially, *Enduring* perceived secular multicultural universities to be anti-faith, yet chose to enter specifically to engage with that worldview from a Christian perspective.

However, *Enduring's* time here has been full of frustrations. Rather than finding critical and insightful minds to debate religious, political, and philosophical ideas with, he largely found a lack of real depth or even interest in those things. Robert Bertrand notes that most people who leave religion do so for passive reasons, such as apathy, boredom, or movement away from family.[45] *Enduring's* experience seems to support this. If most students at UTSC have a nominal Christian identity, as suggested by the high incidence of students expressing belief during conversations, yet are unwilling or unable to intelligently discuss such issues, then this would seem to indicate an apathetic attitude toward faith issues. This might also indicate that if they left faith, it was not due to the strength of secular arguments but rather due to the sense that religious questions were not worth considering.

This may be an offshoot of a secular environment or attitude with an empirical or scientific bias that relegates other fields of study to unimportance. In a 2011 Barna poll, the findings show that 25 percent of Christian teens aged 18 to 25 said they see faith as antithetical to science.[46] Specifically on campus, this apathy may have been influenced by a focus on studies, over-saturation of information, exhaustion, or other factors. Uecker notes that the topic of religion or religious participation appears "crowded out" or rendered "low on the list of most young adults' priorities" somewhere in this period.[47]

Regardless of the cause, an apathetic attitude towards existential questions is not conducive to forming an effective and holistic worldview. In 1966, more than 80 percent of college students identified "developing a meaningful philosophy of life" as an educational goal. That figure dropped to 47 percent by 1996.[48] It is perhaps worth noting that only after the 1960's do we see church attendance dip for 18 to 28 year olds.[49] Something happened in that era.

One of the exceptions to this apathy was a conversation *Enduring* had with an orthodox Muslim student. While coming from very different religious backgrounds, *Enduring* and the Muslim student shared a strong interest in the question of God/Allah and how that intersects with their daily lives. They were able to dialogue over an extended period of time and reaffirmed each other's commitments to the sacred, even while they politely disagreed on the exact nature and identity of that sacred. It was with

---

45. Bertrand, "Limits," 24.
46. Kinnaman, *You Lost Me*, 136–37.
47. Bertrand, "Limits," 14–15.
48. Bertrand, "Limits," 10.
49. Kinnaman, *You Lost Me*, 45.

students from other faiths that *Enduring* has best been able to intelligently discuss the issues that were important to him.

Some of the things that are thought to weaken religion in a university setting are exposure to other religious viewpoints and the breakdown of plausibility structures that this entails.[50] I wonder if this very mindset evidences secular bias—the underlying thought of which is that all religions are false, and that evidence, reason, and exposure to other modes of thinking will thus cause logical collapse.

At least in the case of Christian evangelicals attending secular campuses, the evidence suggests that their religious commitment actually increases while they are at university. This is in contrast to fundamentalist or liberal Christians, who either liberalize or connect to liberal causes while losing their group identity.[51]

Enduring seems to be on that path to strengthened religious commitment, as he increasingly sees his views not being seriously challenged intellectually. His contact with devout Muslim students may actually provide a structural support system, realizing the shared commitment to the divine creates an unintentional bond. While secular challenges to faith may encourage a siege mentality that strengthens faith,[52] it is possible that colleagues of other faiths may also strengthen religious plausibility structures by providing shared belief in the reality and importance of faith.

If not all religions are the same, though, and if one actually does reflect an objectively true deity, then an additional question is how other religions—including secularism, insofar as it is a belief system—would fare in their plausibility structures when confronted with religious truth in a pluralistic setting. As a convert to Biblical Christianity, one of the reasons for my own coming to faith was the realization that the God of the Bible was real. I am entirely open to having that proposition tested and questioned, and the university should be the place for such testing.

It would be interesting to see studies of atheistic, Sunni, Ismaili, Buddhist, Mormon, and other faiths' beliefs through the process of engagement at Western secular universities, especially if those studies include strong interaction with mature Christian peers. Perhaps instead of fearing the secular university, we should truly embrace the opportunity that the intersection of multiculturalism and education provides. While there is a place for private Christian schools, there is definitely a place for more *Enduring*.

---

50. Bertrand, "Limits," 15–16.
51. Bertrand, "Limits," 16–18.
52. Bertrand, "Limits," 16.

UTSC Case 3: The People at the Gate

> *Then the elders and all the people at the gate said, "We are witnesses. May the LORD make the woman who is coming into your home like Rachel and Leah, who together built up the family of Israel. May you have standing in Ephrathah and be famous in Bethlehem."* (Ruth 4:11 NIV)

UTSC has a student council, the Scarborough Campus Students' Union (SCSU), which "democratically unites, represents, and provides avenues for the diverse 14,000 members of the undergraduate student body of UTSC."[53]

Reflecting the ethnic and religious diversity of UTSC, the 2017–18 SCSU was composed of six women of color from Hindu, Muslim, and Christian backgrounds. They and their ethnic and religious groups had come to Canada at some point from Sri Lanka, the Sudan, the Philippines, India, or the tangled diaspora that is increasingly the norm for migrants. In a very real sense, this reflects the Canadian multicultural, secular dream.

SCSU's actions reflect a push back on or a change in direction from the ideals of secularism. In fact, this student council has been aware of and made statements in support of religious, ethnic, and social justice issues. It has chosen to affirm these stances often in specifically religious forums. This is a move away from traditional separation of church and state and harkens to a more fluid interaction between public officials and people of faith.

One example is a statement in support of those affected by the closure of an Islamic high school.[54] The SCSU chose to publish their support statement on Muslimlink.ca, which is a website designed to "inform, connect, inspire, and celebrate Muslims living in Canada."[55] This choice reflects a desire to maintain contact and affinity with faith communities.

Another example is a letter initiated by SCSU to advocate for a multifaith space on campus to fill "religious and cultural gaps in the services and supports provided at UTSC."[56] This letter was worded in the secular and progressive language of multiculturalism and inclusion, but it advocates for religion. Framed within the context of the "large religious and spiritual community" at UTSC, it champions for "students, staff, and faculty of faith."[57] It specifically references the lack of welcome felt by people of faith within the university setting and calls for space to "meditate, pray, perform

---

53. SCSU, "About," line 4.
54. Javed, "Left to Scramble," lines 4–7.
55. SCSU Executive, "Statement in Solidarity," lines 7–22.
56. SCSU, "Multifaith Space," 1.
57. SCSU, "Multifaith Space," 1.

their rituals, and practice their spirituality with other students."[58] It should be noted that the development of faith schools in the UK at the turn of the millennium was also done under a New Labour government waving the banner of diversity.[59]

The reticence to openly identify as part of a faith community discussed in UTSC Case 1 may reflect this lack of perceived welcome. In the West, one of the unspoken assumptions of secularism is that religion is contrary to reason. Where science, rationality, and higher education meet religion, the automatic assumption is that faith will be the loser.[60] Whether it is relegated to private space or taught out of existence by schooling, the expectation is that it will fade. Yet, this was not the thinking of these diaspora offspring, as represented by the SCSU at UTSC.

Rather than adopting the assumption that religion is *de facto* false and that it should not be taught, spread, or encouraged, these six products of multicultural migration chose to advocate for the promotion of religious space and presence on behalf of "students, staff, and faculty of faith." At the very least, this is a move away from the definition of secularism as religious differentiation from other authority structures and demonstrates a rebuilding of those ties—if not an outright strengthening of religious authority.

These twin currents of progressivism (i.e., secularism and multiculturalism) may be working at opposing directions. While the former often seeks to marginalize and limit religion, the latter offers opportunity for an increased engagement with faith. When New Labour brought in increased opportunity for faith-based schools under the aegis of diversity, one of the noteworthy opponents of that measure was the teaching union, which voiced concerns about religious fundamentalism.[61] Secular multiculturalism and traditional agents of progressivism seem to be at odds. This supports Luhmann's contention that secularism can actually lead to religious regeneration.[62]

Secularism has assumed that reason, rationality, science, and—their handmaiden—education would expose religion as a human invention. Meulemann, for instance, states that religion originates this way: "As people are aware of being mortal, they seek to know where they come from."[63] He

58. SCSU, "Multifaith Space," 1.
59. Clements, "Public Attitudes," 954.
60. See Tschannen, "Paradigm," 398, 411–12, and Johnson "Formal Education," 231–33.
61. Clements, "Public Attitudes," 955.
62. Goldstein, "Patterns," 164.
63. Meulemann, "Spontaneous Revival?," 47.

discounts the notion that there is the possibility for deity or deities. From the birth of sociology, Comte "proclaimed the eventual end of religion at the hands of science and the intellect."[64]

This supposition has been so taken for granted as true that it has not been tested thoroughly.[65] What happens if the empirical proof fails to support the hypothesis? As Mark Chaves phrases it: "Religion's stubborn refusal to disappear has prompted a major re-evaluation of inherited models of secularization."[66] What if religious faith stands up well under the rational and intellectual scrutiny of the Western academy? There are those who do not see a contradiction between students, staff, and faculty of faith and higher education, as demonstrated by the multicultural offspring at the SCSU.

Conclusion

There is clearly a perception that the university is a secular space, both by people of faith and students at secular universities. At UTSC, the children of recent immigrants are demonstrating a push back against the marginalization of religion, using the language of multiculturalism and progressivism. Rather than separating religion from public life, highly multicultural and pluralistic settings may offer a platform for reengagement and revitalization of religion in public life and higher education.

Reflection Questions

1. What aspects of multiculturalism might reflect biblical teachings? What interpretations of it do not?

2) Our English word "crisis" comes from the Greek word *krisis* (meaning "judgment") and has evolved into a Latin medical term for the turning point in a disease—that change which indicates either recovery or death. In the crisis of secularism confronting Canadian Christianity, what God-given opportunities for blessings and revitalization do you see?

3) What changes to how we do ministry might be necessary to best grasp these opportunities?

---

64. Schwadel, "Education," 161.
65. Johnson, "Religious Belief," 231.
66. Chaves, "Religious Authority," 749.

Bibliography

Ahmed, Ishtiaq. "Pakistan's National Identity." *International Review of Modern Sociology* 34.1 (2008) 47–59.
Bertrand, Robert L. "The Limits of Secularization through Education." *Journal of Religion and Society* 17 (2015) 1–43.
Bronk, Andrzej. "Secular, Secularization, and Secularism: A Review Article." *Anthropos* 107.2 (2012) 578–83.
University of King's College. *Charter of the University of King's College at York in Upper Canada.* R. Stanton, 1831. https://utarms.library.utoronto.ca/sites/utarms-edit.library.utoronto.ca/files/pictures/uoft-charter.pdf.
Chaves, Mark. "Secularization as Declining Religious Authority." *Social Forces* 72.3 (1994) 749–74.
City of Toronto Social Policy Analysis & Research Unit. "Neighbourhood Profiles Data 2016." https://www.toronto.ca/city-government/data-research-maps/neighbourhoods-communities/neighbourhood-profiles.
Clammer, John. "Secularization and Religious Change in Contemporary Asia." *Southeast Asian Journal of Social Science* 12.1 (1984) 49–58.
Clements, Ben. "Understanding Public Attitudes in Britain towards Faith Schools." *British Educational Research Journal* 36.6 (2010) 953–73.
Global Survey of Evangelical Protestant Leaders. Washington, DC: Pew Research Center, 2011.
Goldstein, Warren S. "Secularization Patterns in the Old Paradigm." *Sociology of Religion* 70.2 (2009) 157–78.
Gören, Erkan. "Economic Effects of Domestic and Neighbouring Countries' Cultural Diversity." *SSRN Electronic Journal* 10.2139 (2013).
Gottfried, Paul. "Thinking About Secularisms." *World and I* 14.7 (1999) 320–29.
Gray, Laura, and Ed Davey. "More or Less: The World's Most Diverse City." *BBC*, 2016. http://www.bbc.co.uk/programmes/p03v1r1p.
Hammond, Phillip E., and James Davison Hunter. "On Maintaining Plausibility: The Worldview of Evangelical College Students." *Journal for the Scientific Study of Religion* 23.3 (1984) 221–38.
Hanson, Eric O. *Religion and Politics in the International System Today.* New York: Cambridge University Press, 2006.
Iqtidar, Humeira. "Secularism and Secularisation: Untying the Knots." *Economic and Political Weekly* 47.35 (2012) 50–58.
Javed, Noor. "Students Left to Scramble after Islamic High School Shuts down." *The Star*, August 23, 2017. https://www.thestar.com/news/gta/2017/08/23/students-left-to-scramble-after-islamic-high-school-shuts-down.html.
Johnson, Daniel Carson. "Formal Education vs. Religious Belief: Soliciting New Evidence with Multinomial Logit Modeling." *Journal for the Scientific Study of Religion* 36.2 (1997) 231–46.
Kinnaman, David. *You Lost Me: Why Young Christians Are Leaving Church.* Grand Rapids: Baker Books, 2011.
Mabokela, Reitumetse Obakeng, and Fatma Nevra Seggie. "Mini Skirts and Headscarves: Undergraduate Student Perceptions of Secularism in Turkish Higher Education." *Higher Education* 55.2 (2008) 155–70.

Meulemann, Heiner. "Enforced Secularization—Spontaneous Revival?: Religious Belief, Unbelief, Uncertainty and Indifference in East and West European Countries 1991–1998." *European Sociological Review* 20.1 (2004) 47–61.

Princeton University. *Minutes of the Proceedings of the Trustees of The College New Jersey 1748*. http://arks.princeton.edu/ark:/88435/7w62f826z.

Mulder, Niels. "Localization and Philippine Catholicism." *Philippine Studies* 40.2 (1992) 240–54.

Ngabo, Gilbert. "Toronto the Diverse: BBC Study Declares City Most Diverse in the World." *Metro News*, May 16, 2016. http://www.metronews.ca/news/toronto/2016/05/16/toronto-the-diverse.html.

Oliverio, Stefano. "The Democratic Public To Be Brought into Existence and Education as Secularization." *Education and Culture* 30.2 (2014) 5–20.

Pelley, Lauren. "US economist touts Scarborough as 'best ethnic food suburb.'" *The Star*, March 18, 2015. https://www.thestar.com/news/gta/2015/03/18/us-economist-touts-scarborough-as-best-ethnic-food-suburb.html.

Rizvi, Ali Amjad. *The Atheist Muslim: A Journey from Religion to Reason*. New York: St. Martin's, 2016.

Romig, Rollo. "Where Islam Meets America." *The New Yorker*, May 13, 2013.

Schwadel, Philip. "The Effects of Education on Americans' Religious Practices, Beliefs, and Affiliations." *Review of Religious Research* 53.2 (2011) 161–82.

Scarborough Campus Students' Union. "About." *SCSU.ca*. http://www.scsu.ca/about.

———. "For Multifaith Space at UTSC." Letter from SCSU, December 2017. Toronto, ON.

Scarborough Campus Students' Union Executive. "A Statement in Solidarity with the Communities Affected by the Islamic Foundation School Closure." *Muslim Link*, August 31, 2017. https://muslimlink.ca/voices/a-statement-in-solidarity-with-the-communities-affected-by-the-islamic-foundation-school-closure.

Story, Ronald. "Harvard and the Boston Brahmins: A Study in Institutional and Class Development, 1800–1865." *Journal of Social History* 8.3 (1975) 94–121.

Taylor, Charles. *A Secular Age*. Cambridge: Belknap Press of Harvard University Press, 2007.

———. "Secularism and Multiculturalism." *Open Mind*. https://www.bbvaopenmind.com/en/article/secularism-and-multiculturalism.

Times Higher Education. "World University Rankings." https://www.timeshighereducation.com/world-university-rankings/2018/world-ranking#!/page/0/length/25/sort_by/rank/sort_order/asc/cols/stats.

Topal, Semiha. "Everybody Wants Secularism—But Which One? Contesting Definitions of Secularism in Contemporary Turkey." *International Journal of Politics, Culture, and Society* 25.1/3 (2012) 1–14.

Tschannen, Olivier. "The Secularization Paradigm: A Systematization." *Journal for the Scientific Study of Religion* 30.4 (1991) 395–415.

University of Toronto Scarborough. *2010–2011 Facts Figures Annual Report*.

———. *U of T Scarborough: By the Numbers, 2015–2016*.

US News & World Report. "Best Global Universities in Canada." https://www.usnews.com/education/best-global-universities/canada.

Vlas, Natalia, and Sergiu Gherghina. "Where Does Religion Meet Democracy? A Comparative Analysis of Attitudes in Europe." *International Political Science Review/Revue Internationale De Science Politique* 33.3 (2012) 336–51.

Yale Corporation. "Yale Corporation Charter and Legislation Printed For The President and Fellows." New Haven: Yale University, 1976. https://www.yale.edu/sites/default/files/files/University-Charter.pdf.

5

The Exodus of Generation Xs and Millennials from Canadian Churches

Implications for Evangelism in a Secular Multicultural Context

DAVID CHEUNG

IN RECENT DECADES, a widespread concern among Canadian churches has been the continuing ascent in the average biological age of local congregants. One dreaded effect of this is the oft-lamented ownership transfers of church real estate to wealthy individuals, property developers, or Eastern religious groups. Meanwhile, ecclesial mergers—whether contemplated or consummated—gain motivation neither initially nor primarily from the cherished ideal of Christian unity but from the raw necessity of congregational life prolongation, even as public statements reserve first place for the former.

This chapter consists of two parts. In the first part, we look at the Canadian situation. In particular, we start with a brief survey of decline patterns among major segments of Canadian Christianity, as well as the massive exodus of Generation Xs and Millennials (GXMs) from the churches. Then, we examine the situational context of today's Canada that features multiculturalism and secularization. The second part of the paper presents four implications for the task of Christian evangelism. As the latter is ultimately something we do, this chapter adopts the dual perspective of an academic and practitioner.[1]

---

1. As an academic for over three decades, the author has been involved in theological education in Europe, Asia, and North America. As a practitioner, he has served as youth pastor in a suburban congregation, solo pastor in an inner city neighborhood, senior pastor of a multilingual church, mission executive, and missions mobilizer.

The Canadian Context

The General Exodus

This brief survey of the general exodus of Canadians from their churches provides the larger historical context for the exodus of GXMs in recent decades. Perhaps we may start with the subjective factor of religious self-identification among Canadians. In the last four decades of the twentieth century, there was a significant decline in this respect.

Table 1. Religious Self-Identification among Canadians (%), 1945–2000[2]

	Protestants	Roman Catholics	Total
1945 May	56.0	33.4	89.4
1955 July	54.1	41.8	95.9
1965 Nov	50.5	42.4	92.9
1975 Nov	44.9	44.5	89.4
1985 Nov	41.8	44.0	85.8
1995 Nov	34.2	42.6	76.8
2000 Nov	28.6	40.5	69.1

For a more visual-friendly presentation, here is the same data in graph form.

Figure 1. Religious Self-Identification among Canadians (%), 1945–2000

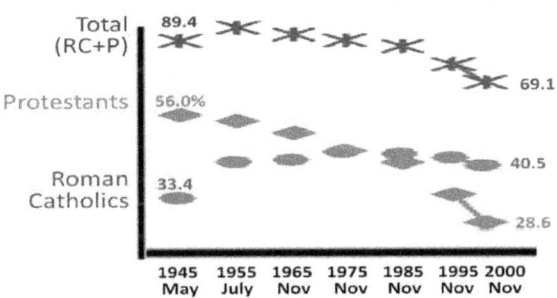

As we can see, the decline started in the 1960s. More worrisome, however, is the acceleration of this downtrend as the new millennium approached. Beyond percentages, we may also look at absolute numbers from the previous decade.

2. Canadian Institute, "Gallup Canada 1945–2000."

Table 2. Religious Self-Identification among Canadians, 2001–2011[3]

		2001	2011	Immigrants 2001–2011
1	Catholic	12,936,905	12,810,705	484,340
2	Protestant	8,654,850	7,265,775	212,285
3	Christian Orthodox	479,620	550,690	107,635
4	Christian NIE	780,450	1,475,575	162,040

In 2001, the national Christian population was 22,851,825 (lines 1–4 of the table). In 2011, it fell to 22,102,745. Thus, broadly speaking, the first decade of this millennium registers a decline of 749,080 or 3.3 percent. But this is including the Christian immigrants (counting 966,300) who arrived over the same ten-year period. If we take this number out, the loss is actually over 1.7 million people. That is, the pre-existing Christian population drops to 21,136,445, a loss of 7.5 percent. This is more than double the 3.3 percent figure.

Aside from the subjective factor of religious self-identification, there is the more objective factor of religious attendance.[4] It is no secret that weekly attendance among Canada's religious groups likewise declined dramatically in the second half of the last century: in 1957, slightly over one half of the Canadian population was attending some religious service on a weekly basis (53 percent); in just three years, that figure dropped to 38 percent; by 1975, it has sunk even further, to 31 percent; after another fifteen years, it slid to 24 percent; and in 2000, the number was down to 21 percent. The table below summarizes the situation, while also providing details pertaining to Roman Catholics, Mainline Protestants, and Conservative Protestants.

---

3. Statistics Canada, "2001 Census"; "Canadian Households in 2011." Considering only the landed immigrants in Canada up to May 09, 2011. Catholic 2011 figure is *contra* Clarke and Macdonald, *Leaving Christianity*, 7 (table 1.2). "Christian NIE" means "Christian not included elsewhere."

4. With regards to measuring personal religiosity, Clark and Schellenberg propose a simple "religiosity index" that combines four factors: affiliation, attendance, personal practices, and general attitude toward religion (see Clark and Schellenberg, "Who's religious?"). The idea is attractive, but it would require a lot of data gathering as well as the buy-in of many researchers.

Table 3. Weekly Religious Attendance among Canadians (%)[5]

	Gallup	Project Canada surveys		
	1957	1975	1990	2000
All-Canada	53	31	24	21
Roman Catholics	83	45	33	26
Mainliners	35	23	14	15
Conservatives	51	41	49	58

Thus, over four decades, the Roman Catholics suffered the greatest losses, falling from 83 percent to 26 percent—a minus-57-percentage-point drain. Mainline Protestants absorbed a minus-20-percentage-point decline. In contrast, Conservative Protestants gained by seven percentage points. The weekly attendance data above corresponds broadly to the surveys on monthly attendance into the twenty-first century.

Table 4. Canadian Religious Service Attendance (%), 1989–2009[6]

	1989	1994	1999	2004	2009
	Monthly	At least monthly			Monthly
All-Canada	38	33	33	31	28
Roman Catholic	49	42	38	40	32
Mainline	33	26	30	30	28
Conservative	59	64	61	64	62
Protestant total (M+C)	39	37	41	45	40

The GXM Exodus

Within the general exodus, we locate the GXM exodus. For this chapter, we bypass the seemingly hopeless variety of defining the birth years of GXMs. Handy and catchy, both terms enjoy great popularity and usage while suffering unregulated reformulation and obfuscation. To move this discussion forward, we may adopt the temporal parameter of Census Canada for Baby Boomers and that of the US Census Bureau for Millennials. These two parameters set the *terminus a quo* and the *terminus ad quem* for the Generation Xs.

---

5. Bibby, *Restless Gods*, 20, 73.
6. Bibby, "Continuing," 835.

Table 5. Birth Years of Generation Xs and Millennials[7]

Generation	Birth Year	Age in Dec 2017
Baby Boomers	1946–1965	53–72
Generation X	1966–1981	36–52
Millennials	1982–2000	17–35

Even during the peak period of Christianity in the mid-1950s, some decline in teen interest in religion has been observed; that is, disinterest relative to the preceding teen generation. When asked to compare, nearly two-thirds of survey respondents said that the newer generation are "not as interested" as their precedents.[8] This impression of receding interest among youth was eventually corroborated by field data from the early 1990s.

Table 6. Weekly Attendance by Age Group (%), 1991[9]

	Age Group		
	18–34	35–54	55 & up
All-Canada	14	23	37
Roman Catholics	15	30	51
Mainliners	22	23	31
Conservatives	54	56	62

Among GXMs, decline is likewise the general feature in the Project Teen Canada surveys (started in 1984). Here are the details on identification and attendance.

---

7. Baby-boomers 1946–1965 from Statistics Canada, "2011 Census." See Colby and Ortman, *Baby Boom*. Millennials 1982–2000 from US Census Bureau. The placing of Millennial birth years at 1982–2000 actually follows the earliest Strauss–Howe formulation (see Strauss and Howe, *Generations*, 297, 335). Later, they moved the endyear to 2002 (see Howe and Strauss, *Millennials Rising*, 14–15). See also Contra Pyöriä et al, "Millennial generation," 3. Scardamalia, *Millennials*, has Millennials born in 1982–2001.

8. That is, 60.8 percent. Meanwhile, 31.6 percent thought their contemporary teen generation is "as interested." See Canadian Institute, "Gallup Canada 1945–2000."

9. Bibby, *Restless Gods*, 25.

Table 7. Canadian Teens (%)[10]

Survey Year		1984	1992	2000
Birth Year		1965–71	1973–79	1981–87
Generation		GX	GX	GXM
Self-Identification				
1	Roman Catholics	51	41	39
2	Protestants (ML+C)	35	28	22
3	Mainliners (ML)	26	17	10
4	Conservatives (C)	9	11	12
Service attendance				
5	All-Canada	23	18	22
6	Roman Catholics	28	21	21
7	Mainliners	17	16	23
8	Conservatives	51	61	70

Strikingly, the Conservative Protestant segment is consistently counter-trending. In comparison, the Mainline Protestant group counter-trends in attendance but not in identification.

While the last data table deals predominantly with GXs, the more recent and much-celebrated *Hemorrhaging Faith*[11] project covers more Millennials.[12] Among Roman Catholics and Mainline Protestants, *Hemorrhaging Faith* reports a loss rate of about 80 percent in terms of weekly attendance. For Evangelical Protestants, the decline stands at 44 percent. The transition after Grade 8 sustains a loss rate (minus 18 percentage points), which is higher than after Grade 12 (minus 13 percentage points). Here are the numbers.

---

10. Bibby, *Restless Gods*, 86, 87, 88. For Data Set 08, the figures for lines 3–4 are derived from the self-identification of Protestant teens for those years (Mainliners at 74, 60, and 46 percent versus Conservatives at 26, 40, and 54 percent).

11. See Penner et al., *Hemorrhaging Faith*.

12. The subjects were raised as Christians or became Christians in young adulthood, being of ages 18–34 in 2010 (born in 1976–1992); that is, Generation X's and Millennials.

Table 8. Decline in Weekly Church Attendance (%)[13]

	Catholic	Mainline	Evangelical	Evangelical Loss rate
K–Gr8	44	54	70	
Gr 9–12	21	19	52	-18
Young Adult	9	12	39	-13

In terms of religious identification in childhood retained during young adulthood, we find alarming loss rates among both Catholics and Protestants.

Table 9. Religious Identification in Childhood Retained in Young Adulthood (%)[14]

Childhood (K–Grade 8)	Young adulthood (After Grade 12)	
	Retention Rate	Loss Rate
Roman Catholic	45	55
Mainline	34	66
Evangelical	63	37

Table 10. Religious Nones by Generation (%), 1971–2011[15]

Birth year	Broadly	2011	Note
Up to 1946		12	4% in 1971
1947–1966	Baby-boomers	20	9% in 1981
1967–1986	Generation X	29	21% in 2001
1987–1995	Millennials	29	

We may now sum up the GXM exodus. Among GXs, there was a general drop in identification and attendance, but Conservative Protestants were a consistent exception. Among Millennials, the decline in both categories is without exception.[16] Therefore, the GMX exodus appears to be growing.

---

13. Penner et al., *Hemorrhaging Faith*, 23n13.

14. Penner et al., *Hemorrhaging Faith*, 25n14. Roman Catholic data is for all of Canada except Quebec. In the latter, the loss rate is 49 percent.

15. Pew Research Center, "Canada's Changing Religious Landscape."

16. As to proposed reasons for decline, the literature is growing, but space does not allow for a full discussion here. For the interested reader, however, we can offer a few titles for a start: aside from Penner et al., *Hemorrhaging Faith*, see Overholt and Penner, *Soul Searching*; Sawler, *Goodbye Generation*; Sawler, *Before They Say*; and Bibby et al., *Emerging Millennials*. For a popular distillation of the latter, see Bibby and Penner, *10*

Multiculturalism

The Canadian context features the combination of secularization and multiculturalism.[17] While many countries share these features, Maple Leaf Land is the first to officially adopt multiculturalism as well as to enshrine the same in its Constitution.[18] In a recent survey of twenty-one countries, Canada ranked second in terms of having the broadest range of multiculturalism policy.[19]

In 1867 Britain's parliament passed the first British North America Act, establishing Canada as a federal self-governing dominion within the British "empire." Patriation was consummated when Constitution Act 1982 was passed, which—among other things—renamed the 1867 act as Constitution Act 1867. By then, Canada had already adopted the federal policy of official bilingualism (1969) and multiculturalism (1971). In 1988 the Multiculturalism Act was passed, giving the policy more defined purpose and direction.[20] Aside from guaranteeing religious and other freedoms, the Canadian Charter of Rights and Freedoms also effectively confesses multiculturalism as a basic Canadian value. Section 27 reads: "This Charter shall be interpreted in a manner consistent with the preservation and enhancement of the multicultural heritage of Canadians." In late fall of 2002, the government designated June 27 as the annual Canadian Multiculturalism Day.

Not without its critics,[21] multiculturalism nevertheless persists as both ideology and policy. Its emergence during the primitive period of national identity formation provided a framework of inclusivity for English Canada, French Canada, First Nations Canada, and the increasingly diverse immigrant Canada (post-1967). Recent surveys indicate that most Canadians support the federal policy of multiculturalism.

Things. Also forthcoming is Bibby, *Latest Emerging*.

17. For a quick introduction, see Fleras and Elliott, *Engaging Diversity*, and Guo and Wong, "Revisiting Multiculturalism in Canada."

18. On the uniqueness of Canadian multiculturalism, see Kymlicka, "Canadian Multiculturalism."

19. See Banting and Kymlicka, "Is There," and Bloemraad and Wright, "Utter failure," 592–99.

20. More in Dewing, *Canadian Multiculturalism*.

21. See Bibby, *Mosaic Madness*; Gwyn, *Nationalism without Walls*; Bissoondath, *Selling Illusions*; Bissoondath, "Failure"; Kay, "Multiculturalism, R.I.P."; Granatstein, *Who Killed Canadian History?*; Ryan, *Multicultiphobia*; Rattansi, *Multiculturalism*; Leung, "Canadian Multiculturalism"; and Wong, "Multiculturalism and Ethnic Pluralism."

Figure 2. Survey Question Result: Canada's Multicultural Makeup Is One of the Best Things about This Country, 2007[22]

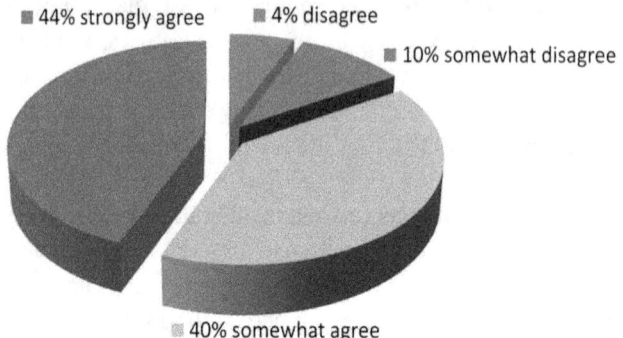

Figure 3. Canadian Perception of Multiculturalism in Relation to National Identity, 2008[23]

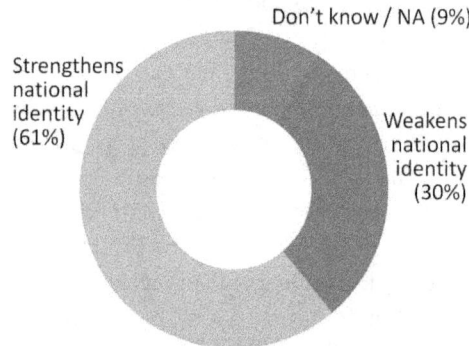

In 1986 Environics asked Canadians what made them most proud of their country and found multiculturalism ranking tenth in frequency. The survey was repeated some two decades later (2006) with multiculturalism emerging second on the list.[24] In a somewhat similar poll in 2010, it came out as the top answer.

---

22. Soroka and Roberton, "Literature Review."
23. Soroka and Roberton, "Literature Review."
24. Adams, *Unlikely Utopia*, 20–21. The number one answer was democracy.

Table 11. Survey Question: "In your view, what is it about Canada that you think most deserves to be celebrated on its 150th birthday?" 2010[25]

	Answer	(%)
1	Multiculturalism	27
2	Charter of Rights and Freedoms	12
3	Natural Beauty/Resources	7
4	Aboriginal History/Heritage/Culture	6
5	Peaceful Country/Absence of Crime /Social Problems	5
6	Nice/Friendly People	
7	Freedom (General)	
8	Independence from US/Other Countries	4
9	Arts & Culture/Literature/Music/Artists	
10	Health Care System	
11	Democracy/Democratic Institutions	
12	Canada's History/Heritage	
13	National Unity	
14	Economic Prosperity/Standard of Living	3
15	Tolerance of Others/Human Rights	
16	Role/Contribution to Peacekeeping/World Peace	
17	Great Canadians	

In 2007 the pro-multiculturalism figure was 84 percent (Data 12 above), which represents a substantial rise of 13.5 percent compared to the previous year.[26] This reveals growing confidence. In 2008 nearly two-thirds of Canadians thought multiculturalism good for the formation of national identity (Data 13). The 2010 poll tells more because multiculturalism emerged the runaway number one when respondent answers were "obtained without prompting" (Data 14).[27] This outcome was echoed in a 2016 poll where multiculturalism emerged as the top answer to the question about what

---

25. Soroka and Roberton, "Literature Review."

26. The 2006 figure was 74 percent. See Bricker, "Canadian Immigration."

27. Likewise, in the 2010 Angus Reid poll, 55 percent of Canadians thought multiculturalism was a good thing for the country, while 30 percent regarded it as bad. See "Canadians Endorse."

makes Canada unique.[28] Clearly, the mosaic vision has won the heart of the nation as a whole.[29] Even as Canada undergoes an identity crisis, multiculturalism, despite the many problems connected with it, enjoys "broad and deep" popular support, having attained the status of "national aspiration" or the very "Canadian dream" itself.[30] Meanwhile, comparative studies of national policies and practices confirm this Canadian pride by celebrating ours as the "success story" of contemporary multiculturalism.[31]

Related in some way to Canadian multiculturalism are certain cherished values of which the evangelistic task needs to be mindful. By no means a comprehensive list, these may be cast into three categories. The first category refers to prerequisite values that are basic or foundational to multiculturalism. In particular, we list inclusivity, diversity, tolerance, and personal freedom (albeit within limits).[32] The second category includes implementation values that are needful for the effective application of multiculturalism. In particular, we list equality, civility,[33] peaceful co-existence, and acceptance or a non-judgmental attitude. Additionally, there is secular pluralism (which theoretically accommodates religion),[34] relativism, and individualism.[35] The third and last category relates to enhancement values that improve the quality or appeal of applied multiculturalism. In particular, we list the values of authenticity, compassion, and pro-minority sympathy.

The values in all three categories above have important implications for evangelism. But aside from the general Canadian support for multiculturalism, an overwhelming majority among the second generation with immigrant parents are also positive toward the policy (as well as toward religious diversity).[36] Given this, it appears the said values are not simply

---

28. Environics Institute for Survey Research, et al. "Canadian Public Opinion," 9.

29. See also Dasko, "Public Attitudes"; Adams, *Unlikely Utopia*, 19–21; "Canadians Endorse"; and Reitz, "Pro-Immigration Canada."

30. Adams, *Unlikely Utopia*, 39–42.

31. See Bloemraad, *Becoming*; Kesler and Bloemraad, "Does Immigration Erode"; and Kymlicka, *Multiculturalism*.

32. "The Canadian Charter of Rights and Freedoms guarantees the rights and freedoms set out in it subject only to such reasonable limits prescribed by law as can be demonstrably justified in a free and democratic society" ("Canadian Charter").

33. See Bibby, *Boomer Factor*, 132–50, and Bibby, *Bibby Report*, 26–34.

34. The *Canadian Charter of Rights and Freedoms* enumerates four "fundamental freedoms," namely: "(a) Freedom of conscience and religion; (b) freedom of thought, belief, opinion, and expression, including freedom of the press and other media of communication; (c) freedom of peaceful assembly; and (d) freedom of association."

35. See also Bibby, *Mosaic Madness*.

36. Beyer, "From Far and Wide," 36–37.

relevant to evangelism but also to dialogue with non-Christians, Christian social engagement, local church ministry, and church planting.

Secularization

The classic secularization thesis was born in the last half of the twentieth century. In 1966 British anthropologist Anthony Wallace boldly announced the coming and the inevitable demise of religion on account of the unstoppable growth and spread of science in the world.[37] In the same decade, the evolutionist and humanist Julian Huxley predicted with dogmatic confidence the sure death of religion by the year 2000.[38] This prophecy quickly gained currency, even as endorsement was claimed of past thinkers such as Comte, Marx, Nietzsche, Durkheim, and Freud.[39] That secularization has won the day became the assumption even of some theologians who proceeded to discard traditional Christianity, replacing it with rather minimalist formulations of the doctrinal essence of the Christian faith. What come to mind are names like John Robinson (bishop of Woolwich), Paul Van Buren, Harvey Cox, John Hick, and Don Cupitt.

While there is wide agreement today that religion has been progressively losing its traditional significance in some societies, most observers do not think it will suffer total extinction. Empirical evidence does exist to support this. Consider, for instance, the many Muslim societies in the Arab world and Southeast Asia, or Turkey, Latin America, South Korea, and rural China, or the case of "exceptional" America in contrast to Australia, Britain, Canada, and Western Europe.[40] Then, just before the turn of the century, the classic thesis suffered a big blow when one of its pioneer thinkers, Peter Berger, changed his mind on the subject.[41] In the same year, tenacious critic Rodney Stark effectively pronounced the very idea to be pure fiction.[42] But be it in the field of sociology or philosophy, proponents of secularization have by no means capitulated.[43] Looking into the future, research will likely

37. Wallace, *Religion*.

38. Elshtain, "Religion and Democracy," 5–6. See also Elshtain, "While Europe Slept."

39 Early formulations include Wilson, *Religion in Secular Society*; Berger, *Sacred Canopy*; and Luckmann, *Invisible Religion*. Critics were not long to respond. See, for instance, Martin, *Religious and Secular*, and Greeley, *Unsecular Man*.

40. See Turner, *Secularization*, and Casanova, "Religion."

41. Berger, "Desecularization," 1–18.

42. See Stark, "Secularization, R.I.P."

43. See Gauchet, *Disenchantment*; Bruce, *God Is Dead*; Bruce, *Secularization*; Norris and Inglehart, *Sacred and Secular*; and Steinvorth, *Secularization*.

intensify on such themes as the sacred-secular border, the definition of religion, the concept of secularization, and the idea of the post-secular.[44] At the same time, case studies will surely continue, whether geographical, sectarian, or comparative.

For our present task, we adopt a sociological definition of secularization.[45] That is, secularization is three things at once: decline in religious beliefs and practices, decline in public expressions of religion, and decline of religious authority in public spheres.[46] The last aspect is easily seen in the "barring" of religious arguments in academic or parliamentary debates;[47] this despite a majority 66 percent believing population (see Data 17 below). Not infrequently, a perspective defended on "secular" grounds is rejected outright simply because it was pre-judged as faith-based or religion-motivated—for instance, the debates on abortion, *LGBTQQIP2SA, and* intelligent-design in cosmology.[48]

Another aspect of secularization is the downturn in religious beliefs and practices. This has been partly discussed when we talked earlier about the Canadian exodus. For now, we simply note that the shrinking of religious identification was accompanied by increases in the number of the so-called *religious nones*. The two data sets below present percentages from the post-second World War, twentieth century and concrete figures from the first decade of this millennium respectively.

---

44. See Latre and Vanheeswijck, "Secularization," and Possamai, "Post-Secularism."

45. See Chaves, "Secularization," and Casanova, *Public Religions*.

46. This definition should allow us to bypass the polarization versus secularization debate over Canadian society. See Bibby, "Religious Polarization"; Eagle, "Changing "Patterns"; Bibby, "Continuing"; and Eagle, "Loosening Bond."

47. For example, in arguing for the traditional family of one husband and one wife, secular discourse allows for appealing to the psychological benefits upon the child but disallows an appeal to the authority of the Bible or other religious texts.

48. See Stith, "Excluding Religion."

Table 12. Religious Self-Identification (%), 1945–2000[49]

	Catholics & Protestants	No religious preference (None)
1945 May	89.4	3.3
1955 July	95.9	—
1965 Nov	92.9	—
1975 Nov	89.4	—
1985 Nov	85.8	10.8
1995 Nov	76.8	16.7
2000 Nov	69.1	20.1

Table 13. Religious Self-Identification, 2001, 2011[50]

Religion		2001	2011	Immigrants 2001–2011
1	Catholic/Protestant/Orthodox/Christian Other	22,851,825	22,228,945	966,300
	A Catholic	12,936,905	12,810,705	484,340
	B Protestant	8,654,850	7,265,775	212,285
	C Christian Orthodox	479,620	550,690	107,635
	D Christian Other	780,450	1,475,575	162,040
2	No religious affiliation (None)	4,900,090	7,850,605	445,130

Beyond the Christian traditions, we should also consider other religious commitments. For what we examine is secularization—not religion versus Christianity but rather belief versus unbelief. In this regard, the field data convincingly demonstrate the reality of decline in religious faith. Proportionalities within the general population from a longitudinal perspective look something like this:

---

49. Canadian Institute, "Gallup Canada 1945–2000."
50. Statistics Canada, "2001 Census"; "Canadian Households in 2011." Immigrants include those who landed in Canada up to May 9, 2011 only.

Table 14. Religious Self-Identification among Canadians (%), 1971–2011[51]

	1971 (%)	2011 (%)	1971–2011 % Point Increase
Catholic	47	39	Minus 8
Protestant	41	27	Minus 14
Other religion	4	11	Plus 7
Religiously unaffiliated	4	24	Plus 20

The last aspect of secularization that needs elaboration is the decline in public expressions of religion or the privatization of religion. A recent poll reveals that 58 percent of Canadians want religion "kept out of public life completely."[52] Popular manifestations of privatization (voluntary or forced) are easy to spot—the general hesitancy or fear of starting a conversation about religion or injecting it into an ongoing conversation, the effort to un-Christmas December 25 and the concomitant acquiescence of Christmas celebrants, and the banning of creationism from science instruction in public schools. More recently, the case of the Toronto atheist pastor Gretta Vosper of the United Church (UC) is most revealing. While the ecclesiastical interview panel assessed her unfit to be a UC minister, a minority of four out of twenty-three panelists dissented, arguing that Vosper's views are shared by her congregation so that her ministry is meeting some real needs.[53] Here, we see secularization contesting not only a public space out there (like the state or education) but also ecclesiastical territory, religion's very homeland—not an invasion by an outsider but a civil war.

The instances are many more. But for our limited space, may we discuss a case with deep symbolisms and broad social significance: the fortunes of our national anthem, *O Canada*. The original French lyrics by Adolphe-Basile Routhier (1880) mentioned God twice and Christ twice; but only in the "additional verses." Today, we use only the first stanza which contains no reference to God. As the Quiet Revolution in Quebec predates the National Anthem Act (1980), this absence of the Divine fit the temper of the times. Here we see clearly the impact of secularization.

Back in 1880, when French Canada was celebrating over what some regarded as their new national anthem, English Canada's *de facto* national anthems were two popular patriotic songs, *God Save the King* and *The Maple Leaf Forever*. As the latter has the line "God save our Queen," both songs

---

51. See the Pew Research Center report, "Canada's Changing Religious Landscape," especially about "other religion" for 1971.

52. See "What makes us Canadian?"

53. See Perkel, "United Church postpones hearing."

confess Christian theism. This is true as well of the English versions of *O Canada* by Richardson (1906), Buchan (1908), Weir (1908), and McCulloch (1909), where reference to God appeared consistently.[54] The Buchan version was quite popular in British Columbia, unabashedly mixing loyalty to colonial master with reliance upon Divine Providence:

> At Britain's side, whate'er betide
> Unflinchingly we'll stand.
> With hearts we sing,
> "God save the King."

Maybe this partly explains why the Weir translation eventually became the best-received English version. The latter was devoid of colonial mentality, reserving loyalty only to God. Its fourth and last verse goes:

> Ruler Supreme, Who hearest humble prayer,
> Hold our dominion within Thy loving care.
> Help us to find, O God, in Thee,
> A lasting, rich reward,
> As waiting for the Better Day,
> We ever stand on guard.

In 1967 the Senate and House of Commons special joint committee recommended the preservation of the original French lyrics as well as two amendments to Weir's English lyrics: namely, to read "From Far and wide" and "God keep our land." The first is geographical, hinting at Canada's heavy dependence upon immigrants. The second is religious, declaring Canada's pious dependence upon God. Both amendments were incorporated into the National Anthem Act. Thus, just as secularized Quebec was allowed a secular *O Canada*, so "religious" English Canada was given a theistic anthem. Meanwhile, recent efforts to remove God from the latter indicate another step toward greater secularization.

Implications for Evangelism

For this chapter, we define evangelism as proclamation evangelism, following the New Testament usage of *euangelizō* (the Greek verb form for proclaiming the good news) and its cognates. The *Lausanne Covenant* preserves this meaning in these words:

---

54. In 1906 Thomas B. Richardson's first English version was meant to be a translation of Routhier, but he in fact added the words, "Holy Cross" and "Almighty God." The translation of Mercy E. Powell McCulloch (1909) contained the phrase "Lord, God of Hosts." The 1908 translation of Robert Stanley Weir underwent some later revisions.

> The nature of evangelism. To evangelize is to spread the good news that Jesus Christ died for our sins and was raised from the dead according to the scriptures, and that as the reigning Lord he now offers the forgiveness of sins and the liberating gifts of the Spirit to all who repent and believe. Our Christian presence in the world is indispensable to evangelism, and so is that kind of dialogue whose purpose is to listen sensitively in order to understand. But evangelism itself is the proclamation of the historical, biblical Christ as Savior and Lord, with a view to persuading people to come to him personally and so be reconciled to God. In issuing the gospel invitation we have no liberty to conceal the cost of discipleship. Jesus still calls all who would follow him to deny themselves, take up their cross, and identify themselves with his new community. The results of evangelism include obedience to Christ, incorporation into his Church, and responsible service in the world.[55]

That we need to do plenty of evangelism is a truism. There are certainly much more important things to say about this subject but space denies us, so we limit ourselves to four implications for the task of evangelism.

1. With GXMs, we expect to do plenty of Incremental Evangelism

By this, we mean that the entire Gospel message is *explained* to an individual or a group a bit at a time over a protracted period of days, weeks, or even years. This is in contrast to the lump-sum presentation of big-tent or crusade evangelism commonly associated with Dwight Moody, Billy Sunday, John Sung, Andrew Gih, Billy Graham, Greg Tingson, Stephen Tong, Christopher Sun, and Luis Palau. Incremental Evangelism (IE) also stands in contrast to prefabricated, formulaic Gospel presentation methods that demands heavy memorization and standardized execution. Not to say that mass evangelism is entirely *passé*[56] nor that other evangelistic methods are not helpful—for both have many fruits to show. Rather, IE seeks to move away from crusade evangelism's preacher-centeredness and evangelism's formulaic method-centeredness in order to be other-centered. This is because contemporary Canadian realities make IE a most useful approach in one-to-one and small-group outreach.

---

55. Stott, *Lausanne Covenant*, 12. The original text also includes Scriptural references (1 Cor 15:3, 4; Acts 2:32–39; John 20:21; 1 Cor 1:23; 2 Cor 4:5; 5:11, 20; Luke 14:25–33; Mark 8:34; Acts 2:40, 47; Mark 10:43–45).

56. See Rice, "Crusade evangelism?"

Note that at the beginning of the previous paragraph, we highlighted the word *explained*. IE does not object to the presentation of the whole Gospel in one go. On the contrary, IE will gladly do so when appropriate. Rather, the emphasis is on the exposition of the elements of the Gospel—such as the Biblical notion of sin, the Divine-human relationship, and the person of Christ. IE favors a prolonged and progressive exposition for the sake of hearer comprehension and *digestion*. Certain characteristics of GXMs[57] make a lengthy staggered approach favorable if not imperative. As the first two generations grow up with remote control TV, one-click-away webpages, real-time audio-visual distance communication, quick-delivery online purchasing, now-you-hear-me-now-you-don't social media chatting, twitter-size conversational exchanges, and clip-length YouTube videos, GXMs are conditioned to expect immediate responses and instant gratification. Though holding high expectations about their own future, they are often unwilling to pay the price of realization, prompting social analysts to describe them as lazy or lacking in self-discipline.

Translated into the context of evangelism, GXMs have a short attention span (though selectively applied) and want the answer to the question instantly, sometimes impatiently. IE means we need offer a twitter-size answer that provokes more questions. That is, we are paying by installments, thereby granting periodic instant gratifications while moving toward the full picture. IE is interactive, just like Candy Crush or LOL (League of Legends), unlike the TV newscaster or the evangelistic crusade preacher. IE is individualized, tailored for the specific person, just like dentures or contact lenses, and unlike *prêt-à-porter* (ready-to-wear) garments or formulaic evangelism. In the IE arsenal, the practitioner keeps a long answer with many shorter points as well as a short answer with a chain of more short answers. The first is handy for a lecture, YouTube video, or blog. The other is handy when a one-to-one or small-setting opportunity shows itself.

2. With GXMs, Incremental Evangelism should do sufficient (likely extensive) pre-evangelism

Our evangelistic field has changed substantially. Alongside the many church dropouts, there is the numerical rise of *other-religion* and *no-religion* groups. In 2011 these comprised nearly a third of the national population (10.5 million out of 34.34 million). For both groups, the main feeder is immigration.

---

57. The literature on Generation X is massive and that on Millennials is growing. For the latter, see two titles for introductory purposes, one on Canada and one on America: Bibby et al., *Emerging Millennials,* and Scardamalia, *Millennials in America.*

Table 15. Other-Religions and No-Religions, 1991–2011[58]

		2001		2011			
	1991	2001	Up by	2011	Up by	Immi-grants 2001–2011	Non-PR
Muslim	253,260	579,640	129%	1,053,945	82%	387,590	39,110
Jewish	318,070	329,995	4%	329,500	-0.2%	21,445	3,725
Buddhist	163,415	300,345	84%	366,830	22%	62,335	9,290
Hindu	157,010	297,200	89%	497,960	68%	153,800	16,105
Sikh	147,440	278,410	89%	454,965	63%	107,000	7,685
No relgn	3,386,365	4,900,090	48%	7,850,605	60%	445,130	99,285

Immigration increases Canadian diversity not just statically but also dynamically. That is, an immigrant who once identified with a particular religion (or with no religion) may no longer do so after residing in Canada for some time.[59] Immigrants always experience both continuity and change. The latter element is the dynamism in the settlement process. An interesting instance of diversity and contrast is worth mentioning here. A common North-American phenomenon is young people losing their Christian faith on going to university. In contrast, there is the oft-seen happenstance of China-born young people becoming more receptive to religion or even adopting the Christian faith during their university years, whether in China or the West.[60] Yet Mainland universities are by no means less secular than their Western counterparts.

Given different states of readiness among its audience, IE strives to be sensitive to the individual's peculiarities, the larger culture, and personal distance from the Gospel. Regarding the last, where the distance is great or

58. Statistics Canada, "1991 Census"; "National Household Survey Profile 2011." "Up by" is in reference to percentage from ten years ago. Immigrants 2001–2011 are those who landed from 2001 to May 9, 2011. "Non-PR" means "Non-permanent residents."

59. See Beyer, "From Far and Wide," 26–37.

60. See Wang and Uecker, "Education," and Nyíri, "Moving Targets."

considerable, a full IE run is needed. In cases where the "harvest is ripe," a full run is obviously no longer required. Personal distance from the Gospel is by no means permanently fixed; it changes in time. IE is sensitive to whether the person is moving toward or away from Christianity, adjusting accordingly. As people do move in either direction, there is a place for hard-sell as well as soft-sell evangelism. Likewise, there is a place for both the missional and the attractional models of doing church.[61]

Consider the no-religion group within the Canadian population. Presumably, these include the "religiously-indifferents" and "religion-rejecters"—or loosely, the neutrals and the hostiles. Theoretically, all other things being equal, the hostile requires a longer and slower IE than the neutral. Presumably pre-existing anti-Christianism gives evangelism a negative starting line. This general, common-sense postulate is confirmed by field experience and actual feedback from ex-atheists born in China in 1930–40 who now reside in Canada. Raised in militant atheism—directly, via indoctrination in school, and indirectly, via conditioning in society—they became life-committed anti-religionists. As the evangelist explains, Divine love and the only-begotten Son of John 3:16, the atheist-hearer is stuck at the second word of the verse, "For *God* so loved the world" (emphasis added). Postponing the proclamation of Christ the Savior in order to first deal with the question of God's existence is doing pre-evangelism. On average, it takes such an individual five to six years to move over to the Christian faith.

In the case of native Canadians who self-identify as "no-religion" people, we face the additional element of inoculation—a common side effect of extended living in an environment with extensive Christian presences or influences. Despite the declining social significance of the churches in our society, their visible ubiquity develops in many Canadians a felt familiarity that is not always congruent with reality. People assume they know what Christianity is so that they also know what they are rejecting or what they are being neutral about. This inoculation complicates things for evangelism, for such a person may pre-empt Gospel presentation by claiming fore knowledge and fore-decision; that is, I know what it is and I have already decided about it. But whether inoculation breeds either hostility or neutrality, it adds to the length of the evangelistic task and thus favors IE.

The matter becomes the more pressing when we consider inoculated dropouts among GXMs in the Roman Catholic, Mainline, and Evangelical churches. Line 4 below shows we are dealing with a challenging number of prospects for re-evangelization.

---

61. For a quick and useful introduction, see Hastings, *Missional God*. Another insightful piece is Nikolajsen, "Beyond Sectarianism." For a Canadian pastoral perspective, see Elkington, "Missional Church."

Table 16. Religious Affiliation in Childhood and Young Adulthood (%)[62]

Childhood	Catholic Quebec	Catholic Rest of Canada	Mainline	Evangelical
Young adulthood (2010)				
1 None	12	17	18	13
2 Agnostic	7	11	13	6
3 Atheist	21	14	15	7
4 (1)+(2)+(3)	40	42	46	26
5 Remained	51	45	34	63

What we face, then, is an immense audience-diversity. This Canadian reality presents equally diverse options for evangelism and pre-evangelism. Take, for instance, apologetics and dialogue as intellectual pre-evangelism. Classical evidentialism fits quicker for those whose tradition of rationality is from the natural sciences. For those who inhabit the arts or literature, the easier fit may be some form of post-liberal or fideistic-presuppositional approach. For the person outside the "ivory tower," combinationalism with its methodological fluidity may be more fitting.[63] In applying multiple apologetic approaches, we do not capitulate to pragmatism. Rather, we are but addressing the subjectivities (or specific faith-obstacles) of a conversation partner. The physician does likewise, prescribing drug X to one patient on Wednesday and drug Y to another patient on Friday, but never, on any day, denying the validity of the un-prescribed drug.

3. Incremental Evangelism requires multiple frontliners

For its individualized and interactive qualities, IE requires a plurality of frontline Gospel presenters. For now, we nominate two reasons among others. One, every person has limited capacity for sustained relationships. Pre-evangelism is not only dealing with intellectual obstacles to faith; it is also building personal trust and friendship over time. But every person has a load limit for relationship maintenance.[64] Even the ablest evangelists and

---

62. Penner et al., *Hemorrhaging Faith*, 25. "Remained" means that the subject retained their childhood affiliation.

63. For an interesting perspective, see Lacoste, "On Knowing."

64. Posterski rides a similar wave when he says the youth worker's "influence is

pastors have a cap on their emotional capital. So if we are to do more, we need to be more in number. This means upping the work of recruitment, training, and mobilization.

Here is a true account to cheer us. In April 2018, at a certain local church in the City Richmond (in Metro Vancouver), its Children Ministry trained a second batch of children to be one-to-one evangelists. Two years ago, the first batch graduated from the nine-month training course, consisting of fourteen children (ages 9–12), fourteen youth (ages 13–15), and two mothers. During the church's Vacation Bible School in the summers of 2016 and 2017, twenty-one children were mobilized to share the Gospel with other children one-to-one. The present batch under training includes six children of ages 10–12. They were not taught to do IE, but their training in formulaic evangelism can be easily converted later into IE application.

The second reason for having multiple front-liners is the diversity of prospects. While having many front-liners is desirable, even more productive is pairing each with the "good-fit" person. To highlight one aspect of a good fit, we may consider how people make decisions. Some do it with the mind, some with the heart. Some operate logically, some relationally. To illustrate relational decision-making, consider A and R, husband and wife, who are new Canadians. R became a Christian because A, the husband, did first. For thirty years now, both have kept the faith with abundant signs of authenticity. In her childhood culture, that is how wives make decisions—they follow their husbands. In this case, evangelism proved fruitful for the couple because the husband came to faith in Christ first.

Now, recall that among immigrants who came in 2001–2011, more than 700,000 self-identified as Muslim, Buddhist, Hindu, or Sikh (Data 18). In 2016 immigrants comprised 21.9 percent of the national population. In short, Canadians are a great diversity, so one front-liner does not fit all groups. Good placement or pairing can yield enhanced results. Having a pool of diverse front-liners is strategic. Having a sea of them is even better.

4. Incremental Evangelism includes waging spiritual warfare

Aside from the intellectual and the relational, there is also the spiritual dimension, for "we do not wrestle against flesh and blood, but against the rulers, against the authorities, against the cosmic powers over this present darkness, against the spiritual forces of evil in the heavenly places" (Eph 6:12 ESV). The *Manila Manifesto* declares: "We affirm that spiritual warfare demands spiritual weapons, and that we must both preach the Word in the

---

limited to just a few young people" (Bibby and Posterski, *Teens Trends*, 257).

power of the Spirit, and pray constantly that we may enter into Christ's victory over the principalities and powers of evil."[65]

Evangelism does not happen apart from spiritual warfare. If the aim of telling people the Gospel is "so that they may turn from darkness to light and from the power of Satan to God" (Acts 26:18 ESV), maybe it is not unreasonable to assume that the invaded party will resist or counter-attack. Without apology, the Bible speaks of angels and demons. The Lord Christ was himself the target of demonic temptation after the days of fasting in the wilderness. In his earthly ministry, he spoke to evil spirits and cast them out of human bodies (Matt 8:28–34). The Bible unambiguously states that "the god of this world has blinded the minds of the unbelievers, to keep them from seeing the light of the gospel of the glory of Christ" (2 Cor 4:4 ESV). It is true what the Lord Himself said: "The thief comes only to steal and kill and destroy. I came that they may have life and have it abundantly" (John 10:10 ESV).

Evangelism should not be undertaken without dealing with the dimension of spiritual warfare. We can prepare and over-prepare for evangelistic work. We can invest and over-invest in both human and material resources. But our over-preparation and over-investment cannot win the war if they deal only with the enemy's army and navy while ignoring his air force. Martially, one meets the opponent in all dimensions. If the other side adds propaganda-war to its repertoire, one adds it too. If they add cyber-war, one adds the same. The point is evangelism must deal with the spiritual dimension of the human, the demonic, and the Divine (Holy Spirit).

We are in the midst of a spiritual war with no possibility of neutrality,[66] escape, ceasefire, or peaceful resolution. We stand (already) with one side and must fight the other—which is not in flesh and blood but oftentimes in utilizing instruments of flesh and blood. Evangelism regards these instruments as potential subjects of Special Grace and their invisible utilizers as true foes. We Canadian Christians must learn to fight the latter or re-learn how to fight. Our national obsession with being nice, being liked, and being popular with the many has made us forget how to fight an unappeasable, non-human enemy in this permanent conflict.

On a Sunday morning many years ago, for a sermon illustration, I talked about the experience of some war veterans. When asked the number one thing motivating a soldier to fight his hardest without care for their very life itself, their answer was not what I was expecting—like love for country, our children, freedom, or democracy; rather, it was this: *They just shot my*

---

65. Lausanne Committee for World Evangelization, *Manila Manifesto*, 5–6.
66. See Schaeffer, *Time*.

friend! A warrior who is trained well is a horrible opponent to face. A warrior who is trained well and angry is worse. A warrior who is trained well, angry, and still disciplined is the worst. If we are to do evangelism, we must wage spiritual warfare and learn to engage the mind, emotion, and spirit. If habituated civility has made us forget how to exercise righteous anger, then tell yourself: *They just shot my friend, who is now bleeding to death.*

Closing Remarks

In many ways, the GXMs are a unique bunch, yet they resemble all other generations in one respect: they need Christ. Because of this, our task has not changed. We must proclaim Christ. The challenge before us is difficult, but the Lord is with his people. And what's more, he has not forsaken Canada. For our Constitution (1982) opens with these words: "Whereas Canada is founded upon principles that recognize the supremacy of God." O, how our souls are lifted up, knowing that in Canada's foundational document, right at its opening line, the Lord "did not leave Himself without witness" (Acts 14:17 ESV).

Bibliography

Adams, Michael, and Amy Langstaff. *Unlikely Utopia: The Surprising Triumph of Canadian Pluralism*. Toronto: Viking, 2007.
Banting, Keith, and Will Kymlicka. "Is There Really a Retreat from Multiculturalism Policies? New Evidence from the Multiculturalism Policy Index." *Comparative European Politics* 11.5 (2013) 577–98.
Beaman, Lori, and Peter Beyer, eds. *Religion and Diversity in Canada*. Leiden: Brill, 2008.
Berger, Peter. "The Desecularization of the World: A Global Overview." In *The Desecularization of the World: Resurgent Religion and World Politics*, edited by G. Weigel, et. al, 1–18. Grand Rapids: Eerdmans, 1999.
———. *The Sacred Canopy: Elements of a Sociological Theory of Religion*. Garden City, NY: Doubleday, 1967.
Beyer, Peter. "From Far and Wide: Canadian Religious and Cultural Diversity in Global/Local Context." In *Religion and Diversity in Canada*, edited by Lori Beaman and Peter Beyer, 9–39. Leiden: Brill, 2008.
Bibby, Reginald W. *The Bibby Report: Social Trends Canadian Style*. Toronto: Stoddart, 1995.
———. *The Boomer Factor: What Canada's Most Famous Generation Is Leaving Behind*. Lethbridge, AB: Project Canada, 2006.
———. "Continuing the Conversation on Canada: Changing Patterns of Religious Service Attendance." *Journal for the Scientific Study of Religion* 50.4 (2011) 831–37.

———. *The Latest Emerging Generation: An Updated Look at Canadian Youth* (forthcoming).

———. *Mosaic Madness: Pluralism without a Cause.* Toronto: Stoddart, 1990.

———. "Religious Polarization in Canada: A Major Empirical Update." Paper presented at the annual meeting of the Society for the Scientific Study of Religion, Newport Beach, CA, October 2015.

———. *Restless Gods: The Renaissance of Religion in Canada.* Toronto: Stoddart, 2002.

———, and D. C. Posterski. *Teens Trends: A Nation in Motion.* Toronto: Stoddart, 1992.

———, and James Penner. *10 things We All Need to Know about Today's Teens, That Is, If We Aare about Them.* Lethbridge, AB: Project Canada, 2010.

———, Sarah Russel, and Ron Rolheiser. *The Emerging Millennials: How Canada's Newest Generation Is Responding to Change and Choice.* Lethbridge, AB: Project Canada, 2011.

Bissoondath, Neil. *Selling Illusions: The Cult of Multiculturalism in Canada.* Rev. ed. Toronto: Penguin, 2002.

Bloechl, Jeffrey, ed. *Christianity and Secular Reason: Classical Themes and Modern Developments.* Notre Dame: University of Notre Dame Press, 2012.

Bloemraad, Irene. *Becoming a Citizen: Incorporating Immigrants and Refugees in the United States and Canada.* Berkeley: University of California Press, 2006.

———, and Matthew Wright. "'Utter failure' or Unity out of Diversity? Debating and Evaluating Policies of Multiculturalism." *International Migration Review* 48.1 (2014) 292–334.

Bricker, Darrell. "Canadian Immigration and Ethnicity—Where Do Voters Stand?" *Ipsos,* January 10, 2006. https://www.ipsos.com/en-ca/canadian-immigration-and-ethnicity-where-do-voters-stand.

Bruce, Steve. *God Is Dead: Secularization in the West.* Oxford: Blackwell, 2002.

———. *Secularization: In Defence of an Unfashionable Theory.* Oxford: Oxford University Press, 2011.

Brynes, Timothy A., and Peter J. Katzenstein, eds. *Religion in an Expanding Europe.* Cambridge: Cambridge University Press, 2006.

"Canadian Charter of Rights and Freedoms." 1982. https://www.canada.ca/en/canadian-heritage/services/how-rights-protected/guide-canadian-charter-rights-freedoms.html.

Canadian Institute of Public Opinion. "Gallup Canada Polls 1945–2000." Carleton University Data Services. https://library.carleton.ca/find/data/gallup-canada.

"Canadians Endorse Multiculturalism, But Pick Melting Pot Over Mosaic." *Angus Reid Institute,* November 8, 2010. http://angusreid.org/canadians-endorse-multiculturalism-but-pick-melting-pot-over-mosaic.

Casanova, José. *Public Religions in the Modern World.* Chicago: University of Chicago Press, 2012.

———. "Religion, European Secular Identities, and European Integration." *Transit: Europäische Revue* 27 (2004) 65–92.

———. "Religion, European Secular Identities, and European Integration." In *Religion in an Expanding Europe,* edited by Timothy A. Brynes and Peter J. Katzenstein, 65–92. Cambridge: Cambridge University Press, 2006.

Chaves, Mark. "Secularization as Declining Religious Authority." *Social Forces* 72.3 (1994) 749–74.

Clark, Warren, and Grant Schellenberg, "Who's religious?" *Canadian Social Trends* 81 (2006) 2–9.
Clarke, Brian P., and Stuart Macdonald. *Leaving Christianity: Changing Allegiances in Canada Since 1945*. Montreal, QC: McGill/Queen's University Press, 2017.
Colby, Sandra L., and Jennifer M. Ortman. *The Baby Boom Cohort in the United States: 2012–2060*. Washington, DC: US Census Bureau, 2014.
Dasko, Donna. "Public Attitudes towards Multiculturalism and Bilingualism in Canada." In *Canadian and French Perspectives on Diversity*, edited by Margaret Adsett, et al., 119–25. Ottawa: Canadian Heritage, 2005.
———. "Public Attitudes towards Multiculturalism in Canada." *Canadian Issues* (2004) 30–32.
Dewing, Michael. "Canadian Multiculturalism." E. Ottawa: Library of Parliament, 2009.
Eagle, David E. "Changing Patterns of Attendance at Religious Services in Canada, 1986–2008." *Journal for the Scientific Study of Religion* 50.1 (2011) 187–200.
———. "The Loosening Bond of Religion on Canadian Society: Reply to Bibby." *Journal for the Scientific Study of Religion* 50.4 (2011) 838–39.
Elkington, Robert Lionel. "A Missional Church Model." *SAGE Open* (2011) 1–11.
Elshtain, Jean Bethke. "Religion and Democracy." *Journal of Democracy* 20.2 (2009) 5–17.
———. "While Europe Slept." *First Things* 191 (2009). https://www.firstthings.com/article/2009/03/while-europe-slept.
Environics Institute for Survey Research, et al. "Canadian Public Opinion on Aboriginal Peoples." June 2016. https://tidescanada.org/wp-content/uploads/2016/06/Canadian-Public-Opinion-on-Aboriginal-Peoples-2016-FINAL-REPORT.pdf.
"The Failure of Multiculturalism." *National Post*, August 25, 2006. A12.
Fleras, Augie, and Jean Leonard Elliott. *Engaging Diversity: Multiculturalism in Canada*. Toronto: Nelson Thomson Learning, 2002.
Gauchet, Marcel. *The Disenchantment of the World: A Political History of Religion*. Translated by Oscar Burge. Princeton, NJ: Princeton University Press, 1997.
Granatstein, Jack L. *Who killed Canadian History?* New York: HarperCollins, 1998. Rev. ed., 2007.
Greeley, Andrew. *Unsecular Man: The Persistence of Religion*. New York: Schocken, 1972.
Guo, Shibao, and Lloyd Wong. "Revisiting Multiculturalism in Canada: An Introduction." In *Revisiting Multiculturalism in Canada: Theories, Policies, and Debates*, edited by Shibao Guo and Lloyd Wong, 1–14. Rotterdam: Sense, 2015.
Gwyn, Richard. *Nationalism Without Walls: The Unbearable Lightness of Being Canadian*. Toronto: McClelland & Stewart, 1995. New updated ed., 1996.
Hastings, Ross. *Missional God, Missional Church: Hope for Re-Evangelizing the West*. Downers Grove, IL: InterVarsity, 2012.
Howe, Neil, and William Strauss. *Millennials Rising: The Next Great Generation*. New York: Vintage, 2000.
Kay, Jonathan. "Multiculturalism, R.I.P. (1982–2007)." *National Post*, April 24, 2007. A16.
Kesler, Christel, and Irene Bloemraad. "Does Immigration Erode Social Capital? The Conditional Effects of Immigration-Generated Diversity on Trust, Membership, and Participation across 19 Countries, 1981–2000." *Canadian Journal of Political Science/Revue Canadienne de Science Politique* 43.2 (2010) 319–47.

Kymlicka, Will. "Canadian Multiculturalism in Historical and Comparative Perspective: Is Canada Unique?" *Constitutional Forum* 13.1 (2003) 1–8.

———. *Multiculturalism: Success, Failure, and the Future*. Washington, DC: Migration Policy Institute, February 2012.

Lacoste, Jean-Yves. "On Knowing God through Loving Him: Beyond 'Faith and Reason.'" In *Christianity and Secular Reason: Classical Themes and Modern Developments*, edited by Jeffrey Bloechl, 127–51. Notre Dame: University of Notre Dame Press, 2012.

Latre, Stijn, and Guido Vanheeswijck. "Secularization: History of the Concept." In *International Encyclopedia of the Social & Behavioral Sciences*, edited by James Wright, 21:388–94. 2nd ed. Amsterdam: Elsevier, 2015.

Lausanne Committee for World Evangelization. *Manila Manifesto*. Pasadena, CA: Lausanne Committee for World Evangelization, 1989.

Leung, Ho Hon. "Canadian Multiculturalism in the 21st Century: Emerging Challenges and Debates." In *Revisiting Multiculturalism in Canada: Theories, Policies, and Debates*, edited by Shibao Guo and Lloyd Wong, 107–19. Rotterdam: Sense, 2015.

Luckmann, Thomas. *Invisible Religion: The Problem of Religion in Modern Society*. New York: Macmillan, 1967.

Martin, David. *The Religious and the Secular: Studies in Secularization*. New York: Schocken, 1969.

Nikolajsen, Jeppe Bach. "Beyond Sectarianism: The Missional Church in a Post-Christendom Society." *Missiology: An International Review* 41.4 (2013) 462–75.

Norris, Pippa, and Ronald Inglehart. *Sacred and Secular: Religion and Politics Worldwide*. 2nd ed. Cambridge: Cambridge University Press, 2011.

Nyíri, Pál. "Moving Targets: Chinese Christian Proselytising among Transnational Migrants from the People's Republic of China." *European Journal of East Asian Studies* 2.2 (2003) 263–301.

Overholt, L. David, and James Penner. *Soul Searching the Millennials: A Guide for Youth Workers*. Toronto: Stoddart, 2002.

———. *Soul Searching the Millennial Generation: Strategies for Youth workers*. Rev. ed. Toronto: Novalis, 2005.

Penner, James, et al. *Hemorrhaging Faith: Why and When Canadian Young Adults Are Leaving, Staying, and Returning to Church*. Richmond Hill, ON: Evangelical Fellowship of Canada, 2012.

Perkel, Colin. "United Church postpones hearing for atheist minister indefinitely." *The Star*, November 14, 2017. https://www.thestar.com/news/gta/2017/11/14/united-church-indefinitely-postpones-hearing-for-atheist-minister.html.

Pew Research Center. "Canada's Changing Religious Landscape." *Religion & Public Life*, June 27, 2013. http://www.pewforum.org/2013/06/27/canadas-changing-religious-landscape.

Possamai, Adam. "Post-Secularism in Multiple Modernities." *Journal of Sociology* 53.4 (2017) 822–35.

Pyöriä, Pasi, et al. "The Millennial Generation: A New Breed of Labour?" *SAGE Open* 7.1 (2017) 1–14.

Rattansi, Ali. *Multiculturalism: A Very Short Introduction*. Oxford: Oxford University Press, 2011.

Reitz, Jeffrey G. "Pro-Immigration Canada: Social and Economic Roots of Popular Views." *IRPP Study* 20 (2011) 1–24.

Rice, Lisa. "Crusade Evangelism? Still Works for Rick Gage." *SBC life: Journal of the Southern Baptist Convention* 15.5 (2007). http://www.sbclife.net/article/1491/crusade-evangelism.

Ryan, Phil. *Multicultiphobia*. Toronto: University of Toronto Press, 2010.

Sawler, David. *Before They Say Goodbye: Thoughts on How to Keep this Generation*. Winnipeg: Word Alive, 2011.

———. *Goodbye Generation: A Conversation about Why Youth and Young Adults Leave the Church*. Winnipeg: Word Alive, 2008.

Scardamalia, Robert L. *Millennials in America*. Lanham, MD: Bernan, 2015.

———. *Millennials in America*. 2nd ed. Lanham, MD: Bernan, 2017.

Schaeffer, Franky. *A Time for Anger: The Myth of Neutrality*. Westchester, IL: Crossway, 1984.

Soroka, Stuart, and Sarah Roberton. "A Literature Review of Public Opinion Research on Canadian Attitudes towards Multiculturalism and Immigration, 2006–2009." Citizenship and Immigration Canada, March 2010. https://www.canada.ca/en/immigration-refugees-citizenship/corporate/reports-statistics/research/literature-review-public-opinion-research-on-canadian-attitudes-towards-multiculturalism-immigration-2006-2009/section-2-1.html.

Stark, Rodney. "Secularization, R.I.P." *Sociology of Religion* 60.3 (1999) 249–73.

Statistics Canada. "1991 Census of Canada." https://www12.statcan.gc.ca/English/census91/data/profiles/Profiles.cfm.

———. "2001 Census of Canada." https://www12.statcan.gc.ca/english/census01/home/index.cfm.

———. "Canadian Households in 2011: Type and Growth." https://www12.statcan.gc.ca/census-recensement/2011/as-sa/98-312-x/98-312-x2011003_2-eng.cfm.

———. "The Canadian Population in 2011: Population Counts and Growth." https://www12.statcan.gc.ca/census-recensement/2011/as-sa/98-310-x/98-310-x2011001-eng.cfm.

———. "The General Social Survey: An Overview." https://www150.statcan.gc.ca/n1/en/catalogue/89F0115X.

———. "National Household Survey Profile 2011." https://www12.statcan.gc.ca/nhs-enm/2011/dp-pd/prof/index.cfm.

Steinvorth, Ulrich. *Secularization: An Essay in Normative Metaphysics*. Cham, Switzerland: Springer Nature, 2017.

Stith, Richard. "Excluding Religion Excludes More than Religion." Paper presented at the international seminar Matters of Life and Death: Religion and Law at the Crossroad, Boston College Law School, 2008. https://ssrn.com/abstract=1477003.

Stott, John R. W. *The Lausanne Covenant: An Exposition and Commentary*. Wheaton, IL: Laussane Committee for World Evangelization, 1974.

Strauss, William, and Neil Howe. *Generations: The History of America's Future, 1584 to 2069*. New York: William Morrow, 1991.

Turner, Bryan S., ed. *Secularization*. 4 vols. London: Sage, 2010.

Wallace, Anthony F. *Religion: An Anthropological View*. New York: Random House, 1966.

Wang, Xiuhua, and Jeremy E. Uecker. "Education, Religious Commitment, and Religious Tolerance in Contemporary China." *Review of Religious Research* 59 (2017) 157–82.

Weigel, G., et al., eds. *The Desecularization of the World: Resurgent Religion and World Politics*. Grand Rapids: Eerdmans, 1999.

"What Makes Us Canadian? A Study of Values, Beliefs, Priorities and Identity." *Angus Reid Institute*, October 3, 2016. http://angusreid.org/canada-values.

Wilson, Bryan. *Religion in Secular Society: A Sociological Comment*. London: C. A. Watts, 1966.

———. *Religion in Secular Society: Fifty Years On*. Edited with commentary by Steve Bruce. Oxford: Oxford University Press, 2016.

Wong, Lloyd. "Multiculturalism and Ethnic Pluralism in Sociology: An Analysis of the Fragmentation Position Siscourse." In *Revisiting Multiculturalism in Canada: Theories, Policies, and Debates*, edited by Shibao Guo and Lloyd Wong, 69–90. Rotterdam: Sense, 2015.

Wright, James, ed. *International Encyclopedia of the Social & Behavioral Sciences*. 2nd ed. 26 vols. Amsterdam: Elsevier, 2015.

6

Millennial Islam and Secularization
Witness Among the Next Generation of Muslims
(Some Preliminary Thoughts)

MATTHEW FRIEDMAN

As THE PLANE TAXIED down the runway and took off for New York, I began conversing with my seatmate, a well-dressed man who appeared to be in his late twenties or early thirties and of South Asian descent. He introduced himself, and over the course of the conversation, he mentioned that he was part of a community that adhered to a well-known but smaller branch of Shia Islam. As the conversation turned toward matters of faith and life, I found myself reaching into my own knowledge of the beliefs of this particular sect of Islam and Islamic mysticism along with the bridges found therein.

The conversation, however, took an unexpected turn: my new friend began describing his own readings from Richard Dawkins and how he has begun questioning whether or not there was a deity at all. I was quite taken aback by this development, not least because I particularly was not expecting this from a *Muslim*. As I mentally began integrating apologetic elements I had learned from Alvin Plantinga's writings, I started to realize that this gentleman was not only a Muslim of South Asian ancestry but *also* an urban North American wrestling with many of the same issues faced by others in his age group and professional status.

I was reminded of an earlier time when I was working among Bengali-speaking Muslim people in South Asia. Prior to my arrival, I had learned a fair amount of material concerning the basics of Muslim beliefs and practices, and even, to a good degree, about folk religion in Muslim contexts. What I discovered then, as I got deeper into the society in which I found myself, was that while Bengali-speaking Muslims were *Muslims*, they were also *Bengalis*, who shared concerns and cultural attributes with the millions of non-Muslim Bengalis. I began to realize that I needed to reapply this understanding in the newer context of Islamic North America.

I am also reminded of another encounter while visiting the Friday *jumua* service at a mosque outside of Minneapolis. I had taken students from my World Religions class for a "tour" of various religious establishments. This was the week prior to election day in 2012, when Minnesota became the first state in the US to approve marriage between people of the same gender by popular vote. There was much to observe and enjoy, along with some expected light debating. What struck me, however, was the manner in which the Friday *khutba* (sermon) bore similarities to what would be preached the following Sunday in many churches across the state: that as society becomes more corrupted, it is important that the youth in our community be given solid grounding in the faith. This spoke to me of parallel concerns in Muslim and Evangelical communities for the upcoming generation and of the influences of secularization in society.

In this chapter we will present some of the broad contours of what secularization has looked like in Muslim populations, especially among younger Muslim millennial generation youth. Following this, I will propose a medieval missional strategy that may be worth exploring in witness given such a North America context.

Secularization Among Muslims in North America

Some of the personal anecdotes that I presented above have echoes in the recent press as well as in discussions taking place among Muslims in the West. These discussions echo those found in previous generations among immigrant communities—questions about assimilation, negotiation between North American and traditional cultural norms, and representation in society. Some of these discussions involve those who wish to be faithful to their understanding of the Muslim tradition, while others reflect those who quietly choose to adopt a more hybrid-like "progressive" version of their faith, or to jettison it altogether.

There are a few well-known public figures who have discarded Islam altogether, such as Ayan Hirsi Ali and the pseudonymous author Ibn Warraq. The novelist Salman Rushdie is ardently antireligious, but he speaks wistfully of memories of a deeply religious, tolerant, and inquiring grandfather while growing up in Indian Kashmir.[1] More recently, the Pakistani-American comedian Kunail Nanjiani's semi-autobiographical film *The Big Sick* explores some of the borders of growing up Muslim in North America

1. See Hari, "Salman Rushdie."

and of rejecting the faith, even while retaining many cultural elements.[2] There is also a stream of edgier, sometimes punk and pop-culture-oriented Muslims of the sort represented by Michael Muhammad Knight's writings, such as his Muslim punk novel *The Taqwacores,* and his travelogues *Blue-Eyed Devil* and *Journey to the End of Islam.*

A recent essay on Muslim assimilation noted that "US Muslims—roughly 60 percent of whom are under 40—are going through a process that's quintessentially American: finding new, diverse, self-constructed identities in their faith, ranging from fully secular to deeply pious."[3] The article quotes Duke Divinity School imam Abdullah Antepli, who notes that while the parents of undergraduates hope their millennial children would focus at some level on the religious side of their identity, they desire for them to also focus on figuring out the balance between their American and Muslim identities. Religious practice has taken a back seat, with less than half of millennial Muslims in the US attending prayers at a mosque on a weekly basis. A young lady in her late twenties is quoted as describing her own practice this way: she cares a lot about certain Muslim traditions, like fasting on Ramadan, but she's not that observant during the rest of the year.[4] Another young Muslim of similar age is quoted as saying, "Too often, the connotation of 'religious' is someone who is very strict and focused on acts. I would say I'm very spiritual and I have a very strong faith."[5] Once again, one can note the parallels between these younger Muslims and many people of the same generation from other backgrounds in North America.

Another figure who has become more influential and visible within and outside the Muslim community in North America is Eboo Patel. A Chicago-based advocate for interfaith cooperation, Patel has written engagingly about the possibilities for such dialogue from the perspective of an educated and Westernized Muslim, and he has advocated for a Muslim community that is integrated into and accepted by American society.[6]

Some of these observations from especially younger Muslims who were raised in North America bring to my mind the insights of University of Notre Dame sociologist Christian Smith. In examining the spiritual lives and thoughts of American youth of various religious affiliations, Smith observed a surprising degree of homogeneity in terms of the manner in which many expressed their beliefs and coined the term "Moralistic Therapeutic

2. See Marantz, "Culture-Clash Comedy."
3. Green, "Transforming Islam."
4. Green, "Transforming Islam."
5. Green, "Transforming Islam."
6. See Patel, *Sacred Ground.*

Deism" (MTD) for the fairly shallow expressions of faith that he found there. He suggested that MTD was actually "colonizing" other religious communities, taking over from the "official" belief systems therein, and found this dynamic at work in Protestant, Catholic, Eastern Orthodox, and Jewish youth.[7] This seems to be at work in the Muslim community, too.

On a recent visit to a mosque in the American Midwest, I spoke briefly with Usman,[8] a Muslim man in his thirties who had a bit of a circuitous back story himself. He had been raised by a fairly strict Muslim father and a mother who was a convert to Islam. As he got older, he began to think of himself as a kind of "spiritual agnostic," marrying an equally nominal Christian woman. Later, however, he ended up returning to Islam and is now involved in outreach. His approach is fairly millennial-friendly, full of disclaimers, and quite engaging. He suggested that resources for understanding how the Muslim community in North America are seeking to better engage North American secularization might be found in two communities that have an online presence; namely, (1) the Ta'leef Collective, founded by Usama Canon and (2) the Yaqeen Institute, founded and led by Omar Suleiman.

I will focus on the second resource since it has a number of posted essays written to address issues of concern for modern Muslim youth—specifically one piece that has a two-part debate concerning the response that North American Muslim communities should have to the growing phenomenon of LGBT+ issues. These issues have become quite visible in the Muslim communities, and, as noted above from my earlier visit in Minneapolis, they are an issue of concern to the Muslim community as a whole.

In an essay entitled "LGBTQ and Islam Revisited: Days of the Donald," Jonathan Brown and Shadee Elmasry debate on what the best *political* response is by the Muslim community regarding the issue of LGBT+ rights, including same-sex marriage. Brown's essay lays out the possible positions available to Muslims in North America, being emphatic that his treatment of this topic is specific to North America. Brown makes a point of differentiating between same-sex attraction and the sexual actualization of these desires in a manner similar to those observed among North American Evangelicals.

Brown lists a spectrum of choices,[9] including "Unquestioned Embrace," "Rejection," "Neutralism," and finally what he calls, "Rights Affirmation/Common Cause/Islamic Orthodoxy (RACCIO)." He advocates for

---

7. See Smith, *Soul Searching*.
8. This name is a pseudonym.
9. Brown and Elmasry, "LGBTQ and Islam Revisited."

the latter, suggesting a kind of *quid pro quo*—since the LGBT+ community has often been perceived to stand with the Muslim community when under pressure in North America (e.g., from anti-immigration rhetoric), this should be reciprocated by the Muslim community. He highlights the Christian community as a kind of "common opponent." Nonetheless, he does not endorse same-sex marriage or the acts themselves but only sees them as a matter of political expediency.

However, Elmasry does not agree that this is acceptable. While he insists that irenic outreach is both possible and advisable, making common cause with the LGBT+ community on issues of legislation cannot be seen as legitimate. Again, the broad contours of this discussion could easily have taken place among Evangelicals, too.

Clearly, we have a good deal in common in terms of concerns. In the midst of these, it is worth asking how might we address our Muslim friends of various stripes in a manner that might be engaging, irenic, and might, using the words of the late Lebanese pastor Fouad Accad, enable us to "build bridges of relationship which can bear the weight of truth."[10] In view of this, I will now turn to one possible model for potentially building such bridges.

An Ancient Approach Worth Exploring: The Irenic Rational-Mystical Witness of Ramon Llull

A figure who makes an appearance in medieval church and mission history is the Spanish mystic and evangelist Ramon Llull (1232–1316). Llull is sometimes given the questionable title of "first missionary to the Muslims."[11] Though he was preceded by many, especially by Middle Eastern Christians, his strategy was influential in his day, and it is worth examining in the context of a more pluralistically-oriented, millennial Muslim people in North America today.

Llull's approach sought to combine the mystical with the rational, seeking to touch the hearts as well as the minds of those with whom he was interacting.[12] His *Art* has been described as originally a semi-mechanical system of determining logical answers to questions of faith. He developed several versions of the *Art*'s original form and presented his principles in

---

10. Standish, "Women," 456. See also Accad, *Building Bridges*.

11. The term "questionable" is used because there were a number of non-Western (and even some Western) missionaries who sought to bring the Gospel to the followers of Islam.

12. Hames, *Art of Conversion*, 12.

narrative form through the *Book of the Gentile and the Three Wise Men*[13] and in Sufi-style devotional poetry form through the *Book of the Lover and the Beloved*.[14]

The *Book of the Gentile and the Three Wise Men* perhaps presented the most accessible form of the *Art*, with its integration into a fairly engaging narrative making it relatively easy to follow. This short book was remarkable for a number of reasons. The time period in which this was written was prior to the modern ideas of "tolerance" and "interreligious dialogue."[15] Under Christian rule, Dominican and Mendicant preachers were often given licenses to preach in the synagogues and mosques. At times, the Jews were compelled to attend church to hear Catholic preaching. What these preachers included in their sermons regarding Jewish people occasionally incited the monks present toward violence.[16]

The *Book of the Gentile and the Three Wise Men* stood in contrast to the prevailing mode of communication and disputation of the day. Having recognized the weakness of polemical arguments based on religious authorities, Llull sought to dialogue initially by finding common beliefs or principles to begin his discussions. Thus, he would begin with the idea that "God is good"—something that both Jews and Muslims held in common with Christians.[17] He understood that Jews and Muslims worship and believe in the same God as the Christians, albeit imperfectly.[18]

Of course, both the triune nature of God and the Incarnation are missed by the Jews and Muslims, which Llull hopes to demonstrate in this narrative.[19] It is worth adding that although this is one of Llull's earlier works, he actually continued to use and recommend it to others in ten of his subsequent writings.[20] Thus, we can observe that, in spite of some of the later openness of Llull to coercive methodologies, he may very well have retained the irenic methodology found here as the *ideal*.

In the book, a Gentile who adheres to none of the monotheistic traditions is wandering in a forest. In the same forest, three *friends* are walking together: a Jew, a Christian, and a "Saracen" (that is, a Muslim). The fact that Llull has them walking together for a stroll and that they are interacting in a

---

13. Bonner, *Doctor Illuminatus*, 78.
14. Bonner, *Doctor Illuminatus*, 175–84.
15. Bonner, *Doctor Illuminatus*, 149–50.
16. Hames, *Art of Conversion*, 113–14.
17. Bonner, *Doctor Illuminatus*, 151.
18. Hames, *Art of Conversion*, 151n137.
19. Hames, *Art of Conversion*, 213.
20. Bonner, *Doctor Illuminatus*, 81.

nonchalant manner is a signal that this is no ordinary book for the period. They converged on a clearing in which is found a fountain, five trees, and a woman among them. The woman named Intelligence was found watering her horse. Written on the leaves of the trees was essentially an abbreviated version of Llull's *Art*: pairing off elements of the seven divine attributes, seven virtues, and seven mortal sins, combining them in various ways. Indeed, these were understood in their day to be generally accepted principles that would not have pointed exclusively to any one faith tradition. The ultimate goal was to aid people to "love, know, and remember God," which "was the goal of all Lullian enterprise," considering himself "a missionary and reformer of Christian society."[21]

The stage was set for the three to discuss their differences according to the rules that are quite neutral and amenable to all three. As they are about to begin, however, the Gentile arrived among them, and they greet him together.[22] *Together*, they convinced him—using the simplified rules of the *Art* elaborated by Lady Intelligence—of the existence of God, the resurrection, and reality of the afterlife.[23]

The conversation progressed when the Gentile realized that the three wise men disagreed among themselves concerning the true path of salvation. In what followed, each figure got a chapter to convince the Gentile (and the reader) regarding which path is the true one.[24] Interestingly, in the initial section, where the three wise men were seeking to explain about the basic principles of God's existence and of the future resurrection, "Llull is purposely vague about which wise man is speaking when the beliefs common to the three religions are under discussion."[25] One suspects that there may be an idea of creating enough intrigue to encourage further reading and investigation.

One of the most surprising elements in the work is the fact that Llull's presentation of the arguments which are put forward by the Jewish and Muslim figures were hardly "straw-man" arguments—those that could have been set-up for them to be knocked down by the Christian figure. These arguments were understood to represent (to a degree) genuine examples of the kind of logical arguments that Jews and Muslims could really have used.[26] For example, one is struck by Llull's agreement—even in an *evange-*

21. Bonner, *Doctor Illuminatus*, 151–52.
22. Bonner, *Doctor Illuminatus*, 152.
23. Bonner, *Doctor Illuminatus*, 152–53.
24. Bonner, *Doctor Illuminatus*, 153.
25. Bonner, *Doctor Illuminatus*, 92n13.
26. Bonner, *Doctor Illuminatus*, 80.

listic work—with a Jewish interlocutor on the *superbia* (pride) of Christians as well as Muslims.[27]

Perhaps the most surprising element of the *Book of the Gentile* is its ending. After summarizing the arguments of all three wise men and concluding with a prayer that could have been prayed by a follower of any of the three traditions, the Gentile said that he was ready to announce his decision. The wise men, however, *did not wish to know* what his decision was! What they agreed to do was to return regularly to begin the discussion of their *own* faiths with one another, in light of the system laid out by Lady Intelligence, with the hope of one day coming to a united conclusion.[28]

This did not imply some sort of easy universalism for Llull; indeed, Bonner subsequently points out that in his *Book of the Beloved and the Lover*, Llull later implied that the system presented ultimately pointed to the truth of the Christian faith.[29] But in the *Book of the Gentile*, Llull clearly offered a rhetorically neutral means for those of different faiths to dialogue and debate in a non-threatening manner in order to come to their own conclusions. Such restrained balance would be remarkable in *any* age but much more so in Medieval Spain. Bonner writes:

> With this, we have seen how Ramon Llull has constructed an ingenious and highly innovative edifice, and how he has operated a kind of short circuit in all the problems of the inter-religious controversy and of the hostile attitudes of one group against another. He has found a dirty slate of insulting graffiti, of defenses and attacks, of hermeneutic discussions that can never end, and with a masterful stroke he has made it clean, with a methodological proposal to which it was difficult not to pay attention. Instead of wanting to deny the problems of lack of understanding or of violence, he has said simply, let us "enter through another door," which was the door of his Art.[30]

Thus, we can see here that while Ramon Llull was no stranger to controversy and debate, having written works designed to refute the Jewish and Muslim traditions,[31] he made it clear that his preference would be to engage the religious "other" in as irenic a manner as possible. Perhaps this approach would at least be one more tool worth having in order to engage in dialogue

---

27. Hames, *Art of Conversion*, 173.
28. Bonner, *Doctor Illuminatus*, 154.
29. Bonner, *Doctor Illuminatus*, 155.
30. Bonner, *Doctor Illuminatus*, 155.
31. Bonner, *Doctor Illuminatus*, 80n21.

and witness the emerging and often secularizing Muslim communities in North America.

Reflection Questions

1. How has secularization in described Muslim communities been similar to and different from secularization among Christian and especially Evangelical communities?
2. Sociologist Christian Smith mentioned that the spiritual lives of North American teenagers are actually connected to what he terms "Moralistic Therapeutic Deism." How has this affected Muslim youth?
3. What elements of Ramon Llull's approach might be useful in interaction with Muslims in the West today?

Bibliography

Accad, Fouad Elias. *Building Bridges: Christianity and Islam*. Colorado Springs: NavPress, 1997.
Ali, Ayaan Hirsi. *Nomad: From Islam to America*. New York: Free Press, 2010.
Bonner, Anthony. *Doctor Illuminatus: A Ramon Llull Reader*. Princeton: Princeton University Press, 1993.
Brown, Jonathan, and Shadee Elmasry. "LGBTQ and Islam Revisited: Days of the Donald." *Yaqeen Institute*, December 14, 2017. https://yaqeeninstitute.org/en/jonathanbrown/lgbtq-and-islam-revisited-the-days-of-the-donald.
Green, Emma. "How America Is Transforming Islam." *The Atlantic*, December 31, 2017. https://www.theatlantic.com/politics/archive/2017/12/muslims-assimilation-weddings/549230.
Hames, Harvey J. *The Art of Conversion: Christianity & Kabbalah in the Thirteenth Century*. Leiden: Brill, 2000.
Hari, Johann. "Salman Rushdie: His Life, His Work and His Religion." *The Independent*, October 12, 2006. https://www.independent.co.uk/news/people/profiles/salman-rushdie-his-life-his-work-and-his-religion-419902.html.
Knight, Michael Muhammad. *Blue-Eyed Devil: A Road Odyssey Through Islamic America*. Brooklyn: Autonomedia, 2006.
———. *Journey to the End of Islam*. Berkeley, CA: Soft Skull, 2009.
———. *The Taqwacores*. Brooklyn: Autonomedia, 2004.
Marantz, Andrew. "Kumail Nanjiani's Culture-Clash Comedy." *The New Yorker*, May 8, 2017. https://www.newyorker.com/magazine/2017/05/08/kumail-nanjianis-culture-clash-comedy.
Patel, Eboo. *Sacred Ground: Pluralism, Prejudice and the Promise of America*. Boston: Beacon, 2012.
Smith, Christian. *Soul Searching: The Religious and Spiritual Lives of American Teenagers*. New York: Oxford University Press, 2009.

Standish, Alberta, "With Women in the West." *Encountering the World of Islam*, edited by Keith Swartley, 455–57. 2nd ed. Colorado Springs: BottomLine Media, 2014.

Warraq, Ibn. *Why I am not a Muslim*. New York: Prometheus, 1995.

Part 3

Mission in Global Christianity

7

How Africa Might Save Global Christianity

GLENN MARTIN

Introduction

THIS CHAPTER IS BORN of an optimism rooted in a faith-filled reading of Scripture. Though global mission advance has suffered some setbacks through the centuries, Scripture is clear that "this gospel of the kingdom will be preached throughout the whole world, as a testimony to all nations, and then the end will come" (Matt 24:14 RSV). The prophetic utterance affirmed that, though the Messiah's Kingdom began as a stone, it would become "a great mountain" and fill "the whole earth" (Dan 2:35 RSV). Isaiah also declared that "of the increase of his government and of peace there will be no end" (Isa 9:7 RSV).

I write as a missionary practitioner, in academic terms, and as a generalist. A generalist is not unlike an undisciplined animal that escapes pasture and grazes gladly and widely in fields not his own. In my wide grazing, I came to see that most of what I suggest here has already been said and has often been said better. I hope to contribute something by connecting points already made in distinct fields of inquiry with the benefit of a practitioner's perspective.

As an introduction, a sweeping review will serve us well. Increased secularization as a consequence of modernization seems self-evident to many and has been widely argued for a long time—not least by Peter Berger in his landmark *The Sacred Canopy* in 1967. His arguments for modernization's inevitable lead to secularization held dominance in the field at least until Finke and Stark's 1988 publication of alternate theories based on an economic market model or what has been known as rational choice theory.[1] The evidence of religion's decline in Europe was more than enough for some theorists while the resurgence of religion in unexpected places prompted counter-arguments. Berger himself later retracted much of his theory of secularization,[2] while scholars in various corners have argued for and against it.[3] Moreover, Reginald Bibby provides a brief but nuanced history of that process of inquiry with a pointed summary.[4]

As the dust of the twentieth century settled behind us, Zurlo and Johnson looked at the numbers and contended that secularization theory has been "largely debunked" and that "despite increased modernity the world has in fact become *more* religious."[5] They note that the percentage of the world's population self-reporting religious affiliation increased from 80.8 percent in 1970 to 88.1 percent in 2010. Rather than decreasing, this number is expected to increase to 91.5 percent by 2050. Africa is far and away the continent with the least secularization: over 99 percent of the population self-identified with religion both in 1970 and 2010, and that number is expected to stay over 99 percent through 2050.[6] That contrasts significantly with Asia's 1970 figure, at the height of Communism's attack on religion, when only 74.3 percent of Asia's vast population were identified as "religionist."[7] The fact that Africa's share of global population is increasing due to its higher-then-average birthrate also increases the significance—not only statistically—of its relative resistance to secularization.

In resonance with the above numbers, a fiftieth-anniversary treatment of Berger's *The Sacred Canopy*, considering perspectives from different continents, continues both a contention for secularization theory's ongoing validity[8]—notably an American contribution to the research—and a statement from Africa that "within African ontology and cosmos, secularization never happened either during or after colonial modernity."[9]

---

1. Finke and Stark, *Religious Economies*, 41–49.

2. See Berger, "Secularism in Retreat," 3–12, and Berger, *Many Altars of Modernity*.

3. See Anderson, "Transformation of World Christianity"; Bruce, "Secularization and Impotence"; Norris and Inglehart, *Sacred and Secular*; Schnabel and Bock, "Persistent American Religion"; Stark, "Secularization, R.I.P."; Stark, *Triumph of Faith*; and Warner, "Work in Progress."

4. See Bibby, "Religious Polarization in Canada."

5. Zurlo and Johnson, "Unaffiliated, Yet Religious," 50.

6. Zurlo and Johnson, "Unaffiliated, Yet Religious," 68.

7. Zurlo and Johnson, "Unaffiliated, Yet Religious," 69.

8. Gorski and Guhin, "Ongoing Plausibility," 1118–31.

9. Ukah and Wilks, "Theorizing the African Context," 1150.

Global perspectives aside, the narrative of secularization theory resonates with so much of what we see happening in Europe and North America, where the native-born white population in particular is most noticeably less attached to Christian Church and creed than were their parents or grandparents.[10] Whether or not one agrees that modernization drives secularization, statistics stubbornly indicate that European and North American culture—quite arguably Western civilization as a whole—are increasingly post-Christian. Church attendance by the emerging generation is at an all-time low in the US, for example.[11] The composite picture is one of a decaying influence of the Church in society, at least in the West. That said, it does not necessarily follow that Christianity is dead, or, much less so, that God is dead. Stark and Bainbridge pointedly state, "The scholars in the heart of Christendom who proclaim the death of God have been fooled by a simple change of residence."[12] Bibby argues that the data points not to secularization versus de-secularization but rather to polarization.[13] Furthermore, Bibby comes to precisely the same conclusion that I argue for in this paper, as we shall see.

Whatever be the theory we accept as more plausible, certain pressures are being exerted upon the status quo of Christian life and faith in the early twenty-first century, especially in the West. Whatever be the threat to Christianity's existence, it may be instructive to draw a parallel with the experience of the Church at the dawn of the Middle Ages. At that time, the Christian faith—at least on its western end—was mostly limited to the Roman Empire, and both Empire and Church despaired of surviving the extended onslaught of the barbarian hordes from the north.[14] As Cahill so famously argues, Ireland's relative isolation from the processes at work in the heart of the Empire positioned it to be a stable reservoir of the Church, from which creative, renewing energy would be drawn after the broader crisis had passed.[15] A similar process may be observed in our day.

The argument of this chapter is that just as the Christians and Christianity of Ireland were uniquely positioned to be a source of renewal to Europe in the early Middle Ages, the Church of Africa may be positioned

10. See Kinnaman and Hawkins, *You Lost Me*; Pew Research, "America's Changing Religious Landscape"; and Twenge, *iGen*.

11. Dreher, *Benedict Option*, 9.

12. Stark and Bainbridge, *Future of Religion*, 529.

13. See Bibby, "Beyond No Religion Panic," and Bibby, "Religious Polarization in Canada."

14. See Latourette, *History of Christianity*, 1:327–73; Neill, *History of Christian Mission*; and O'Grady, *Beyond the Empire*.

15. See Cahill, *Irish Saved Civilization*.

to lead global Christianity into the next era beyond post-modernism. Statistics on Church growth indicate that this might be the case: Africa is the continent with the highest growth rate of Christianity, the continent with the most Christians, and at the current rate, will become the continent with the majority of the world's Protestants before 2050.[16] If this be so, we may well ask what kind of Christianity will spring forth anew from Africa, as it gives increasing leadership to the global Church.

The rest of this chapter seeks to answer that question by weaving together two threads of analysis. First, I will consider literature across disciplines on the contribution of Africa to global Christianity; second, I will incorporate interviews of African Christians serving in Church leadership outside Africa. The latter input was solicited by a simple process of emailed questions to a few friends about the unique characteristics and contributions of African Christianity, with the further invitation that they forward the email to other African Christians in their network who serve outside Africa.

African Church and Global Christianity

The general thrust of this chapter is not original to me and has been capably suggested elsewhere. Philip Jenkins's *The Next Christendom: The Coming of Global Christianity*, originally published in 2002, presages much of what has recently developed as well as what I suggest here. Jenkins argues that "the growth of Black spirituality has powerful implications for the wider picture of world Christianity in the new century. Not only will Africa itself be the religion's spiritual center within a few decades, but hundreds of millions of other Christians will belong to the wider African diaspora in the Americas, the Caribbean, and on the soil of Europe itself."[17] And again, Jenkins says: "We can even imagine Southern Christians taking the initiative to the extent of evangelizing the North, in the process changing many familiar aspects of belief and practice, and exporting cultural traits presently found only in Africa or Latin America."[18]

More recently, Jenkins reports on projections of African religious developments toward 2050, saying: "Not only will there be many more African Christians and Muslims, but they are also likely to be active and devoted in their religious practice and strongly resistant to secularization. African religiosity emerges strongly in most surveys, even if it is not quite uniform.

---

16. Johnson et al., "Christianity 2017," 41–52.
17. Jenkins, *Next Christendom*, 75.
18. Jenkins, *Next Christendom*, 14.

Nowhere are there significant minorities rejecting or questioning the religious consensus, especially not such fundamental assumptions as the belief in God."[19] A young woman from Congo serving in leadership of a worship and discipleship ministry in Atlantic Canada observed the same thing: "In Africa, most of the world believes that there is a God, creator of heaven and earth. Even if these people are not Christians, they consider it a folly not to believe that there is a God. Here it is the opposite, people consider it a folly to believe in God."[20]

Andrew F. Walls, drawing on sixty years of scholarship on the African contribution to Christianity, notes that "the Christian Church is now multicentric, its centers of energy widely dispersed across the world, so that major initiatives in mission—whether that mission be expressed in evangelism, social action, theological reflection or radical spirituality—may arise in any part of the world and be directed to any other part of it."[21] Again, he notes that "Christianity is in process of becoming again what it was in its origins—a non-Western religion. Africa has a special significance in this picture, since it is in Africa, during the twentieth century, that the largest accession to the Christian faith has taken place."[22]

Walls harks back to an earlier authority: "That wise old owl, Henry Venn of the Church Missionary Society, reflecting on the Great Commission in 1868, argued that the fullness of the Church would only come with the fullness of the national manifestations of different national churches."[23] The contribution from Africa is well on its way.

Contribution and Description of African Christianity

What then is to be the unique contribution of African Christianity to the global mission task? Jenkins argues that "the most important trend in African Christianity has been toward especially enthusiastic, charismatic, and Pentecostal expressions of faith."[24] The general sense of African Christianity is that it is alive. Noting the contrast in Canada, a Cameroonian missionary-entrepreneur told me, "I sometimes have the impression that church is not a happy place for some Canadians."

---

19. Jenkins, "African Faith Going Global," 29.
20. Personal correspondence with the author, March 6, 2018.
21. Walls, "World Christianity," 235.
22. Walls, "World Christianity," 237.
23. Walls, "Gospel," 102.
24. Jenkins, "African Faith Going Global," 28.

What might we identify as salient characteristics of African Christianity, potentially reproducible elsewhere, inasmuch as our situation parallels that of the Irish Christianity of the early Middle Ages? What does the literature from Africa tell us? There is a lot of material to consider: John Mbiti wrote in 1979 that already at that time he had access to over 300 articles and books written by African theologians.[25] Much of this content has been directed to questions of African Christianity's relationship to Africa's pre-Christian past. This is perhaps our best point of departure: cultural characteristics may be transformed by the Gospel, but they always remain in some sense what they were previously. This is true of individuals and of cultures, as we come to Christ. In general terms, what might we see then as essential to African religion that could shape the expression of Christianity from Africa? In his 2015 preface to the enduring *Introduction to African Religion*, Mbiti gives us some clues to the nature of African Christianity, in his description of the African religions that, at least south of the Sahara, predated Christianity's long history in Africa:

> African Religion ... evolved without "founders" or "reformers," growing and spreading spontaneously.... It survived and flourished in different historical, geographical, sociological, cultural, and physical environments. It is the experiences and reflections of people in their total life situations, recording their encounters and their interactions with one another and with their total life setting. It is not a book religion, but it is wrapped up in the oral traditions and cultures of the people.... This was a creative process that took place spontaneously, accommodating changes that added new ideas and practices, as well as abandoning those that no longer applied to the individual and community lives.[26]

Mbiti's description is of African religion in general, but it is of course applicable to African Christianity and stands in contrast to much of what is seen in Western Christianity. I suggest that it is not at all a caricature of African Christianity to describe it first of all as decentralized; secondly, as spontaneously adaptive; thirdly, as primarily oral; and fourthly, as holistic. We can add the following fifth and sixth descriptions of African Christianity—theologically, ethically, and culturally conservative, and supernaturalist.

I posit that the first three of the above relate to physical and technological issues—we might say "material culture"—and position African Christianity to positively shape the globalized, post-literate world of today, while the second set of three characteristics together position African Christianity

---

25. Mbiti, "Biblical Basis," 83.
26. Mbiti, *Introduction to African Religion*, ix.

perhaps better than most of global Christianity as antithesis to the (arguably Western) tendencies of secularism, scientific materialism, and extreme individualism.

Decentralized African Christianity

What then do we mean by saying that Christianity in Africa is "decentralized"? In looking at the panorama that is African Christianity, one is struck by the diversity of it all. Pew Forum found thirty-two African countries in which Christianity is the majority religion, nineteen countries with a Muslim majority, and five with no one religion having a majority (including Nigeria, which is strategic in many ways to the continent as a whole).[27] Notably, the Christian-majority countries—for the most part—do not have one monolithic expression of Christianity. They are religiously diverse, with strong independent churches and both Catholic and Protestant representation across sub-Saharan Africa. Catholic sources indicate that apart from four small island nations, only four African countries have a Catholic majority, and none have a higher percentage of Catholics than Burundi's 65 percent of the population.[28]

Consistent with the above characterization of diversity, Christianity in Africa has given rise to the much-studied "AICs," sometimes spelled-out as African Independent Churches (and alternately as African-Initiated Churches or African Indigenous Churches). Though they do not represent a majority of African Christians, their ubiquity and vitality are in themselves a statement: Christianity in Africa has no one head but Christ. While this may be in part attributed to the missionary process of the colonial era under diverse European states with their respective privileged religions, it may perhaps have more to do with the ethnic and linguistic plurality to which the missionaries came. We must also emphasize that there are African expressions of Christianity that pre-date by more than a millennia and a half the colonial European missionary initiatives to Africa. The first missionary movement between Europe and Africa was not north to south but south to north, as Oden so passionately reminds us.[29] African Christianity then has the rich legacy of Alexandria in the north and the faithful witness of its Ethiopian and Nubian expressions complementing the broad presence of Roman Catholics, Protestants, and AICs south of the Sahara.

27. See Pew Research, "Future of World Religions."
28. "Statistics by Country."
29. Oden, *Africa Shaped Christian Mind*, 29.

Whatever the cause of this decentralization, it is hardly a bad fit for the globalized world of today, where who you are or where you are matters less than how connected you are. In a religious context, without an established hegemony, are there any limits to quantitative growth? And what might be the qualitative implications of there being so much locally-initiated Christianity? In South Africa, Öhlmann, Frost, and Gräb contend that AICs now number half the country's population and that both because of their size and their posture on matters of individual and societal transformation, their potential contribution to development of the nation is enormous.[30] What might be the transformational implications beyond Africa?

Spontaneously Adaptive African Christianity

Secondly, the spontaneity and creative adaptivity that Mbiti finds in African religion in general is also strongly visible in its Christianity. It is important to note that if this is the way of African religious expression from time immemorial it is not to be dismissed as being simply due to the youthful vigor of a young Church or a "sect." That said, the spontaneity and creativity are not without order. As Walls says, "African life is ordered, has a sense of the appropriate time, place, and person; but it is also spontaneous, improvisatory, responsive. What is both more ordered and more spontaneous than the dances of Africa?"[31]

Jenkins likewise affirms the innovative initiatives of African faith this way: "Many of the newer churches use highly entrepreneurial forms of marketing and evangelism to spread that faith, commonly employing the most advanced technology. Little-known in the West, one of the main expressions of popular evangelical faith in Africa is the Nigerian-based video industry."[32]

Oral African Christianity

Thirdly, the identification of African Christianity as fundamentally oral juxtaposes it with much of Western Christianity since the time of the Reformation and the widespread use of printed media. The global context, however, has changed much in recent decades. The primary orality of African

---

30. See Öhlmann et al., "African Initiated Churches' Potential."
31. Walls, "Anabaptists of Africa," 51.
32. Jenkins, "African Faith Going Global," 28.

Christianity might be less a handicap today than an advantageous positioning to impact a global digital culture that is increasingly post-literate.[33]

Oral cultures make good use of stories to impart vital truths. A Zambian church-planter in a small town in central Alberta told me, "The art of telling stories has been a vital aspect of my African heritage that has benefitted ministry in Canada. Bible truths and teachings are often encased in stories, and African culture is one that transports culture and customs in the vessels of stories. I have also found that First Nations peoples share these aspects, so I have been able to engage and connect with First Nations peoples with my storying." Perhaps especially in the digital age, storying is a gateway to influence.

Holistic African Christianity

Fourthly, we noted the African religious emphasis on a holistic approach in relation to the applicability of faith to all of life. Noting the contrasting ways our cultures affect our interpretation of Scripture, Walls mentions theological debate in Africa about worship during menstruation.[34] An African faith is expected to apply to health, to marriage and family, to fertility and prosperity, and to the spirit world. All of this African faith application is especially interesting in light of the contrast it represents with a compartmentalized, "sanitized" separation of private conviction from public life, such as what is widely accepted as civil religion in Western Christianity.

In the Western context, the influence of secularism and individualism produces, on the one hand, a defensiveness in the public sphere such that any intrusion of religion in that sphere is suspect and, on the other, a defensiveness in the private sphere such that no one can tell me what to do. In the face of this Western separation of religion from life, what does African mission work in Canada look like? Our Zambian friend in Alberta says, "The African diaspora is characterized by passionate, very serious, disciplined, and sacrificial living out of their faith." He mentions specifically the exercise of hospitality in discipleship, letting people get close to us: "We directly engage with our broken world by bringing people into our world." It is not hard to see the contrast between that and what goes for normal Christianity in the West.

---

33. Willis et al., "Making Disciples," 6.
34. Walls, "Gospel," 101.

Conservative African Christianity

In fifth place, African Christianity manifests a marked conservatism in its approach to biblical interpretation and ethics or morality. Lamin Sanneh notes the adverse Western reaction to the African bishops' stance on the ordination of homosexuals in the Anglican communion.[35] Jenkins also contends that African Christianity exhibits "a more conservative Christianity and traditional view of Scripture . . . a much greater respect for the authority of Scripture, especially in matters of morality; a willingness to accept the Bible as an inspired text and a tendency to literalism."[36]

This marked conservatism in African Christianity is consistent with its identification as a "culture of honor" in the extensive research of values brought together by Miguel Basáñez. Cultures of honor "are motivated by respect for traditions, hierarchies, and authority."[37]

Supernaturalist African Christianity

Finally, in sixth place, African Christianity is markedly supernaturalist in its outlook. That this is relevant to our argument is underscored by Stark and Bainbridge: "Far from marking a radical departure in history and an era of faithlessness, secularization is an age-old process of transformation. In an endless cycle, faith is revived and new faiths born to take the places of those withered denominations that lost their sense of the supernatural."[38] That African Christianity is supernaturalist posits it to thrive where more secularized Christianity has languished. As a young woman from the Republic of Congo who now leads a worship ministry in Atlantic Canada noted, "I think that in Africa, because of poverty in some areas, people put their trust in God because only he can help them. But here, people put a lot more trust in themselves and God comes in last place, even when they are Christians."

No doubt, the life and death realities of the relatively unstable African context contribute to the development of this passionately supernaturalist approach. As I wrote this chapter, I found myself sitting at a table with an African mission colleague at one of our larger training centers in the US. He had just finished a week of teaching young candidates for missionary service, when his visit to the US was cut short by news that a terrorist rampage a few hundred meters from the mission center in Africa had ended the

---

35. Sanneh, "Current Transformation," 213.
36. Jenkins, "Reading the Bible," 68.
37. Basáñez, *World of Three Cultures*, 13.
38. Stark and Bainbridge, *Future of Religion*, 529.

lives of thirty people. He needed to return immediately to accompany the people at the ministry center in a time of acute crisis—not the first they have suffered. African Christianity has faced great trials and has developed a posture of dependence on God and passionate pursuit of divine intervention in everyday life that stands in contrast to our relative passivity in the West.

Conclusion

It is of course also true that every one of African Christianity's strengths has its corresponding vulnerabilities. A decentralized church can also be a divided church. A synergistic adaptability can show a vulnerability to syncretism. However, my point is that the strengths of African Christianity seem in so many ways to complement wonderfully the vulnerabilities of Western Christianity. If African Christianity is a reservoir from which the global Church will draw in the post-postmodernist era, we have much reason to celebrate the fact that this is so.

Canadian sociologist Reginald Bibby has made a lifetime study of religion in Canada. His writings indicate a process of discovery and (frankly) changing opinions about the impact of secularization on Canadian life and society.[39] He has come to the same conclusion as that of this chapter—expecting a "rejuvenation of religion as a result of immigration."[40] Reflecting on the implications specifically for French Canada of the consistently higher indicators of religious participation and commitment of immigrants, Bibby says: "As in the rest of Canada, much of the hope for the revitalization of the Catholic Church in Quebec [and] Montreal lies with immigration."[41] That certainly resonates with the intent of missionary immigrants. As Aechtner notes, the vision of the African diaspora is to "help bring Christianity back to Canada."[42] Lastly, in the words of the Zambian church-planter in small-town Alberta, the vision is "to remind the church that we are God's hands and feet" and "that spiritual battles are won not in academia but on our knees." May God grant them success, and may we be wise enough to celebrate it.

---

39. See Bibby, "Beyond No Religion Panic," and Bibby, "Religious Polarizations in Canada."
40. Bibby, "Being Pro-Religious," 54.
41. Bibby, "Being Pro-Religious," 74.
42. Aechtner, *Health, Wealth, Power*, 2.

Reflection Questions

1. "Christianity is in the process of becoming again what it was in its origins—a non-Western religion." Do you find this statement to be encouraging, incredible, or frightening? Why?
2. How do you think a more conservative approach to theology, ethics, and culture would be received in your local context?
3. How can you better position your local context to get maximum benefit from renewal and growth in other parts of the global Church?

Bibliography

Aechtner, Thomas. *Health, Wealth, and Power in an African Diaspora Church in Canada*. New York: Springer, 2015.
Anderson, Allan H. "The Transformation of World Christianity: Secularization, Globalization and the Growth of Pentecostalism." Paper for the Society for Pentecostal Studies 44th Annual Meeting, Southeastern University, Lakeland, FL, March 2015.
Basáñez, Miguel. *A World of Three Cultures: Honor, Achievement, and Joy*. Oxford: Oxford University Press, 2016.
Berger, Peter L. *The Many Altars of Modernity: Toward a Paradigm for Religion in a Pluralist Age*. Boston: de Gruyter, 2014.
———. *The Sacred Canopy: Elements of a Sociological Theory of Religion*. Garden City: Doubleday, 1967.
———. "Secularism in Retreat." *The National Interest* 46 (1996) 3–12.
Bibby, Reginald W. "Being Pro-Religious, Low Religious, and No Religious in Montreal: A Mirror of Canada and the World." Paper presented to the Catholic Archdiocese of Montreal, November 2017. http://reginaldbibby.com/images/MONTREAL_ARCHDIOCESE_Thurs_Nov_30_FINAL.pdf.
———. "Beyond the 'No Religion' Panic in the United States." *Annual Meeting of the Pacific Sociological Association*, Portland, OR, 2014.
———. "Religious Polarization in Canada: A Major Empirical Update." *Annual Meeting of the Society for the Scientific Study of Religion*, Newport Beach, CA, 2015.
Bruce, Steve. "Secularization and the Impotence of Individualized Religion." *Hedgehog Review* 8.1/2 (2006) 35–45.
Cahill, Thomas. *How the Irish Saved Civilization*. New York: Anchor, 2010.
Dreher, Rod. *The Benedict Option: A Strategy for Christians in a Post-Christian Nation*. New York: Penguin, 2017.
Finke, Roger, and Rodney Stark. "Religious Economies and Sacred Canopies: Religious Mobilization in American Cities, 1906." *American Sociological Review* 53.1 (1988) 41–49.
Gorski, Philip, and Jeffrey Guhin. "The Ongoing Plausibility of Peter Berger: Sociological Thoughts on The Sacred Canopy at Fifty." *Journal of the American Academy of Religion* 85.4 (2017) 1118–31.

Jenkins, Philip. "African Faith is Going Global." *Trends* 1 (2016) 26–32. http://trend.pewtrusts.org/en/archive/trend-summer-2016/how-africa-is-changing-faith-around-the-world.

———. *The Next Christendom: The Coming of Global Christianity*. Oxford: Oxford University Press, 2002.

———. "Reading the Bible in the Global South." *International Bulletin of Missionary Research* 30. 2 (2006) 67–73.

Johnson, Todd M., and Brian J. Grim, eds. *World Religion Database*. Leiden/Boston: Brill, 2015.

Johnson, Todd M., et al. "Christianity 2015: Religious Diversity and Personal Contact." *International Bulletin of Missionary Research* 39.1 (2015) 28–30.

Johnson, Todd M., et al. "Christianity 2017: Five Hundred Years of Protestant Christianity." *International Bulletin of Mission Research* 41.1 (2017) 41–52.

Kinnaman, David, and Aly Hawkins. *You Lost Me: Why Young Christians are Leaving Church . . . and Rethinking Faith*. Grand Rapids: Baker, 2011.

Latourette, Kenneth S. *A History of Christianity*. Vol. 1. New York: Harper, 1953.

Mbiti, John S. "The Biblical Basis for Present Trends in African Theology." In *African Theology en Route*, edited by Kofi Appiah-Kubi and Sergio Torres, 83–94. Maryknoll, NY: Orbis, 1979.

———. *Introduction to African Religion*. Long Grove: Waveland, 2015.

Neill, Stephen C. *A History of Christian Missions*. New York: Penguin, 1964.

Norris, Pippa, and Ronald Inglehart. *Sacred and Secular: Religion and Politics Worldwide*. Cambridge University Press, 2011.

Oden, Thomas C. *How Africa Shaped the Christian Mind: Rediscovering the African Seedbed of Western Christianity*. Downers Grove, IL: InterVarsity, 2007.

O'Grady, Desmond. *Beyond the Empire: Rome and the Church from Constantine to Charlemagne*. New York: Crossroad, 2001.

Öhlmann, Philipp, Marie-Luise Frost, and Wilhelm Gräb. "African Initiated Churches' Potential as Development Actors." *HTS Theological Studies* 72.4 (2016) 1–12.

Pew Research. "America's Changing Religious Landscape." May 12, 2015. http://www.pewforum.org/2015/05/12/americas-changing-religious-landscape/.

———. "The Future of World Religions: Population Growth Projections, 2010–2050." April 2, 2015. http://www.pewforum.org/2015/04/02/religious-projections-2010-2050/.

Sanneh, Lamin. "Conclusion: The Current Transformation of Christianity." In *The Changing Face of Christianity: Africa, the West, and the World*, edited by Lamin Sanneh and Joel A. Carpenter, 213–24. New York: Oxford University Press, 2005.

———. *Translating the Message: The Missionary Impact on Culture*. Maryknoll, NY: Orbis, 2015.

Schnabel, Landon, and Sean Bock. "The Persistent and Exceptional Intensity of American Religion: A Response to Recent Research." *Sociological Science* 4 (2017) 686–700.

Stark, Rodney. "Secularization, R.I.P." *Sociology of Religion* 60.3 (1999) 249–73.

———. *The Triumph of Faith: Why the World is More Religious than Ever*. New York: Open Road Media, 2015.

Stark, Rodney, and William Sims Bainbridge. *The Future of Religion: Secularization, Revival, and Cult Formation*. Berkeley: University of California Press, 1985.

"Statistics by Country." *Catholic Heirarchy*. http://www.catholichierarchy.org/country/sc1.html.

Twenge, Jean M. *iGen: Why Today's Super-Connected Kids are Growing Up Less Rebellious, More Tolerant, Less Happy—and Completely Unprepared for Adulthood (and What This Means for the Rest of Us)*. New York: Atria Books, 2017.

Ukah, Asonzeh, and Tammy Wilks. "Peter Berger, The Sacred Canopy, and Theorizing the African Religious Context." *Journal of the American Academy of Religion* 85.4 (2017) 1147–54.

Walls, Andrew F. "The Anabaptists of Africa? The Challenge of the African Independent Churches." *Occasional Bulletin of Missionary Research* 3.2 (1979) 48–52.

———. "The Gospel as the Prisoner and Liberator of Culture." *Missionalia: Southern African Journal of Mission Studies* 10.3 (1982) 93–105.

———. "World Christianity, Theological Education and Scholarship." *Transformation* 28.4 (2011) 235–40.

Warner, R. Stephen. "Work in Progress Toward a New Paradigm for the Sociological Study of Religion in the United States." *American Journal of Sociology* 98.5 (1993) 1044–93.

Willis, Avery, et al. "Making Disciples of Oral Learners." Lausanne Occasional Paper 54. https://www.lausanne.org/docs/2004forum/LOP54_IG25.pdf.

Zurlo, Gina A., and Todd M. Johnson. "Unaffiliated, Yet Religious: A Methodological and Demographic Analysis." *Annual Review of the Sociology of Religion* 7 (2016) 50–74.

8

Do Missionaries Destroy Culture?

JOANNE PEPPER

THROUGHOUT THE HISTORY AND across the breadth of our nation, certain missiological currents have been the focus of repeated, intense inquiry and scrutiny. Indeed, in the last half-decade, many in our country have jumped into a centuries-old, global debate concerning worldview change. As the findings of the report produced by the Truth and Reconciliation Commission (TRC) of Canada[1] were made openly available, socially concerned persons arose as one to query whether Christian missionaries bore culpability for the destabilizing or the euthanizing of indigenous cultures. Disquieted citizens wanted to know: "To what degree has Christianity been a mechanism of conflict, injustice, and secularizing colonialism in Canada?"

The discussions that ensued across broad segments of Canadian society as a result of the release of the TRC report serve as an example to underscore the inevitability that the painful query—"Do missionaries destroy culture?"—is a legitimate question that must be addressed by each new generation of Christ-followers, standing in its particular moment of global history.

An Honest Question

Criticism is often aimed at missionaries over the validity of their work. Some of this criticism has been—and, in some case remains—sadly justified. But other criticisms come from a stereotypical image of missionaries in popular culture that has distorted the perception of who missionaries actually are and what they do.

Do missionaries destroy culture? Posed as an honest and humble inquiry, this question becomes a vital and significant focus of investigation.

---

1. Truth and Reconciliation Commission of Canada, "Honouring the Truth." See also the research work and publications of the Aboriginal Healing Foundation.

But when the same query is postured with skeptical disdain and contempt, the question becomes rhetorical, from someone whose ideology does not value the transformation that the Gospel brings.

Do missionaries destroy culture? Each part of this question needs careful examination and elaboration.

To begin with, who are *missionaries*?

Without a doubt, some persons who self-identify as Christians have been instruments of harm to cultures foreign to them. However, are missionaries careerists who have extensive culture and language training and have labored long among a people group, or are these persons who, perhaps for the very first time, are experiencing a second culture and may go for a short excursion into a new cultural milieu to do something loosely termed as "ministry"? And do all persons between the two ends of this spectrum qualify to be designated as missionaries? Does self-identifying alone make "missionaries"?

Do missionaries *destroy*?

Destruction connotes an ultimate, un-reclaimable, and negative dismantling of persons, natural or manufactured properties, or ideas. The vast majority of missionaries would see such activity as incompatible with the sacredness of divine creation and of the *imago Dei*. However, some missionaries have acted in a culture-destroying manner. The onlooking world, especially those eager to discredit Christ's name, has often been quick to notice these mistakes and brand Christian workers as cultural imperialists.

The question "Do missionaries destroy culture?" is simplistic, prejudicial, and needs to be replaced by a more fundamental query. That is, "Does the change brought about by the Gospel—the message proclaimed by the missionary—bring positive or negative transformation to cultures?" Can the change represented by the Gospel and the method by which it is introduced enhance rather than undermine culture? Can personal—and therefore societal—transformation caused by the introduction of the Gospel bring a *desirable* result and therefore be a benefit and not a detriment? If so, how can that be measured and judged?

The Gospel powerfully affects cultures. It should—it is designed to. But good-news culture change is meant to be *positive*; that is, it is meant to lead humankind toward what God has intended them to be: to restore and to complete the good for which they were originally designed and created.

Part of the Gospel is that humans are endowed with free will. Even the United Nations Declaration of Human Rights acknowledges that people have a basic human right to decide for themselves the religion that they believe and wish to practice.² So, conversion (or its prevention) by coercion—whether at the point of a sword, by economic bribe, or through emotional manipulation—removes this free choice from persons and is morally wrong. There is cause for genuine concern when individuals are forced to convert to a particular religious faith against their free will. Occasionally, Christian missionary work has stumbled significantly in this area—evident in the residual fallout of First Nations residential schools in Canada—but by and large, Christian outreach does not involve those routinely forced conversions fondly imagined in some literature. Indeed, from the perspective of Evangelical Christian theology, it is the choice of the person freely made, not adherence to a particular religious structure, which brings that person into right standing with God. Forced conversions are no conversions.

At the same time, to oppose missionaries' rights to call people to conversion is likewise to undermine people's freedom of choice, thus denying them the right to decide for themselves what religion they wish to follow. This is a form of paternalism that subtly implies "we know what is best for you." Such a position—often taken primarily by atheistic Westerners or by political or religious rulers who feel threatened by dissent in society—effectively denies others the right to choose what they themselves have rejected.

Linked to this is the occasionally expressed idea that persons of a particular social, cultural, or economic background cannot or do not understand the Christian message—or that the message of the Gospel is irrelevant to them. At best, this is an ignorant perspective; at worst, a racist one. Very often, persons deemed unlikely to appreciate or understand the message of Christ are acutely aware of ideas that are key biblical concepts. For example, many in the Majority World have a much better grasp of the context behind the message of the Gospel than most supposedly learned Westerners. Sacrifice, judgment, and salvation are familiar notions in much of the world beyond the West.

Even today, a remarkable majority of the world remains firmly religious. Earth-wide, belief in God remains the norm. In spite of its association with the richest and most powerful nations on earth, secular materialism—which seeks to overrun the world through globalizing economic forces—is actually a recent, minority worldview. Indeed, people throughout the world are frequently most enlivened when talking about spirituality and religion. Globally, the Christian church is mostly non-Western in its composition, and in many locales, it is expanding at a rate faster than world population

---

2. United Nations, "Human Rights." The Universal Declaration of Human Rights was adopted by the United Nations General Assembly on December 10, 1948, at the Palais de Chaillot in Paris.

growth. This alone is a logical indicator that the peoples of the earth still want to hear the story of Jesus.

In light of the positive impact of the Gospel on culture, the empowering of missionaries to continue evangelizing should be encouraged with a view *toward* enhancing culture change rather than seeking to avoid it. As powerfully displayed in the New Testament book of Acts, a Gospel impact on society results in new goals in life, new economic relations, new leadership qualifications and leadership styles, and a new political agenda—not just new hearts.

Time and time again throughout history, Gospel-based changes have positively influenced global societies. Examples may be seen in Francis of Assisi's confronting the power and wealth of the thirteenth-century Catholic church, William Wilberforce's role in stopping England's participation in the slave trade, William Carey's influence in ending widow-burning in India, or John Wesley's call to revival and social reform in eighteenth-century England. Culture change has been a powerful apologetic for Christian faith. But where there have been less known or less-often-seen indications of righteous change in society due to a lack of Christian witness, conversion has slowed. In fact, in the early decades of the twentieth century in China, leading intellectuals rejected Christianity precisely because they saw it as a merely privatized faith with little or no public impact.[3]

An Honest Response

Do Missionaries destroy culture? Some have; some do. Sometimes, this harm has even been intentional. Are missionaries a secularizing force, drawing converts away from and permanently re-establishing them apart from their first culture? In certain places and times, they are. It is only right and honest to own responsibility on the part of those who have gone (and who continue to go) "in the name of Christ" into cross-cultural mission work and actively and systematically worked to dismantle the cultural self-identity of a people. Don Richardson laments for his fellow-laborers when he says, "Whether through misinterpreting the Great Commission, pride, culture shock, or simple inability to comprehend the values of others, we have needlessly opposed customs we did not understand. Some, had we understood them, might have served as communication keys for the Gospel."[4] While it may be possible to see a kind of spiritual sincerity in the actions of missionaries who support cultural genocides thinking they are honoring God, their disregard

3. Ling, *Chinese Intellectuals*, 165.
4. Richardson, "Missionaries," 461.

for the dignity of those to whom they were sent is an affront both to God and to his people.

However, even among Christian workers who support the cultural identities of local peoples, there are yet points of tension—sometimes sharply felt—between missionaries and those to whom they have brought the good news. Why might culturally aware and culturally sensitive missionaries be perceived as secularizing agents? One possible answer is that they may be directing people to do what offends cultural or personal conscience.

Robert Priest's observation helps to elucidate this idea: though the faculty of conscience is a cultural universal, the content of conscience is fallible and variable.[5] That is, the content of conscience is directly dependent on learned cultural meanings, norms, ideals, and values. In intercultural situations, there are bound to be both significant overlaps and marked discontinuities between the consciences of interacting persons or groups. But it is not the overlap that those who interact will tend to notice. Rather, it is in the area of discontinuity—specifically where one's own conscience speaks, and the other's does not. Therefore, in an intercultural situation, a person may be likely to morally condemn another for behaviors about which the other has no conscience.

Furthermore, while human consciences do in large part agree with and overlap with moral tenets as revealed in the Word of God, there are also significant areas of discontinuity between consciences shaped by culture and what is revealed in the text of Scripture. On its own, conscience is not a completely sufficient guide for biblical and moral understandings.

Scripture as well as culture shape a missionary's conscience, but the Christian worker may seldom distinguish clearly between the two, so missionary preaching and teaching that stresses wrongdoing with reference to that which the missionary's conscience deems sinful—but local social conscience does not—has the effect of calling the listeners' attention to cultural discontinuity. To the hearer, this dissonance implies that an invitation to conversion is actually a call to abandon one's own culture for that of the foreign messenger.

The ensuing confusion of Gospel and culture typically yields two possible results. First, persons may refuse to convert because it appears that that conversion is a process that leads away from one's own culture, which is familiar and believed to be good, to the missionary's national culture, which is alien and may even seem immoral. Second, people may choose to convert precisely because conversion is a turning from their own culture to that of

---

5. Priest, "Conscience," 291–315. Priest appeals to the Apostle Paul's discussion on the matter (Rom 2:1–15; 2 Cor 4:2; 1 Cor 10:25–27).

a novel foreign worldview. But the latter scenario—even if undertaken in response to one who claims to speak for God—becomes predominantly a cultural conversion rather than genuine conversion to Christ. Missionaries must understand the role that culture has played in the formation of their own conscience. Furthermore, they need to distinguish between morals grounded in transcendent biblical truth and those morals shaped, at least in part, by conventional cultural meanings.

Is it possible to avoid destroying culture while also challenging culture to uphold biblical norms? If so, how? Certainly, cross-cultural mission workers must first of all seek to live exemplary lives in terms of the virtues and social norms stressed by the people group among whom they live. Moreover, the missionary methods used to disciple local converts must be grounded in a commitment to reject all authority except that of Scripture. Cultural expatriates must acknowledge with sincere humility that they are not in prime positions to unilaterally declare how biblical principles should be applied to cultural particulars.

A contemporary case study from experienced Wycliffe Bible Translators (WBT) in the South Pacific well-illustrates this conundrum of conscience and culture. The WBT missionaries' dilemma was whether or not to directly intervene as cultural change agents in social practices and in the development of indigenous Christian theologizing over matters of physical health. Specifically, the issue they wrestled with was: "Should a Christian smoke?" Like many Evangelicals, these missionaries did not smoke. They understood the negative physical health risks posed by smoking, and they took seriously Paul's counsel to care for the human body (1 Cor 6:19–20).

Christians from the Bahinemo indigenous group, among whom the missionaries spent many years in Papua New Guinea, were eager to obey God and his commands. Bahinemo believers had been taught to go to God's Word rather than to the foreign church workers for answers to their life questions. The missionaries knew they would only be with the Bahinemo for a limited number of years and wanted them to fully depend on Christ for help. Much to the consternation of the missionaries (and when reporting on their outreach ministry to mission co-workers, an endless source of embarrassment), the Bahinemo tribespeople saw no command against smoking in the Bible and had no conviction that it was a sin. This was in a context of God clearly convicting them of other wrongdoings in their lifestyle.

Bahinemos knew that the Bible commanded the care of the human body, but they saw no relationship between smoking and disease. In fact, the concept of a slow, incremental cause and the statistical concept of risk were alien to their worldview. Without the demonstration of a direct cause and effect relationship, they were unwilling to accept the idea that the lung diseases and coughs they had were the result of smoking. Furthermore, locally grown tobacco provided one of the few pleasures Bahinemos experienced in a world full of insects and discomfort. It was also one of the few ways they could afford to provide hospitality to visitors, a very high value in Bahinemo society. Only a few persons who were very ill from lung diseases quit smoking for medical reasons, despite concerted efforts of the missionaries to teach on this point.[6]

It would have been possible for the WBT couple to have told the local tribespeople, "You cannot smoke and be a Christian." After all, these mission workers were their initial evangelists and, in the early years of the Bahinemo Christian community, the source of all they knew about biblical teachings. But to do so would not have tied the teaching to Scripture. Rather, it would have convinced the new Christians that there are some things for which you do not go to Scripture at all. The result would have been a lessened willingness to submit to God's Word as the primary source for knowing his will. It also might have increased their susceptibility to self-styled prophets who came along.

Perhaps, as the Wycliffe workers imply, missionaries do best when they resist being voices agitating for culture change based on their personal, cultural conscience. Mission work entails faith—not only to believe for salvation but for the ensuing sanctification of oneself and others as well.

Clearly and biblically, the culture of all peoples should be respected. Culture gives members of society a sense of shared identity, belonging, and values. But no culture is perfect or unchanging. Indeed, demonstrating respect for individuals and communities while honoring culture underscores the importance of seeking to facilitate personal and communal development in such a way that it also positively impacts wider culture.

Mission work can legitimately be a force for change without harm. It is right to advocate for Christian conversion knowing that a change in religion—the core institution of society—will cause an unpredictable ripple-effect change throughout all of society.

Why is it possible to be optimistic and open toward culture change due to conversion? In part, the reason is because culture is not static. It is always changing. It is only a question of how it changes and by which influence it does so. Today, media and commerce ensure that almost no place on earth remains isolated from the outside world. In fact, the most powerful forces for change are those of globalization and the values they promote. With an unrelenting push toward uniformity in both manufactured products and philosophical ideas—disseminated via conduits such as the internet, pop

---

6. Dye, "Definition of Sin," 27–41.

music, and Hollywood movies—Western-influenced global consumerism that champions "life, liberty, and the pursuit of stuff"[7] has little regard for or interest in preserving local cultures or fostering their development.

Theory and Theology

Clearly, not all features of human cultures are good for human flourishing. The social science notion of cultural relativism argues that no culture or worldview can exclusively claim to possess a set of absolute standards by which other cultures and worldviews may be judged.[8] But there is a need to consider biblical absolutism. That is, the Word of God delivers to humankind principles that are God-honoring and also honor each culture in which they are enacted. A key example is the set of ten great rules of God (the ten commandments). These simple statements have become the foundation of jurisprudence and law in much of the world, serving to universally benefit *all* peoples and cultures.

In some global cultures, slavery, forced prostitution, child labor, revenge killings, or female genital mutilation are proven to be adaptive practices. In other global cultures, industrial and personal pollution, income tax evasion, racial discrimination, and materialism are advocated and approved. But what moral foci make these actions right or wrong? Should these practices be legitimized simply because they are already entrenched in certain social and historical locales? Part of the missionary role is to bring positive alternatives for the development of specific cultures, something other than the default options already in place.

Helpful insights in the debate on culture change come from Bruce Olson, a present-day American missionary among the South American Motilone peoples. Olson posits principles concerning culture change that have guided him through his social and spiritual encounters with tribes in Latin America. Firstly, he observes that contact between peoples of the earth is inevitable and ongoing: "One can neither stop the clock nor go back in time."[9] He proceeds by noting that minority groups and culturally remote peoples are often in a weak position in this contact, even though their morals and culture are in many ways superior to those of the wider world. Because of this, the unity, self-esteem, and pride of the weaker group must be strengthened, so that they will want and be able to defend their own future.

---

7. Postman, *Amusing Ourselves*, 39.

8. See Boas, "Museums," 589; Kluckhohn, *Mirror for Man*; and Renteln, "Relativism," 56–72.

9. Kung, *Missionary or Colonizer?*, 147. See also Olsen, *Bruchko*.

Furthermore, Olson warns that no people can be stopped from changing and developing in myriads of different ways. But changes must not be forced and have to be executed within the framework of the people's own norms and traditions—that is, change is best when it is self-initiated and not a result of external pressure. Olson strongly advocates that "cultural shock and cultural collision must be prevented at all costs. Transitions must be made as softly and as free-willingly as possible."[10] Finally, Olson argues that Christian mission as culture change is the highest hope for global society, declaring: "Frankly, you don't help other human beings very much if you don't help them find Jesus Christ."[11] These are wise words to ponder.

Do missionaries destroy culture? The painful but honest truth is that some have, and some do—and some probably will continue to do so. But the wanton dismantling of culture is wrong because God himself is the author of culture and his image is present in every person, giving each human being intrinsic value.

When pursued as Christ intended, missionary work is not simply meant to not destroy culture; rather, it is designed to strengthen, enrich, and uplift global cultures. Thus, the message and mission of Christ remains to be good news for all people.

Reflection Questions

1. How can a missionary discern whether their impact on the culture is positive (due to the Gospel) or potentially negative (because of personal or cultural biases)?

2. While condemning coercion, the author suggests that calling people to conversion provides freedom of choice so that people may "decide for themselves which religion they may follow." How would you describe "best practices" for evangelism that are ethically appropriate and that avoid coercion?

3. Do different cultures have different nuances of conscience? What is one lifestyle behavior that your first culture considers to be morally wrong (or right), but which other cultures do not believe is wrong (or right)? How and why might differing concepts of conscience arise?

---

10. Kung, *Missionary or Colonizer?*, 176.
11. Kung, *Missionary or Colonizer?*, 176.

Bibliography

Boaz, Franz. "Museums of Ethnology and their Classification." *Science* 9.228 (1887) 587–89.
Dye, Wayne. "Toward a Cross-Cultural Definition of Sin." *Practical Anthropology* 4.1 (1976) 27–41.
Kluckhohn, Clyde. *Mirror for Man*. Greenwick, CT: Fawcett, 1944.
Kung, Anders. *Bruce Olson: Missionary or Colonizer?* New York: Christian Herald, 1977.
Ling, Samuel. *Chinese Intellectuals and the Gospel*. Phillipsburg, NJ: Horizon, 1999.
Olson, Bruce. *Bruchko*. Lake Mary, FL: Charisma House, 2006.
Postman, Neil. *Amusing Ourselves to Death: Public Discourse in the Age of Show Business*. New York: Penguin, 1985.
Priest, Robert J. "Conscience and Culture." *Missiology* 22.3 (1994) 291–315.
Renteln, Alison. "Relativism and the Search for Human Rights." *American Anthropologist* 90.1 (1988) 56–72.
Richardson, Don. "Do Missionaries Destroy Culture?" In *Perspectives on the World Christian Movement*, edited by Ralph D. Winter and Stephen C. Hawthorne, 460–68. 3rd ed. Pasadena, CA: William Carey, 1999.
Truth and Reconciliation Commission of Canada. "Honouring the Truth, Reconciling for the Future: Summary of the Final Report of the Truth and Reconciliation of Canada (2015)." www.trc.ca.
United Nations. "Universal Declaration of Human Rights." *Department of Public Information*. http://www.unhchr.ch/udhr/lang/eng.htm.

Part 4

Mission and Strategy for a Changing Context

9

Tentmaking

Creative Mission Opportunities within
a Secularizing Canadian Society

JAMES W. WATSON AND NARRY F. SANTOS

Introduction

CANADIAN SECULARIZATION PRESENTS CHALLENGES to the church and mission. The *missio Dei* (mission of God) can overturn expectations to uncover new opportunities presented by challenging environments. While current countertrends to secularization in Canada seem limited in overall effect, exploration of their potential may bring to light new ways of engaging in mission. Consideration is given to the pragmatic incentives and missiological ideals for tentmaking ministries. Frequently, if the church can engage with central theological issues, both the motivation and direction for new ventures flow most naturally. While this is primarily a conceptual exploration, it raises concerns for further research and development.

What Tentmaking Is

Tentmaking has been variously called bivocational or covocational[1] ministry and dual role/career work.[2] It has also been closely identified with "business as mission," "marketplace," or "workplace" ministry.[3] Tentmak-

---

1. Brisco, *Covocational Church Planting*, 23–24.

2. Ott and Wilson, *Global Church Planting*, 319. In light of the biblical and long-term use of "tentmaker" in the history of mission, this chapter chooses to continue this tradition. See "Local Church in Mission," 23.

3. For distinctions in the use of the three terms (tentmaking, marketplace ministry, and business as mission), see Li, "Marketplace Ministry," 9–10. See also Tunehag et al.,

ing refers to the practice of Christian workers and professionals who support themselves financially (fully or partially) by working as employees or by engaging in business. Thus, it infers the integration of work and witness. The more common discussion of tentmaking is in cross-cultural and international missions. In the 1989 Congress in Manila of the Second Lausanne Committee for World Evangelization, tentmakers are described as believers in all people groups who have a secular identity and who—in response to God's call—proclaim Christ cross-culturally. Tentmakers witness with their whole lives, and their jobs are integral to their work for the Kingdom of God. In our current secularizing world, particularly in our Canadian context, tentmaking can provide great opportunities for mission with its greater flexibility and possibility of financial independence. It can be a part of what Orlando E. Costas describes as mobilization, particularly the mental transformation of understandings about leadership, the willingness to engage in sacrificial action, and a comprehensive faith perspective of all of life continuing to be within God's agenda.[4]

As has been mentioned, tentmaking can be applied in the role of a bivocational pastor, whom Dennis Bickers defines as a minister who serves in a paid ministry position and has income from another source.[5] That source may be a full-time or part-time job or another form of income. Tentmaking pastors may receive larger salaries from their second jobs than they do from their churches. The second job may not be ministry related. The intentional combination may provide options that facilitate basic financial viability for new congregational initiatives and allow creative engagement for challenging ministry contexts.

Canadian Society and Secularization

Current discussion of secularization in Canada considers the rate, nature, and effects of secularization but concedes a general trend towards less religious participation and influence in society. Sociologist Joel Thiessen summarizes a basic argument of secularization theory this way: "Individuals and entire societies are less religious today than in my parent's generation, whose cohort was less religious than their parent's generation."[6] Discussions of secularization or issues indicative of secularization are affecting all lev-

---

"Business as Mission," 13.

4. Costas, *Integrity of Mission*, 25–33.

5. Bickers, *Art and Practice*, 5.

6. Thiessen, "Sociological Description," 97. See also Reimer, "Conservative Protestants," 187–208.

els of Canadian society. Debates on issues that have impact on the activity or expression of values for certain religious groups have been recurring in popular and academic discourse.[7] While there are various debates on secularization in Canada that consider a broad range of societal structures and political influence, this reflection will be primarily concerned with the decrease in congregational participation in general, the increase in individuals who identify with no religion in particular, and how strategic tentmaking ministries can respond.

Sociologist Reginald Bibby noted that an early national Gallup poll (1945) of Canadians who are over twenty years old indicated that 65 percent attended a religious service in the three weeks after Easter Sunday; in the province of Quebec, nine out of ten stated they had attended Mass during that time frame.[8] However, the weekly national attendance figures[9] have declined from 67 percent in 1946 to 11 percent in 2015.[10]

This decline in attendance is accompanied by a rise to almost 25 percent of the population that indicate "no religion" (that is, people who decline to affiliate with any religious tradition). This contrasts with almost 10 percent who identify with conservative Protestantism, 15 percent with mainline Protestantism, and 40 percent with the Catholic religion.[11] Projections to 2036 anticipate that between 28.2 percent and 34.6 percent of the Canadian population will identify with no religion (compared to an increase of 13 percent to 16 percent affiliation with a non-Christian religion).[12] As successive generations are raised in non-religious homes, current research suggests that there will be a cumulative increase over time.[13] The term "religious nones" has become attached to these individuals in both academia and popular discourse.

Interviews conducted by Thiessen with city of Calgary (Alberta) residents who were religious nones revealed some themes that are important

7. One example relates to the challenges negotiating zoning for houses of worship (no property tax, parking/transit, and proximity to industrial sites) with urban planning authorities. See Hackworth and Stein, "Collision of Faith," 37–63.

8. Bibby, *Resilient Gods*, 12.

9. Different samples, sources, and analysis offer differences in numerical decline; however, the general pattern of decline remains. See Reimer and Wilkinson, *Culture of Faith*, 48–66.

10. Reimer, "Conservative Protestants," 187–208. Weekly attendance is being questioned in academic and denominational leadership circles as a measure for congregational participation or religious faithfulness, in part because of its rarity among individuals who consider themselves regular attendees.

11. Thiessen, "Sociological Description," 97–124.

12. Morency et al., *Immigration and Diversity*.

13. Thiessen and Wilkins-LaFlamme, "Becoming a Religious None," 64–82.

for missiological reflection. While extensive review of the research in not possible here, a few themes are illustrative of the challenges for mission. Thiessen notes that religious nones will identify themselves as open-minded and free because of the lack of affiliation with a religion.[14] He found that two-thirds of religious nones are unsure or do not believe in life after death, their emphasis being on a meaningful life in the here-and-now.[15] While these are only a couple of conversation topics that can emerge with non-religious Canadians, there are obvious issues that would require substantial dialogue to engage. Thiessen suggests that it "would be wise for church leaders as missionaries in the Canadian context to invest in trying to understand religious nones for how they view the world, not how church leaders think or wish religious nones would view the world."[16]

Countervailing Factors for Consideration

Two current trends that counter or respond to the prevailing trajectory of secularization are new congregations started by newcomers to Canada and experimental forms of congregational mission. Discussion of secularization in the popular media and academic literature has not been encouraging from a church leader's perspective, so it is important to reflect on how the trend might be countered. Anthropology and sociology of religion have considered implications of globalization, which suggests a countering effect. Observation and interaction with creative expressions of congregational mission suggest options for future developments. An overview of these two areas will allow for a focus on the development of new congregations by recent immigrants to Canada[17] and new expressions of congregational outreach with the implications for tentmaking ministry.

Immigration has been a life-changing experience for many Canadians with implications for all levels of society. The acceptance of about a quarter of a million immigrants a year is the result of federal policy[18] and requires provincial accommodations and municipal settlement. At the global level, the secularization thesis that modernization will lead to greater secularization has been questioned based on growth of religious engagement in

---

14. Thiessen, *Meaning of Sunday*, 110.
15. Thiessen, *Meaning of Sunday*, 116–20.
16. Thiessen, "Sociological Description," 106.
17. Reimer et al., "Christian Churches and Immigrant Support," 495–513, and Janzen et al., "Integrating Immigrants," 441–70.
18. Hiebert, *What's So Special?*

different regions.[19] Immigrants and refugees come to Canada from all over the world, bringing their religious commitments with them. Pew Research Center's Phillip Connor has investigated the relationship between immigration and religion and found that 59 percent of immigrants in Canada are Christian, while 17 percent are unaffiliated with any religion (and 24 percent represent other religions).[20] As the total number of individuals indicating no religious affiliation has climbed to almost one quarter of all Canadians,[21] this is a significant difference. Immigration is not reversing secularization in Canada, but it could be considered as partially countering or slowing secularization.[22]

The influx of Christian adherents to Canada creates a need for new churches. Some individuals are called specifically to Canada as missionaries, while others arrive and expect some form of congregation with elements of Christian spirituality familiar to them. This ability to gather and mobilize the diaspora is an important factor that is noted by both practitioners and academics alike.[23] While churches of recent immigrants can specialize in reaching people who share the same language or cultural background as they do, others view Canada as a mission field and create a more multicultural strategy for outreach.[24] The vibrancy of faith and particular missiological perspectives of the diaspora can enrich Western understandings of the church and strategies for mission.[25] Global networks are formed and sustained through migration[26] that can facilitate mission opportunities. How current rates of immigration would continue to bolster participation in Canadian congregational life, or how the second and third generations would interact with the faith of their parents and grandparents[27] will remain to be seen. This generational issue shares some similar concerns about the rate of retention of young adults in long established Canadian congregations.[28]

Experimental forms of congregational mission may include initiatives by recent immigrants, but some Canadian-born leaders are also exploring

19. Berger, "Further Thoughts," 313–16.
20. Connor, *Immigrant Faith*, 20.
21. Morency et al., *Immigration and Diversity*.
22. Thiessen, "Sociological Description," 97–124.
23. Wan and Casey, *Church Planting*.
24. Santos, "What's a Missionary Doing," 97–110.
25. Chapman and Watson, "Common Actions," 63–86. See also Costas, *Christ Outside the Gate*, 81–83.
26. Wilkinson, *Spirit Said Go*.
27. Thiessen, "Sociological Description," 97–124. See also Caron-Malenfant et al., "Religious Switching of Immigrants."
28. Penner et al., "Hemorrhaging Faith."

new approaches that may connect with Canada's religious nones. Three forms will be considered as theoretical types or models—missional groups, small church plants, and larger church initiatives. These categories are exploratory and anecdotal but provide a framework for discussion of engagement with people who are not connected to a church.

Missional groups include new initiatives that are smaller than most churches and that do not have a stated intent of ongoing sustainability as a congregation. Small church plants are intentionally developing a sustained faith community and are started for the purpose of reaching a parish, neighborhood, or niche population. Larger church initiatives are generally developed by an established congregation for a specific purpose that may include approaches to mission such as missional groups and small church plants. There are no strict categories of mission engagement; this framework is only useful to allow for consideration of certain ranges for a broad spectrum. These definitions can show some overlap and interaction between the categories to allow for the complexity of innovation to be considered.

Missional groups may include intentional outreach programs imported from other countries (such as Alpha, Messy Church, and Celebrate Recovery), providing a potential forum for religious nones to explore faith and experience certain forms of Christian community. They may also be experimental in a "made-in-Canada" fashion, such as the MoveIn movement,[29] as well as other forms of "incarnational living" or "missional small groups."[30] Generally, there is a specific concern being addressed by this small group of Christians. In some cases, there is a particular type of Canadian in focus (religious nones or affiliates to other religions) or there may be a need to address a particular life issue (such as addiction, poverty, or youth gang involvement).

There is a high degree of intentionality in connecting with individuals where they live, work, study, or engage in recreation in meaningful ways. There are also three common elements among these forms of discipleship groups that are valuable—they are highly relational, spiritual, and focused on the surrounding community (rather than their own needs). While they may prioritize prayer or spiritual disciplines, they continually engage with people around them and build relationships. These groups may actually be embryonic church plants that further develop into ongoing and sustainable congregations, or they might be supported by larger churches. As an example, MoveIn groups in neighborhoods within close distance to an

---

29. See "MoveIn."
30. Davidson, "How to Make."

established church may engage in worship and share outreach with that congregation.

From a 2015 study of Canadian church plants, the respondents indicated that in year one, average worship attendance was forty-one, and by year three, this number rose to sixty-one, which indicates a limited number of people immediately available to fund the plant.[31] Starting small may create a bias towards part-time paid leadership but can also facilitate experimentation with intentional design or focus that incorporates tentmaking. Church plants often develop with a core group of people committed to sustained mission within a specific geographic area or network of relationships that allow for creative contextualization.

Not all church plants start small; some may have well over the average number of people at their beginning, perhaps as either a satellite or daughter congregation of a larger church (and, in this manner, may serve as a mission initiative of that church). Some will develop into larger congregations over time while others will seek to retain their particular flavor or style by intentionally remaining small (possibly spinning off additional missional groups or small church plants).

Intentional research, reflection, and writing—which are necessary for shared learning—are developing with a focus on these "pioneering"[32] or "emergent expressions of Christianity."[33] In the 2015 Canadian study, both "evangelistic visits" and "municipal involvement" were factored into Canadian plants that incorporated unchurched people,[34] thus showing the value of being spiritually engaged in the community. Some develop a community-center form of presence while others explore methods for having a complementary business interest that allows for a different form of relational connection than most Canadians might anticipate for a church.[35] Others even introduce worship into atypical public spaces.[36] While new churches may start for a variety of reasons, connection with religious nones (or "dones")[37] can be the distinctive drive for new plants.

Larger church initiatives may take a myriad of forms intentionally focused on creating opportunities for connection with religious nones. The

---

31. Stetzer and Im, *Church Planting in Canada*, 23.
32. Siebert, *Gutsy*.
33. Studebaker and Beach, "Emerging Churches," 862–79.
34. Stetzer and Im, *Church Planting in Canada*, 17.
35. See "We Make Craft Beer."
36. As an example, "Church at the Manor" meets in an adult entertainment establishment and reaches out to performers, customers, and nearby social housing.
37. Religious "dones" refers to individuals who have been affiliated with a congregation but have ceased any meaningful participation in it.

term "larger" is used quite broadly with the understanding that it could refer to any church that has achieved a level of financial sustainability and leadership allowing it to branch out and intentionally develop creative initiatives. In the Canadian large church survey coordinated by Leadership Network, 55 percent of the churches with Sunday attendance of 1,000 or more indicated that they had started another church.[38] While Canada has a limited number of churches with worship attendance over 1,000 on any given weekend, these churches—as well as those with less than fifty regular attendees—can create new initiatives by leveraging part-time staff or empowering volunteer leaders to engage communities. The extent of creativity is generally only limited by the holy imagination of leaders as initiators or sponsors of mission.

Sam Reimer and Rick Hiemstra note that of the approximately 24,000 congregations in Canada (45 percent of which are identified as evangelical), there is an increase in part-time staff.[39] From their analysis, they observe an increase in the reporting of part-time staff of 3 percent from 2003 to 2011 (that is, from 56.1 percent to 59.1 percent). This does not necessarily mean that part-time staff should be considered equivalent to tentmakers—not all part-time priests, ministers, or pastors will necessarily engage in other paid work and not all church staff are serving pastoral roles (administrative and janitorial staff are included in the study). It is suggestive, however, that tentmaking may be a rising consideration.

Reimer and Hiemstra tend to credit declining church participation and limited budgets related to secularization as a reason for this trend. Differences between volunteer leadership ("appointed more often because of availability than for their ability")[40] and intentional engagement in ministry (which is bivocational) should be explored. Further research may be needed to determine the extent of reactive rather than creatively proactive responses to secularization. Reimer and Hiemstra offer some suggestions for training which are generally applicable: "The traditional model of full-time, on-site training at a seminary is less viable for part-time, second career, or bi-vocational clergy and other staff. Non-residential, modular programs that target specific part-time roles (i.e., a certificate in worship leading or in children's ministry) may better serve part-time staff."[41]

---

38. Bird, *Large Canadian Churches*.
39. See Reimer and Hiemstra, "Rise of Part-time," 1–22.
40. Reimer and Hiemstra, "Rise of Part-time," 4.
41. Reimer and Hiemstra, "Rise of Part-time," 14.

New opportunities for ministry can benefit from volunteer and part-time leaders who are intentionally engaged in the church and community with appropriate training and support.

Tentmaking Opportunities

Newcomers to Canada can face unique challenges with regards to congregational leadership. Some congregations are small, and while immigrants may arrive with substantial financial resources or have arranged employment before arrival, others come with few resources (entry to Canada as a refugee being one example) and employment can be challenging to obtain in a new country.[42] Combinations of these factors may make it difficult for new congregations to provide a full salary to a pastor or minister, thus creating incentive for tentmaking arrangements. In addition to the practicality of additional revenue, the global connections and entrepreneurial spirit of leaders who were willing to engage in a journey to a new country may foster creative forms of work and mission.

Experimental forms of congregational mission in Canada are intentionally created to explore new forms of faithfulness and fruitfulness in an era of increasing secularization. Sustainability will commonly be an issue in early stages of development. Tentmaking arrangements for alternative employment may be necessary. Beyond pragmatic reasons for employment, some individuals are highly strategic in engaging with work that facilitates their calling to mission. Entering into workplaces that provide the necessary flexibility and opportunity for good community connections or for creating such forms of employment may in itself be some of the current "research and development" required of the Canadian church.

Given the context of urban communities with substantial population density and cultural diversity or the different situation of less population and diversity in rural Canada, leaders with biblical understanding and some missiological training may be well positioned to bridge between disconnected relational networks. The leaders' ability to connect in settings outside of their regular ministry involvement can allow them to connect to a broader range of community members, some of whom are normally disinclined to visit a church. These opportunities raise issues of conceptual clarity.

Biblical and theological reflection on the issues related to having both sacred and secular employment provides opportunities for exploring the ideas that might contribute towards a national missiology of tentmaking. In light of the Canadian realities of immigration influx, missional initiatives

---

42. Kaushal et al., "Immigrant Employment," 1249–77.

and small or large church plant efforts in a secularizing context, the potential for tentmaking becomes more pronounced. Missiologist Stuart Murray suggests that bivocational church planting or ministry needs to be normal in a post-Christendom world.[43]

Biblical Inputs on Tentmaking from Paul's Model

Biblically, tentmaking takes up the Pauline model of using one's skills to gain access to mission fields (local or global) and to maintain support as a means of becoming "all things to all men so that by all possible means I might save some" (1 Cor 9:22b NIV). As a bivocational minister, the Apostle Paul supported his ministry by literally making tents[44] (Acts 18:3), just as his ministry partners, Aquila and Priscilla, were also tentmakers (Acts 18:1–2). For Paul, being a tentmaker was in accordance to the custom that required every rabbi to have a trade in order to support himself. William Barclay comments that rabbis were not "detached scholars and always knew what the life of the working man was like."[45]

Hock has shown that, far from being peripheral to Paul's life, tentmaking was central to it: "More than any of us has supposed, Paul was *Paul the Tentmaker*. His trade occupied much of his time. . . . His life was very much that of the workshop . . . of being bent over side-by-side with slaves."[46] This indicates that Paul's work was physical and arduous, requiring hard labor that began before sunrise: "Surely you remember . . . our toil and hardship; we worked night and day" (1 Thess 2:9a NIV).

---

43. Murray, *Post-Christendom*, 263.

44. As a native of Tarsus in Cilicia, Paul may have learned about *cilicium*, a goat's haircloth used especially by sailors and soldiers, or he may have been a leatherworker, since in Hellenistic times, many tents were constructed of leather. See Boraas, "Tent," 1031; and Marshall, *Acts*, 293.

45. Barclay, *Acts of the Apostles*, 135. See also Longnecker, *Acts*, 989. Barnett cites a rabbinic quote from Rabbi Gamaliel III, who wrote: "An excellent thing is the study of the Torah combined with some secular occupation, for the labor by them both puts sin out of one's mind. All study of the Torah which is not combined with work will ultimately be futile and lead to sin (Pirque 'Abot 2.12)" (Barnett, "Tentmaking," 924). However, Hock contends that Paul probably learned tentmaking later in his life, in order to put his teaching into practice. See Hock, "Paul's Tentmaking," 555–64; and Hock, "Workshop as Social Context," 438–50.

46. Hock, *Social Context*, 67.

Paul intentionally kept his tentmaking or leather-working[47] trade during his missionary journeys.[48] He did this in order to model how it was to "work with your hands, just as we told you, so that your daily life may win the respect of outsiders and so that you will not be dependent on anybody" (1 Thess 4:11b–12). While Paul performed his trade, he reasoned with the Jews and God-fearing Greeks in the synagogues "as well as in the marketplace day by day with those who happened to be there" (Acts 17:17b NIV).

Paul's tentmaking was part of his intentional strategy to fulfill his mission. In his letters, Paul mentioned that he often supported himself financially by practicing a trade within the community (1 Cor 9:14–15; 2 Cor 11:9; 1 Thess 2:9). Along with Silvanus and Timothy, Paul recounted his labor of working "day and night in order not to be a burden to anyone" (1 Thess 2:9b NIV). His tentmaking also avoided giving potential converts any reason to suspect that he was after their money. Once a church was established, however, he would draw upon its resources to support his ministry in other locales (2 Cor 11:8–9; Phil 4:15–16).[49]

Paul's use of tentmaking as part of his strategic mission had three purposes.[50] First, tentmaking served the purpose of establishing his credibility (that he might not be an obstacle or stumbling block to the Gospel). Paul argued that he could have availed of his rights in receiving his living from the Gospel (1 Cor 9:1–14) but chose not to (1 Cor 9:15) so that "in preaching the gospel I may offer it free of charge, and so not make use of my rights in preaching it" (1 Cor 9:18b NIV). He did not want to be identified with itinerant lecturers with no scruples, like his Corinthian opponents who would "peddle the word of God for profit" (2 Cor 2:17a NIV). Instead of accepting payment for his ministry, Paul worked and cared for the congregations (1 Thess 2:5–10).

Second, Paul used tentmaking for the purpose of identification with those he sought to reach. From Ephesus, Paul wrote: "To this very hour we go hungry and thirsty, we are in rags, we are brutally treated, we are

---

47. Throckmorton, "Tentmaker," 573. Throckmorton argues that, though the etymological meaning of the Greek word *skenopoios* is "tentmaker," the term possibly meant "leatherworker." In addition, Elwell argues, "The Greek term for tentmaker may have served to denote a range of activities in cloth and leather" (Elwell, *Baker Encyclopedia*, 2092). Thus, "Paul's work need not have been restricted to the manufacture of tents, especially if he was a leatherworker" (Smith, "Tentmaker," 523). Since Paul worked as a tentmaker in Thessalonica, Ephesus, and Corinth, it is possible that Paul could "have manufactured and repaired various kinds of booths, canopies, and awnings for city use" (Barnett, "Tentmaking," 924).

48. Bruce, *Book of Acts*, 236–37.

49. See Powell, "Paul," 753; and Weima, *1–2 Thessalonians*, 151.

50. Siemens, "Vital Role of Tentmaking," 123–24.

homeless. We work hard with our hands" (1 Cor 4:11–12a NIV).[51] He did not only adapt to the general culture of each host city but also to the people he hoped to win—such as the "weak," day laborers, and slaves. This laboring class, which belonged to the social and economic bottom of society, comprised the majority of the residents of the Roman Empire.[52] Paul worked as an artisan, using his trade to make connections. Even though his contemporaries generally regarded work as appropriate for slaves but not for free citizens, and even though they looked down upon artisans and manual laborers,[53] Paul still engaged in tentmaking. Though he was a Roman citizen who might have had affluent background in provincial Cilicia (Acts 22:28), Paul still worked as tentmaker for the sake of the people whom God called him to reach.

Third, Paul employed tentmaking for the purpose of modeling a biblical work ethic. Talking about his own work ethic, he instructed the Thessalonians: "For you yourselves know how you ought to follow our example. On the contrary, we worked night and day, laboring and toiling . . . in order to offer ourselves as a model for you to imitate" (2 Thess 3:8b–9 NIV). Because of his own tentmaking model, Paul could command the Thessalonians to also have a strong work ethic—warning them against idleness and being busybodies, telling them to work for the food they eat, and giving them the rule of not eating when one is unwilling to work (2 Thess 3:6–12). In this list of instructions, Paul clearly expressed his conviction that idleness, which was endemic in Greco-Roman society, was inappropriate for Christian believers.

Significantly, Paul knew how to connect his tentmaking with his ministry: "We worked night and day . . . while we preached the gospel of God to you" (1 Thess 2:9c NIV). Such link of work and preaching probably means that Paul talked with people while he worked and "also, almost certainly, that on some days, or during part of the day, he laid aside his apron and tools and taught the gospel."[54] In other words, Paul lived out the value of combining work and witness well.

---

51. On the other hand, Paul was able to identify with the educated and upper class in society (e.g., the philosophers at the Aeropagus; the upper-class converts in Corinth; and the Asiarchs in Ephesus). Paul's tentmaking occupation could have placed him among the more fortunate members of the Roman Empire's impoverished population. He was poor, but he may have been a step above those who were living at a mere subsistence level (or worse). See Powell, "Paul," 754.

52. "Seventy percent of the population in the provinces were slaves, and 90 percent in Rome and Italy" (Siemens, "Vital Role of Tentmaking," 124).

53. Barnett, "Tentmaking," 927.

54. Barnett, "Tentmaking," 926. See also Weima, *1–2 Thessalonians*, 151.

Theological Insights on Tentmaking

Almost a hundred years ago, Studdert Kennedy asserted in relation to his Anglican denomination: "A very large number of the people who attend our services and partake of the sacrament are disassociated personalities. They are one person on Sunday and another on Monday. They have one mind for the sanctuary and another for the street. They have one conscience for the church and another for the cotton factory. Their worship conflicts with their work, but they will not acknowledge the conflict."[55]

There are many contributing factors to the "Sunday–Monday" gap. These factors can be categorized as distortions of Scripture, Christian history, and questionable application of secular social structures.[56] While there are many ways to address and bridge the "Sunday–Monday" gap,[57] this chapter proposes three theological paradigm shifts: (1) a shift from the "sacred-secular" divide; (2) a shift from the "clergy-laity" divide; and (3) a shift from the "church-community" divide.

The sacred-secular divide can be bridged through the understanding of the Lordship of Jesus in all of life, realizing the unhealthy nature of compartmentalizing life (into family, work, church, recreation, finance, social, and private aspects of life). When we learn to see our lives according to the three-word Gospel worldview, "Jesus is Lord," we realize that there is no part of our lives or the world that does not fall under the loving lordship of Jesus.[58] At the Cape Town Commitment of Lausanne III, this statement on truth and the workplace is affirmed: "The falsehood of a 'sacred-secular divide' has permeated the Church's thinking and action. This divide tells us that religious activity belongs to God, whereas other activity does not. Most Christians spend most of their time in work which they may think has little spiritual value (so-called secular work). But God is Lord of all of life."

The "clergy-laity" divide can be bridged through the understanding of the priesthood of all believers (as Martin Luther passionately taught it). We need to recognize that we are all *kleros* (from which the word "clergy" is derived). We must also comprehend that we are called and we are all *laos* (from which the word "laity" is derived) or God's people.[59] As Ott argues,

---

55. *Report of Anglican-Catholic Congress* cited in Kenneth Leech, *Eye of the Storm*, 2.
56. "Marketplace Ministry," 13–18.
57. "Marketplace Ministry," 19–36.
58. Wegner and Magruder, *Missional Moves*, 36.
59. Clement's first letter to the Corinthians (ca. AD 96) is the first use of the clergy-laity distinction. See Stevens, *Abolition of the Laity*.

"We must avoid communicating that professional pastors and missionaries are the only, or even the best, way to reach the world for Christ."[60]

The "church-community" divide can be bridged through the understanding of the "gathered" and "scattered" natures of the Church. As citizens of the city of God, we are called not to spend all our time "gathering" in the *ecclesia* or town hall like a Christian ghetto. Instead, we meet there to rehearse how we might help to humbly transform our city and workplace in the light of the coming city of God.[61] We are to be engaged in the "scattered" aspect of Church during the week for our ministry to the community while we also take part in the "gathered" aspect during the weekend of our Church worship. As we are called to care as a community, we are also called to care for the community.

These three paradigm shifts help us to see the potential for tentmaking to address the different cultural realities related to secularization and immigration. Though tentmaking has its unique challenges such as effectively handling two major vocations (aside from marriage and family) or condescending attitudes towards it as a second-class ministry, its potential for effective ministry in the Canadian context is promising. Possible benefits including increased relevance in identifying better with the people, speaking their heart language, use of incarnational lifestyle, practice of more hospitality through the relational connections, and active witness through word and deed.[62]

Conclusion

While the challenges created by secularization are daunting, opportunities exist to discern faithful responses. Understanding the current realities being faced and gathering insight from current experiments in mission as well as biblical and historical precedents can offer ways forward. The challenge is primarily contextualization, wrestling with the theological priorities we have identified in such a way that we effectively partner with the *mission Dei*. While the concepts require further refinement and research is required to better understand the current experience of tentmaking, this initial exploration points to further pathways for discovery. Multicultural research into the lived experience of tentmaking and the corresponding adaptation of training and support methods could be one strategic approach to

60. Ott, "Let the Buyer Beware," 287.
61. See Cole, "Doctrine of the Church," 2–17.
62. Lai, *Tentmaking*, 171–73. See also Murray, *Church Planting*, 224–26, and Murray, *Planting Churches*, 170.

addressing this particular contemporary issue in Canadian society. Paul's example in the biblical text and theological reflection resonating with the issues raised can guide the process of discovery and provide spiritual depth to strategy. This form of integrated missiological reflection and intentional action can assist in the process of identifying opportunities in the midst of the challenges.

Reflection Questions

1. What are meaningful ways to encourage and support newcomers to Canada who are functioning as missionaries?

2. With the wide range of experimental forms of congregational mission available, how can local leaders be encouraged to engage in innovative outreach and affirmed when they do?

3. If you were called to tentmaking, what would be the biblical images and themes that would motivate you?

Bibliography

Barclay, William. *The Acts of the Apostles*. Philadelphia: Westminster, 1976.
Barnett, P. W. "Tentmaking." In *Dictionary of Paul and His Letters*, edited by Gerald F. Hawthorne, et al., 657–58. Downers Grove, IL: InterVarsity, 1993.
Berger, Peter L. "Further Thoughts on Religion and Modernity." *Society* 49 (2012) 313–16.
Bibby, Reginald W. *Resilient Gods*. Vancouver: UBC Press, 2017.
Bickers, Dennis. *The Art and Practice of Bivocational Ministry: A Pastor's Guide*. Kansas City, MO: Beacon Hill, 2013.
Bird, Warren. "Large Canadian Churches Draw an Estimated 300,000 Worshippers Each Week: Findings from a National Survey." *Leadership Network*, October 13, 2015. https://leadnet.org/large-canadian-churches-draw-an-estimated-300000-worshippers-each-week-findings-from-a-national-study.
Boraas, Roger S. "Tent." In *Harper Collins Bible Dictionary*, edited by Mark Allan Powell, et al., 1030–31. New York: Harper Collins, 2011.
Brisco, Brad. *Covocational Church Planting: Aligning Your Marketplace Calling and the Mission of God*. Alpharetta: SEND Network, 2018.
Bruce, F. F. *The Book of the Acts*. The New International Commentary on the New Testament. Grand Rapids: Eerdmans, 1979.
Caron-Malenfant, Éric, et al. "The Religious Switching of Immigrants in Canada." *Journal of Ethnic and Migration Studies* 44.15 (2017) 2582-602.
Chapman, Mark D., and James W. Watson. "Common Actions: Participatory Action Research as a Practice for Promoting Positive Social Action among and between

New Canadian Church Planters and Denominational Leaders." *Ecclesial Practices* 4 (2017) 63–86.

Connor, Phillip. *Immigrant Faith: Patterns of Immigrant Religion in the United States, Canada and Western Europe*. New York: New York University Press, 2014.

Costas, Orlando E. *Christ Outside the Gate: Mission Beyond Chrsitendom*. Maryknoll, NY: Orbis, 1984.

———. *The Integrity of Mission*. San Francisco: Harper & Row, 1979.

Davidson, Sean. "How to Make Small Groups Missional." *The Institute of Evangelism Wycliffe College*, September 10, 2017. https://institute.wycliffecollege.ca/2017/09/how-to-make-small-groups-missional.

Elwell, Walter A., ed. *Baker Encyclopedia of the Bible*. Grand Rapids: Baker, 1988.

Hackworth, Jason, and Kirsten Stein. "The Collision of Faith and Economic Development in Toronto's Inner Suburban Industrial Districts." *Urban Affairs Review* 48 (2012) 37–63.

Hiebert, Daniel. *What's So Special about Canada? Understanding the Resilience of Immigration and Multiculturalism*. Washington, DC: Migration Policy Institute, 2016.

Hock, R. E. "Paul's Tentmaking and the Problem of His Social Class." *Journal of Biblical Literature* 97 (1978) 555–64.

———. *The Social Context of Paul's Ministry: Tentmaking and Apostleship*. Philadelphia: Fortress, 1980.

———. "The Workshop as a Social Context for Paul's Missionary Preaching," *Catholic Biblical Quarterly* 41 (1979) 438–50.

Janzen, Rich, et al. "Integrating Immigrants into the Life of Canadian Urban Christian Congregations: Findings from a National Survey." *Review of Religious Research* 53 (2012) 441–70.

Kaushal, Neeraj et al. "Immigrant Employment and Earnings Growth in Canada and the USA: Evidence from Longitudinal Data." *Journal of Population Economics* 29 (2016) 1249–77.

Leech, Kenneth. *The Eye of the Storm, Living Spiritually in the Real World*. New York: Harper Collins, 1992.

Li, Wong Siew, ed. "Marketplace Ministry." Lausanne Occasional Paper 40. Lausanne Committee for World Evangelization, 2004. https://www.lausanne.org/content/lop/marketplace-ministry-lop-40.

"The Local Church in Mission: Becoming a Missional Congregation in the Twenty-First Century Global Context and the Opportunities Offered through Tentmaking Ministry," Lausanne Occasional Paper 39. Lausanne Committee for World Evangelization, 2004. https://www.lausanne.org/content/lop/local-church-mission-lop-39.

Longnecker, Richard N. *Acts*. The Expositor's Bible Commentary. Grand Rapids: Zondervan, 2007.

Marshall, I. Howard. *Acts*. Tyndale New Testament Commentaries. Grand Rapids: Eerdmans, 1980.

Morency, Jean-Dominique, et al. *Immigration and Diversity: Population Projections for Canada and its Regions, 2011 to 2036*. Ottawa: Statistics Canada, 2017.

"MoveIn is a Movement of Regular Christians Prayerfully Moving in Among the Unreached, Urban Poor." *MoveIn*. https://movein.to.

Murray, Stuart. *Post-Christendom: Church and Mission in a Strange New World*. Carlisle: Paternoster, 2004.
Ott, Craig, and Gene Wilson. *Global Church Planting: Biblical Principles and Best Practices for Multiplication*. Grand Rapids: Baker Academic, 2011.
———. "Let the Buyer Beware: Financially Supporting National Pastors and Missionaries May Not Always Be the Bargain It's Cracked Up to Be," *Evangelical Missions Quarterly* 29 (1993) 286–91.
Penner, James, et al. "Hemorrhaging Faith: Why and When Canadian Young Adults are Leaving, Staying and Returning to Church." Foundational Research Document, commissioned by The EFC Youth and Young Adult Ministry Roundtable. n.p., 2011.
Powell, Mark A. "Paul." In *Harper Collins Bible Dictionary*, edited by Mark Allan Powell, 748–62. New York: Harper Collins, 2011.
Reimer, Sam, et al. "Christian Churches and Immigrant Support in Canada." *Review of Religious Research* 58 (2016) 495–513.
———. "Conservative Protestants and Religious Polarization in Canada." *Studies in Religion* 46 (2017) 187–208.
Reimer, Sam, and Michael Wilkinson. *A Culture of Faith: Evangelical Congregations in Canada*. Montreal: McGill-Queen's University Press, 2015.
Reimer, Sam, and Rick Hiemstra. "The Rise of Part-time Employment in Canadian Christian Churches." *Studies in Religion* 44 (2015) 1–22.
Santos, Narry. "What's a Missionary Doing in Canada?" In *Green Shoots out of Dry Ground: Growing a New Future for the Church in Canada*, edited by John P. Bowen, 97–110. Eugene, OR: Wipf & Stock, 2013.
Siebert, Jared. *Gutsy: (Mis)Adventures in Canadian Church Planting*. Mississauga: New Leaf Network, 2016.
Siemens, Ruth E. "The Vital Role of Tentmaking in Paul's Mission Strategy." *International Journal of Frontier Missions* 14 (1997) 123–24.
Smith, Abraham. "Tentmaker." In *The New Interpreter's Dictionary of the Bible*, edited by Katharine Doob Sakenfeld, 523. Vol. 5. Nashville: Abingdon, 2009.
Stetzer, Ed, and Daniel Im. *The State of Church Planting in Canada*. Nashville: LifeWay Christian Resources, 2016.
Stevens, R. Paul. *Abolition of the Laity: Vocation, Work and Ministry in Biblical Perspective*. Carlisle: Paternoster, 1999.
Studebaker, Steven, and Lee Beach. "Emerging Churches in Post-Christian Canada." *Religions* 3 (2012) 862–79.
Thiessen, Joel. *The Meaning of Sunday*. Montreal: McGill/Queen's University Press, 2015.
———. "A Sociological Description and Defence of Secularization in Canada." *Post-Christendom Studies* 1 (2016) 97–124.
Thiessen, Joel, and Sarah Wilkins-LaFlamme. "Becoming a Religious None: Irreligious Socialization and Disaffiliation." *Journal for the Scientific Study of Religion* 56.1 (2017) 64–82.
Throckmorton, B. H. "Tentmaker." In *The Interpreter's Dictionary of the Bible*, edited by George A. Buttrick, 573. Vol. 4. Nashville: Abingdon, 1962.
Tunehag, Mats, et al., eds. "Business as Mission," Lausanne Occasional Paper 59. Lausanne Committee for World Evangelization, 2004. https://www.lausanne.org/content/lop/lop-59.

Wan, Enoch, and Anthony Casey. *Church Planting among Immigrants in US Urban Centres*. Portland, OR: Institute of Diaspora Studies–USA, 2014.

"We Make Craft Beer in Sarnia, Ontario." *Refined Fool Brewing Co.* https://www.refinedfool.com.

Wegner, Rob, and Jack Magruder. *Missional Moves: 15 Tectonic Shifts that Transform Churches, Communities, and the World*. Grand Rapids: Zondervan, 2012.

Weima, Jeffrey A. D. *1–2 Thessalonians*. Baker Exegetical Commentary of the New Testament. Grand Rapids: Baker Academic, 2014.

Wilkinson, Michael. *The Spirit Said Go: Pentecostal Immigrants in Canada*. New York: Peter Lang, 2006.

10

Technology as Loose Cannon on the Deck of Secularization's Ship

Glenn Martin

Introduction

Technological development may be alternately understood as handmaid to mission progress or as agent of secularization. It is perhaps best understood as both/and, much like the proverbial loose cannon on board a sailing vessel of wartimes past. If not fixed adequately to its mounting, a cannon could move around with the roll of the vessel, pointing anywhere and being as dangerous to oneself and to one's enemies. This chapter reviews literature around this conversation—considering especially the growing impact of social media—and argues for the leverage of technology for mission. I write in academic terms as a generalist but also with the heart of a missionary practitioner, for whom technology matters.

In light of the challenges of mission and evangelism in an arguably secularizing world, the relationship between technology and secularization is worth our attention. Is technology friend or foe? Has technology weakened the hand of religion in our lives? While making space for argument from the social sciences, I wish to pay heed to David Hesselgrave's admonition to missiologists at the dawn of the third millennium, when he turned a phrase of Augustine's and exhorted missiology not to be enamored with "Egyptian gold," which was to say, social science.[1] Our mandate on mission comes not from social science research but from solid biblical moorings, as is our hope and confidence in a favorable end.

---

1. See Hesselgrave, "Third Millennium Missiology."

"It's Complicated"

That said, two points should be briefly noted to frame the conversation, though for reasons of space, we cannot develop them. First, it must be said that even in the academy, secularization theory has been significantly called into question and must not be taken as a sure thing.[2] It is not a sure thing that modernization leads unequivocally to secularization. Secondly, it is equally simplistic to think of technology's influence on culture in concretely deterministic ways. Danah Boyd reminds us—her comments pointed especially to social media—that technological determinism "assume(s) that technologies possess intrinsic powers that affect all people in all situations the same way."[3] Such views, whether in the dystopian or utopian versions, do not adequately take into account that "reality is nuanced and messy, full of pros and cons."[4] The nuances, variables, and complexities are too many for easy generalizations. It is equally naïve to think that technology has no influence on us and that we are simply and always its master. Three significant books on this subject, the subtitles of which give away the author's perspectives, are David Landes's *Revolution in Time: Clocks and the Making of the Modern World*, Neil Postman's *Technopoly: The Surrender of Culture to Technology*, and Nicholas Carr's *The Shallows: What the Internet is Doing to our Brains*.

Within the broad spectrum of technological advance, it is perhaps of most interest for us as missionaries to consider the fields of technological development that have so much to do with going and preaching and with our connectedness—specifically, the technologies of transportation and communication. In our day, this brings to mind internet and social media technologies, but in the past century, this line of development has given us the automobile, commercial air transportation, television, radio, and telephone. The printing press is in the same vein. Neil Postman considers the telegraph a pivotal innovation—messages could finally travel faster than people. Postman notes: "For the first time, transportation and communication were disengaged from each other," giving us "context-free information" with all of its potential for good and evil.[5] Separating the message from its carrier did not only give rise to mass media communication and new opportunities to get the message out but also inevitably to the misrepresenta-

---

2. See Anderson, "Transformation of World Christianity"; Berger, "Secularism in Retreat"; Berger, *Many Altars of Modernity*; Bibby, "Religious Polarization in Canada"; and Stark, *Triumph of Faith*.

3. Boyd, *It's Complicated*, 15.

4. Boyd, *It's Complicated*, 16.

5. Postman, *Technopoly*, 67.

tion and trivialization of the message. Technological developments usually carry implications far beyond the immediately obvious.

Technology as Handmaid to Gospel Advance in History

Technological progress has generally been understood in mission history as a handmaid to Gospel advance. Three classic examples come to mind in Church and mission history; namely, the first-century Church, the Reformation era, and the nineteenth century (sometimes referred to as the "Great Century" of mission advance).[6] We consider these three classic examples and then rejoin the question of technology's relationship to secularization and mission in our era.

First of all, the technology of the Roman Empire—most notably the Roman system of roads and the common Greek language—created a context for the efficient and rapid spread of Christianity in the first three centuries of the Church. The hegemony of Rome and the subsequent *Pax Romana* were vital to the early Christians' maximizing their use of the available technology. Good roads and a common language are much less useful without social stability. On the other hand, the concentration of political power that provided social stability also turned out to be a peril when the tide of opinion in the palace turned against the early Christians. It was an imperfect context, a mixed bag, but Christians seized the day and the Church grew.

In the Reformation era, it is readily acknowledged that the advances in printing technology were pivotal in setting the stage for the relative success of Martin Luther's work, especially in contrast with efforts of Reformers just ahead of him in history. As in the early centuries of the Church, the decision to use a particular language was key to the effective dissemination of ideas. In the Reformation era, the printing of Luther's works in vernacular German was instrumental in spreading his radical ideas. In contrast with the early Christian era, it was not the centralizing tendency of an empire that came as an auxiliary to facilitate the impact of technology but rather the indigenizing principle of a German nationalism that gave impetus to Reformation initiative. This, too, was an imperfect context, a mixed bag. Critics of Luther make much of his interaction with the political issues of his day, especially in regard to the Peasant Revolt.

In our third example, we find Europe in the era of colonial expansion. Now, it is not one empire but multiple competing empires that form the geopolitical backdrop for the "Great Century" of missionary advance to the four corners of the earth. We see the significance of technology in the life

6. Latourette, *History of Christianity*, 2:1063.

and work of William Carey at the dawn of that era. The accessibility of print and printed media were key not only to his early formation and to the broad dissemination of his argument for missionary initiative (*An Enquiry into the Obligations of Christians to Use Means for the Conversion of the Heathens*) but also for his formidable work in translation and printing of Scriptures in Asia. What is more, the technology of sea transportation had advanced enough to allow for greater ease, speed, and precision in trans-oceanic travel—all of which were vital in getting thousands of laborers to far-flung corners of the globe, including places in the Pacific unknown to Europeans until that era. The military strength of Britain had created what came to be known as *Pax Britannica*, but it was in many ways a fragile *pax*; missionary initiative was always vulnerable, caught in the restless struggle between the powers. Missionaries lived a precarious relationship with politics, depending on governments and trading companies for transportation and protection, even though they often found themselves in opposition to the posture those entities took with the local population. In all of the missionary advance of the "Great Century," technology was more handmaid than hindrance, but to take advantage of the available technology, the missionaries often had to work in the shadow of the empire—always at risk of being painted with the same brush as that with which the other passengers stepping off the boat were painted. It was, again, a mixed bag. Missionaries did not maneuver that imperfect context perfectly, but they did courageously use the *means* that their advance afforded.

Returning to the twentieth century, we see that even in spite of catastrophic evil wrought by totalitarian exploitation of technology, the Gospel of Jesus Christ continued its relentless spread through the creative, daring, and often mundane use of available technologies. How much of the fruitfulness of Trans World Radio, HCJB, Open Doors, Wycliffe Bible Translators, and the Jesus Film were enhanced by improved technologies? The Jesus Film was already widely disseminated in the analog era (positioned for explosive advance) when digital technology came on the scene, on its way to becoming the most-watched film in history.[7]

Even so, technological advantage is not always strategic advantage in missionary endeavor. Missionaries can be too quick to assume that their more "efficient" methods are better. Patrick Johnstone notes: "We must not be dazzled by the wonders of technology, and think that the need for mighty intercessory prayer is obviated, the need for the cross and suffering nullified, or the value of real-life acculturation and incarnation of expatriate missionaries within the culture lessened. Technology lessens our sole dependence

---

7. See Eshleman, "Jesus Film," and Johnstone, "Covering the Globe," 549.

on physical nearness and direct personal contacts, but does not lessen its value."[8] If we allow ourselves to imagine that—because the message can get there without us—we do not need to go, then the true Gospel of the incarnated Christ has suffered a terrible loss.

As we transition back to our own digital era, it is pertinent to wonder whether technology's inherent bent is more toward a centralizing or decentralizing orientation and why that might matter. I suggest that it does matter. To illustrate from Scripture, does digital technology have more in common with pre-Babel mono-cultural reality or with the multi-form expression of Pentecost? Lammin Sanneh argues that Pentecost is representative of something vital about Christianity—its affirmation of linguistic diversity and the validity of the Gospel message in the vernacular. Sanneh notes: "The 'many tongues' of Pentecost demonstrate that God accepts all cultures within the scheme of salvation, reinforcing the position that Jews and Gentiles are equal before God. . . . In mission, the church applied this insight by recognizing all cultures and the languages in which they are embodied as lawful in God's eyes, making it possible to render God's word into other languages without reservation."[9]

Value of Digital Technology

Digital technology seems a good fit for such aims. Given this very biblical emphasis on the adaptability of the message to its context and the similarly biblical emphasis on individual decision to faith in Christ, much advantage to mission lies with a technology readily adaptable to local expression. In every field of communication, the move to digital technologies lowers the threshold to access. In printing, one can do at home with little cost what was once much harder to acquire or to hide when made available. For over a decade, friends in Cuba have run a campus ministry distributing homemade tracts designed on their laptops, even when these tracts were banned. Audio and video connectivity are similarly widespread, such that the next viral video could come from anywhere. This decentralizing effect of digital media has had a parallel significance in political movements for change, when those resisting totalitarian force used social media to organize.

The significance of digital technology to Christian mission is hard to over-emphasize. In every field of our endeavor, its impact favourably shapes progress. Negatives appear but they seem to pale in comparison to the positives. Mission mobilization and networking of resources have been

8. Johnstone, "Covering the Globe," 551.
9. Sanneh, *Translating the Message*, 53–54.

tremendously enhanced through communication technology. Fieldwork in Bible translation has sped up incredibly, thanks to technological advances. As Wycliffe Global Alliance notes on their website: "We embrace the vision that by the year 2025, a Bible translation project will be in progress for every people group that needs it."[10]

What about evangelism? Increased broadband access across the globe and the persistent creativity of God's people have hugely increased the reach of the message. Evangelism and discipleship efforts can be both global and people-group specific, as with the evangelistic cartoon videos on indigitube.tv. As of this writing, Youversion.com reports over 300 million installs and 16.7 billion Bible chapters read. Faithcomesbyhearing.com has Bible recordings available online in 1,145 languages. Who can measure the reach of these and the literally millions of other websites in terms adequate to capture their mission significance? Clearly, digital technology has facilitated an ever-expanding proliferation of tools and strategies for global missions.

Downsides of Advances in Technology

Can all these technological advances have any downsides? Two questions come readily to mind. How much does it matter that this technology is not only available to us but also to those of a different mindset and agenda? Secondly, what can be said of the inherent impact of technology itself, apart from the content that the technology might deliver? At this juncture, we now consider these questions.

How much does it matter that these technological advances are also available to those who work against the Christian missionary impulse? A global missions leader recently commented, "In just the last forty-eight hours, I went through three airports on two continents. The first one, a developing country, scanned my passport and took my picture. The second one scanned my passport, took my picture, put me through a body scanning machine, and took a picture of my eyes. The third one did all of the above, as well as taking my fingerprints. Of course, this information is widely exchanged among countries. The scary thing is what countries are doing with this technology to attempt to shut down Christianity."[11]

How much should this concern us? Our concern must lead us to be proactive. We must not be careless or lazy in the use of the means that have become available to us. The opportunities we have today may not be ours tomorrow. Persecution of the Church and restrictions on evangelism and

---

10. Wycliffe Global Alliance, "Vision 2025."
11. Promotional email from call2all.org, Feb 1, 2018.

discipleship are not just a thing of the past. Christians must proactively "seize the day," including the development of both more and better evangelistic and nation-discipling content that reflects God's shalom values in the promotion of holistic human well-being in order, abundance, and beauty.[12] The global internet community's voracious appetite for new content is truly astounding, and messengers of the faith must ever seek to express eternal truth again, in ways both winsome and relevant.

What about the influence of communication technology itself, apart from the content delivered? To answer this question, we have to consider two distinct but related issues: the influence of the *process* by which technological development happens, and the influence of the *product* of that technological development. Again, we consider them in turn.

Technologies do not arrive by themselves or develop uniformly across populations. Along the way to widespread usage, they highlight and exacerbate inequalities of status and economics. A new technology is first the privilege of the elite before it becomes the prerogative of the masses. One thinks of the horseless carriage, the telephone, the television, the personal computer, and the smartphone as representative examples in the living memories of older North Americans. In our connected world, most of what we hold in our hands was made elsewhere, and it is impossible to adequately evaluate the impact of new digital technologies without addressing their manufacture and distribution and the symbiotic relationship between globalization, consumerism, and pop culture. For reasons of space, we cannot give this adequate treatment here except to affirm that our globalized geopolitical context today is, like the historical contexts referred to earlier, rife with ethical complexity and profoundly imperfect.

In considering the impact of the *product* of technological development, it is relevant to ask whether communication technologies inherently favor collectivization or favor individualization. The record appears mixed. Not all technologies point to the same direction. We can obviously find images of totalitarian use of state media, wire-tapping, propaganda, and violations of privacy, but totalitarian regimes existed before these technologies did, and we may legitimately ask if the technologies have tended to strengthen or weaken their force and control.

Once we get a new technology in our hands, we use it to advance a certain set of goals in our life agenda, but it also inevitably shapes us. I suggest that the general direction of that influence has favored individual autonomy. There is little doubt that technological advances in transportation and communication, for example, have greatly facilitated individualism. To

---

12. See Jethani, *Futureville*.

take a case in point, the automobile significantly altered the dating life of most North American young adults, giving them the freedom to leave the front parlor behind. The telephone's development offers a similar picture. I am old enough to remember "party lines" in rural Ontario, Canada, where our home phone line was shared with a few neighbors—each house having a distinct ring, indicating for which house an incoming call was meant. All of us knew the tell-tale "click" that gave away that someone else had picked up the phone in a neighboring home while you were still on the line. I remember my father insisting that our conversations be short and to the point, partly for reasons of cost but also in light of the shared nature of the line. And, of course, the phone handset was wired to the wall. Privacy was relative. In our home at least, conversations were rarely out of earshot of family. I distinctly remember my sister stretching the cord to its maximum length to step into the stairwell while talking with her boyfriend. How much has cellular technology facilitated our individual agenda, our not needing to negotiate shared usage, and bypassing, in many cases, what have been traditional gatekeepers of communication (such as parents or tribal elders)? Who remembers the fights over the TV remote, when everyone can now watch what they want to on their own device?

It seems appropriate here to distinguish between the influence of technology having to do with the devices themselves and technology having to do with platforms of connectivity, including social media. While device development consistently seems to favor individual user-friendliness and autonomy, the unintended influence of platform development—by which I mean structures like Facebook or Instagram—and their capacity to allow users to "participate in and help create" what might be called "networked publics"[13] is often quite the opposite. Social media is perhaps the most important case in point.

An abundance of research in the past decade has generated lots of opinions but few definitive conclusions,[14] as Boyd suggests by the title of her book, "It's complicated." Even so, common threads emerge. Stephen Marche's question "Is Facebook making us lonely?" hits a nerve.[15] This generation has coined the term FOMO (that is, the fear of missing out) to speak of the underlying angst felt as one scans the social media feed to see what one's friends are posting and doing. Recent studies indicate that adolescent

---

13. Boyd, *It's Complicated*, 5.

14. See Boyd, *It's Complicated*; Carr, *Shallows*; Turkle, *Alone Together*; and Twenge, *iGen*.

15. Marche, "Is Facebook Making Us Lonely?"

females are particularly vulnerable.[16] High social media use and depression are strongly linked[17] and teen suicide in the US is up.[18] Social media exacerbates the widespread and enduring tendency of adolescents to compare themselves with others. This is not likely limited to adolescents. While the greater danger among adolescents may be cyber-bullying, the greater danger among adults may be a self-inflicted FOMO. Internet technology's impact on culture is mixed; even when two factors appear more or less in sequence, it is very difficult to substantiate causation.

Perhaps the heart of the matter—especially inasmuch as mission is concerned—is that the promise of technology is in its ability to connect us while the threat of technology is in its potential to isolate us. Technology is a handmaid of mission only inasmuch as it serves as a bridge to individuals, communities, ethnicities, and their mediums of language and communication. Inasmuch as technology separates or isolates individuals and communities, it is no longer serving the mission cause. Perhaps it really is all about relationships. That said, Vriens and Van Ingen contend from their research on social media use in the Netherlands that we "can conclude with more certainty that—rather than with erosion of strong ties—social media use is associated with more and more dynamic interaction with our strong ties. This should temper some of the worries about negative consequences of the Internet."[19]

Does Technology Inherently Secularize?

Is there any indication that technology inherently secularizes? Medical technology is an interesting case in point. While it is a biblical imperative to save and heal whenever we can, and technological advance has given us huge benefits in medicine, we can readily discern an inherent ambivalence in the relationship between medical technology and religion. Conscious pursuit of the divine in healing is more prevalent where less medical care is available. Moses's admonition of Israel not to forget God when they come into their prosperity (Deut 6:10–12) still applies.

Even as new advances in medicine may marginalize the transcendent to issues of deep crisis, Neil Postman suggests that new communication media may do the same. He cautions: "A preacher who confines himself to considering how a medium can increase his audience will miss the significant

---

16. See Twenge, *iGen*.
17. See Twenge et al., "Increases."
18. See Twenge, *iGen*.
19. Vriens and Van Ingen, "Rise of Internet," 14.

question: In what sense does new media alter what is meant by religion, by church, [and] even by God?"[20] Postman argues, by way of illustration, that advancements in astronomy under Copernicus, Galileo, and Kepler shaped theological developments in ways totally unexpected by them. Though these astronomers were very interested in God, their work, argues Postman, "left the Western world to wonder if God had any interest in us at all."[21] While we may see that as a non sequitur, we can understand why Postman says it.

While it is premature to make definitive declarations about the long-term impact of digital media on our society, families, and individual development—or even on our mission task—we can draw a parallel with the eras we mentioned earlier. The context of mission advance has never been a perfect one. The relationship with the sociopolitical context is always rife with risk. Will we seize the day? Will we heed William Carey's exhortation to "use means"?

In our globalized and digitally-mediated context, both the medium itself and the content remind us in many ways of our connectedness, our need for one another (Facebook "likes" have to come from someone else), our limits and inadequacies, and our need for the transcendent. Through the ages, the very human reality of perceived loneliness has often been a portal to the pursuit of God. On the other hand, the greatest negatives of our digital technology may lie with its power to distract us from what is truly important, its powerful addictive tendencies, and the fact that by placing such a premium on titillating new content, it easily marginalizes the old. What long-term impact the new technologies will have on our brains and structures of thought is beyond the scope of this paper, but it is also a matter of tremendous significance.

Application of Technology for Mission

We come to the focus of our argument and the point of application for mission. Some leading mission researchers argue that the most significant mission statistic today is that 86 percent of the world's Muslims, Buddhists, and Hindus do not personally know a Christian.[22] This is not expected to change much anytime soon. According to their estimates, even by 2050, the percentage of non-Christians who personally know a Christian is still expected to be below 16 percent![23] Of course, God can reveal himself to

---

20. Postman, *Technopoly*, 19.
21. Postman, *Technopoly*, 29.
22. Johnson et al., "Christianity 2015."
23. Johnson et al., "Christianity 2015," 29.

the lost in their dreams; they can download the Jesus Film or find an audio Bible online in their language—but the significance of a human connection can hardly be overstated.[24] At the same time, the "degrees of separation" between every human being on the planet continue to drop. Facebook claimed in 2016 that between members of the global Facebook community of 1.59 billion users, the average number of intermediaries was only 3.57.[25] In other words, on average, between any of us that uses Facebook and the most unrelated Facebook user you can find in the world, there are less than four intermediaries. How many of those potential intermediaries might be immigrants in our communities, recently arrived and well connected relationally to broad networks in the lesser-reached corners of the globe? How much more connected are we today, now that the number of monthly Facebook users has passed two billion?[26]

Why should you care about this? Might you be one connection away from sowing into a people movement to Christ on the far side of the globe? Might more connectedness facilitate mission? Research indicates that "between-group" interaction (that is, you and a circle of your friends interacting with a circle of friends from the other group interacting in ongoing ways—for example, hosting a quarterly international potluck for immigrants) reduces out-group prejudice, even for others of that circle not personally part of the interaction. The study found that extended contact, "knowing that another ingroup member has positive outgroup contact, can also reduce outgroup prejudice" and that even "individuals experiencing no direct, face-to-face intergroup contact can benefit from living in mixed settings where fellow ingroup members do engage in such contact."[27] What this means is that your friendship with unreached people group members in your neighborhood can open doors for the Gospel in all of their circle of influence, even beyond persons of your own acquaintance. Think of it this way: a recent immigrant talking by Skype with family overseas about her interactions with you not only affects how they see your group but may also soften their hearts for that moment when they encounter a Jesus follower where they are. Of course, the flow goes both ways: your friendship with immigrants can help your whole circle of non-immigrant contacts see immigrants differently. You may help address the widespread anxiety many feel about relating to immigrants. In a recent survey of one thousand pastors, researchers in the US found that "churches are twice as likely to fear

24. Fleischmann, "How Outsiders Find Faith."
25. Bhagat et al., "Three and a Half Degrees."
26. Chaykowski, "2 Billion Users."
27. Christ et al., "Contextual Effect," 3996.

refugees as they are to help them."[28] Researchers remind us that the benefits of inter-group contact will only be realized "when members of different groups take up those opportunities and engage in more frequent, positive, face-to-face contact."[29]

How much can social media bridge us to those face-to-face contacts? In a fascinating study of the use of social networking sites (SNSs) by first-generation immigrants to the Netherlands, Damien and Van Ingen found that "SNS usage is positively related to the number of outgroup ties" and "online activities may help establish relations with natives, which is known to be an important success factor in acculturation processes."[30] In other words, immigrants found that Facebook (and Hyves, a now-defunct networking platform unique to the Netherlands) helped them connect with the non-immigrant community. The researchers continue, "SNSs can be tools that help establish and maintain outgroup contacts, but only in the hands of someone who has the desire to use them that way. Nonetheless, it is plausible that the rise of social Internet applications has made life a bit easier in this regard."[31] Damien and Van Ingen are on to something relevant to us here. They also note: "Our second conclusion is that the use of SNSs has a positive effect on the quality of social relationships. Our findings extend previous studies in this regard, because as far as we know, this has never been tested among migrants before. Again, the effects among migrants may even be greater than among non-migrants, since they are still establishing a personal network with resourceful contacts."[32]

In its mercenary march for progress, globalization has placed communication technology in the hands of an ever-widening body of people and has lumped us together with others very different from us—not only in physical spaces like schools and neighborhoods but also in virtual communities. Canada is very diverse. Leveraging technology for friendship with people unlike us may build bridges toward unprecedented global harvest and may potentially counteract some of technology's arguably inherent bent toward secularization. If technology were a loose cannon, let us tie it down. Let us use it as a means for mission purposes.

Perhaps very much like biblical Abram in his pilgrimage from Ur of the Chaldeans to the land of Canaan, we have been brought in our day to a place of much traffic, where continents come together. Why are we here?

28. Smietana, "Churches Fear Refugees."
29. Christ et al., "Contextual Effect," 4000.
30. Damien and Van Ingen, "Social Network Site Usage," 648.
31. Damien and Van Ingen, "Social Network Site Usage," 649.
32. Damien and Van Ingen, "Social Network Site Usage," 649.

The imperative in our day is like that of Esther, to understand that we have been brought to a place of influence "for such a time as this" (Esth 4:14).

Reflection Questions

1. In what ways is technological development a mixed blessing in your context?
2. Who are the people you hope to reach, for whom the first threshold of contact might more readily be accomplished via social media?
3. How might technology be used to encourage the pursuit of God without also encouraging an increased dependency on technology?

Bibliography

Anderson, Allan H. "The Transformation of World Christianity: Secularization, Globalization and the Growth of Pentecostalism." Paper for the Society for Pentecostal Studies 44th Annual Meeting, Southeastern University, Lakeland, FL, March 2015.

Berger, Peter L. *The Many Altars of Modernity: Toward a Paradigm for Religion in a Pluralist Age*. Boston: de Gruyter, 2014.

———. "Secularism in Retreat." *The National Interest* 46 (1996) 3–12.

Bhagat, Smriti, et al. "Three and a Half Degrees of Separation." *Facebook Research Blog*, February 4, 2016. https://research.fb.com/three-and-a-half-degrees-of-separation.

Bibby, Reginald W. "Religious Polarization in Canada: A Major Empirical Update." Paper presented at the Annual Meeting of the Society for the Scientific Study of Religion, Newport Beach, CA, 2015.

Boyd, Danah. *It's Complicated: The Social Lives of Networked Teens*. New Haven: Yale University Press, 2014.

Carr, Nicholas. *The Shallows: What the Internet is Doing to our Brains*. New York: Norton, 2011.

Chaykowski, Kathleen. "Mark Zuckerberg: 2 Billion Users Means Facebook's 'Responsibility is expanding.'" *Forbes*, June 27, 2017. https://www.forbes.com/sites/kathleenchaykowski/2017/06/27/facebook-officially-hits-2-billion-users.

Christ, Oliver, et al. "Contextual Effect of Positive Intergroup Contact on Outgroup Prejudice." *Proceedings of the National Academy of Sciences* 111.11 (2014) 3996–4000.

Damian, Elena, and Erik Van Ingen. "Social Network Site Usage and Personal Relations of Migrants." *Societies* 4.4 (2014) 640–53.

Eshleman, Paul A. "The 'Jesus' Film: A Contribution to World Evangelism." *International Bulletin of Missionary Research* 26.2 (2002) 68–72.

Fleischmann, Mike. "How Outsiders Find Faith." *Leadership Journal* 31.3 (2012) 79–82.

Hesselgrave, David J. "Third Millennium Missiology and the Use of Egyptian Gold." *Journal of the Evangelical Theological Society* 42.4 (1999) 577–89.

Jethani, Skye. *Futureville: Discover Your Purpose for Today by Reimagining Tomorrow.* Nashville: Thomas Nelson, 2014.

Johnson, Todd M., et al. "Christianity 2015: Religious Diversity and Personal Contact." *International Bulletin of Missionary Research* 39.1 (2015) 28–30.

Johnstone, Patrick. "Covering the Globe." In *Perspectives on the World Christian Movement*, edited by Ralph D. Winter and Steven C. Hawthorne, 541–52. Pasadena: William Carey, 1999.

Landes, David S. *Revolution in Time: Clocks and the Making of the Modern World.* Cambridge: Belknap, 2000.

Latourette, Kenneth S. *A History of Christianity.* Vol. 2. New York: Harper, 1953.

Marche, Stephen. "Is Facebook Making Us Lonely?" *The Atlantic* 309.4 (2012) 60–69. https://www.theatlantic.com/magazine/archive/2012/05/is-facebook-making-us-lonely.

Postman, Neil. *Technopoly: the Surrender of Culture to Technology.* New York: Vintage, 1993.

Sanneh, Lamin. *Translating the Message: The Missionary Impact on Culture.* Maryknoll, NY: Orbis, 2015.

Smietana, Bob. "Churches Twice as Likely to Fear Refugees Than to Help Them." *LifeWay*, February 29, 2016. https://lifewayresearch.com/2016/02/29/churches-twice-as-likely-to-fear-refugees-than-to-help-them.

Stark, Rodney. *The Triumph of Faith: Why the World is More Religious than Ever.* New York: Open Road Media, 2015.

Turkle, Sherry. *Alone Together: Why We Expect More From Technology and Less From Each Other.* New York: Basic, 2012.

Twenge, Jean M. *iGen: Why Todays Super-Connected Kids are Growing Up Less Rebellious, More Tolerant, Less Happy—and Completely Unprepared for Adulthood (and What This Means for the Rest of Us).* New York: Atria Books, 2017.

Twenge, Jean M., et al. "Increases in Depressive Symptoms, Suicide-Related Outcomes, and Suicide Rates Among US Adolescents After 2010 and Links to Increased New Media Screen Time." *Clinical Psychological Science* 6.1 (2018) 3–17.

Vriens, Eva, and Erik Van Ingen. "Does the Rise of the Internet Bring Erosion of Strong Ties? Analyses of Social Media Use and Changes in Core Discussion Networks." *New Media & Society* 20.7 (2017) 2432–49.

Wycliffe Global Alliance. "Vision 2025." http://www.wycliffe.net/about-us/more?id=7988.

11

Their Eyes Were Opened

A Holistic Epistemology for Missional Discipleship

STEVEN SHETTERLY AND RHONDA M. MCEWEN

Introduction

HOW DOES THE WAY in which we *know* influence the way we *live*? To put it in philosophical terms, how does our epistemology impact our ethics? Whether explicitly stated or implicitly assumed, one's epistemology in fact provides an undergirding and foundation to all other disciplines; as such, it has a tremendous, unseen impact on all aspects of life. As Parker Palmer asserts, "Epistemology *becomes* our ethic."[1] Knowing and being are intrinsically linked.

Further, how does knowing relate to discipleship, and what are the implications for mission, especially within our current secular context? This chapter will seek to show, through reference to the Emmaus Road encounter in conversation with the work of Michael Polyani, that knowing, particularly for Christians, is a process far different, more personal, and more mysterious than our Western-trained minds initially comprehend. Further, this more holistic epistemology invites several implications for missional discipleship that are especially relevant to the prevailing secularism in our present global context.

The modern, secular worldview—increasingly influential in contemporary global contexts—offers a decidedly lopsided epistemology, one which privileges certain ways of knowing over others: favoring facts over feelings, objectivity over subjectivity, and reason over faith. Moreover, it has inadvertently contributed to an anemic understanding of discipleship

---

1. Palmer, *Know As We Are Known*, 21.

within Christian mission—one that is only focused on "spirituality" or learning facts about the Bible, prayer, and other religious activities.

Contrary to this more limited view of discipleship, a consequence of the prevailing secular worldview separating what is "Christian" or "holy" from everyday knowledge, a biblical worldview is more than sufficient to offer a compelling counter-narrative. This narrative includes an inextricable ethical dimension. As Christopher Wright asserts, discipleship involves knowing "what it means to walk in God's ways and demonstrate righteousness and justice."[2] Knowing in this respect represents so much more than mere knowledge about God and his laws, but rather, this sort of knowing is incarnational. Following Wright's emphasis, this chapter refers to "missional discipleship" as the whole-life transformation of individuals into the likeness of Christ through active participation in a community of believers devoted to cooperating with God in the *missio Dei*.[3]

Indeed, epistemology has an intrinsic connection to discipleship as our understanding of knowledge has a formative role in how we live our lives. To explicate this relationship even further, however, we first must take a closer look at the concept of knowing, for, as Palmer asserts, we cannot amend our approach to discipleship until we have first transformed our epistemology.[4]

In an effort to provide a roadmap of sorts for the rest of our chapter, we will focus on a passage from the Gospels that reveals the importance of epistemology in the discipleship of the Twelve. The Road to Emmaus offers a particularly illuminating account of an epistemological shift in the lives of Jesus' disciples:

> He said to them, "How foolish you are, and how slow to believe all that the prophets have spoken! Did not the Messiah have to suffer these things and then enter his glory?" And beginning with Moses and all the Prophets, he explained to them what was said in all the Scriptures concerning himself. . . . When he was at the table with them, he took bread, gave thanks, broke it and began to give it to them. Then their eyes were opened and they recognized him, and he disappeared from their sight. They asked each other, "Were not our hearts burning within us while he talked with us on the road and opened the Scriptures to us?" (Luke 24:25–26, 30–32 NIV)

---

2. Wright, *Mission of God's People*, 95.

3. Wright's focus on the *Missio Dei* as an overarching narrative for God's work in the world offers significant implications for the task of the church, especially as it concerns Christian discipleship.

4. Palmer, *Know As We Are Known*, xvii.

This encounter between the risen Christ and two distraught disciples is both strange and stirring, revealing a resurrected Jesus who is somehow mysteriously different and unrecognizable to his followers until the climactic moment at the breaking of the bread. Utilizing the Road to Emmaus encounter in conversation with Polanyi's scholarship, the following exploration invites Christians to consider a fresh approach to "knowing."

Without intending to draw a sharp dichotomy between rational-empirical and more holistic approaches, we will sketch the major contours of an epistemology that has been developed over the last several decades in counterpoint to the prevailing Western, rationalist-empiricist model. Though not specifically Christian in its origins, this model has been adopted and modified by a number of Christian thinkers (including Meek, Newbigin, Wright, Smith, and others) as a practical way forward in the face of modern, "scientific" objections to the faith. The key claims of this approach are that knowing involves an integrative, intuitive, and subjective process. It is practical before it is theoretical, and it is dynamic rather than static. Speaking to the core of Trinitarian faith, knowledge is both incarnational and interpersonal. As this more holistic epistemology invites several implications for missional discipleship, these will be interwoven throughout the chapter.

An Integrative, Intuitive, and Subjective Process

In the face of a modernist epistemology which is purportedly objective, explicitly rational, and concerned with deconstructing and classifying reality into its constituent parts, coming to know something is actually often an integrative, intuitive, and subjective process. Over the last several decades, in a growing reaction to logical positivism and empiricism, knowledge has come to be seen by many as inherently subjective. It is now widely (though certainly not universally) conceded that there is no objective or unaligned stance from which to neutrally observe and record reality. Polanyi used the term "tradition" or "tacit knowledge" to describe this phenomenon.

For example, a child can only learn how to think and communicate her thoughts by submitting herself to the authority of the community in which she is raised—first and foremost, through the act of acquiring a language.[5] When told that the small, white, fluffy, and energetic creature bounding around her house is "dog," she does not question whether or not "dog" is the appropriate nomenclature for such a creature nor does she consider whether or not this "dog" actually exists in any objective sense of the word. And

---

5. Mitchell, *Michael Polanyi*, 65.

when told later on that the much larger, brown, growling, and brooding creature that lives in her neighbor's yard is also "dog," she does not question why two such obviously different creatures should both be called "dog." She simply trusts what she is told and perhaps modifies her conception of what actually is a "dog" based on the varying, concrete examples she has seen.

As Polanyi says: "Traditionalism, which requires us to believe before we know, and in order that we may know, is based on a deeper insight into the nature of knowledge and of the communication of knowledge than is a scientific rationalism."[6] In order to acquire knowledge of "dog," the child from our example was required to submit herself to the tradition of her elders; any further exploration of the concept of "dog" for her will necessarily be subjective, based as it is on this inherited tradition. More to the point, this process of submitting herself to tradition will prove just as important, whether she is learning Spanish, Euclidian geometry, or particle physics.

Once it can be asserted that all knowledge is based on the subjective grounds of inherited tradition, N. T. Wright contends that the last thing one should do is to attempt to return to a sort of "chastened positivism" that tries to differentiate between knowledge which is subjective and that which can still be objectively determined, based on empirical sense-data and reasoning. Rather, he proposes a stance of critical realism in which "knowledge takes place . . . when people *find things that fit* with the particular story . . . to which they are accustomed to give allegiance."[7] Missionary anthropologist Paul Hiebert arrived at a similar conclusion in his evaluation of the profound impact that changing epistemological assumptions can have on the missionary enterprise. He asserted that it is critical realism that "affirms the presence of objective truth but recognizes that this is subjectively apprehended."[8] In other words, the way in which human beings understand truth is necessarily informed by the social, cultural, and historical contexts in which they are situated. The importance of narrative and of subjective personal experience leads to another of Polanyi's primary emphases: the integrative and "top-down" nature of knowing.

In his theory of knowledge, Polanyi speaks of "subsidiaries" or details of which we are aware in any given situation. These discrete, seemingly unrelated data points are formed into a "focal pattern" through an act of integration in the knower's mind[9]—the "a-ha!" moment at which an individual connects the dots, seeing *through* the subsidiaries to grasp a bigger

---

6. Polanyi, *Tacit Dimension*, 61–62.
7. Wright, *New Testament*, 37.
8. Hiebert, *Implications of Epistemological Shifts*, 69, 106.
9. Meek, *Longing to Know*, 47–48.

truth beyond them. There are countless examples of this sort of knowing in everyday life. Take, for instance, the act of recognizing a loved one's face. This focal pattern is achieved instantaneously, based on a number of subsidiary data points: the shape of a mouth, color of eyes, curvature of a chin, and so forth. Yet facial recognition is not a logical process of assembling and assessing various bits of sense data; instead, it is an instant, integrative leap of perception. After it has been achieved, the knower is aware not of a collection of familiar facial features in his general vicinity but simply of the whole, integrated *presence* of his loved one. Knowledge is thus an integrative process in which the whole is greater than the sum of the parts.

In addition to being integrative, knowledge is also intuitive in the sense that large swaths of what we know is "informal, undefined, and in large measure inarticulate, yet still of critical significance in explicit thought and conceptual formulation."[10] Torrance held that significant advances in knowledge are made by "unformalizable leaps of creative insight,"[11] while in his theory of knowledge, Polanyi speaks of a *prolepsis*, or an intuitive insight that leads to integration. Prolepsis is achieved by indwelling a given field of inquiry—living within it, trying it on for size, and soaking it in—until it suddenly and quite inexplicably makes sense. Polanyi stresses that this insight is *extra logical* (though not illogical).

Meek helpfully describes this process of prolepsis as being analogous to riding a bicycle; though it is theoretically possible to explain all of the mathematical and physical forces that go into riding a bicycle, the rider does not consider these—he simply "embodies the act of bike riding."[12] At the same time, it should be noted that the bike rider could not "intuit" or "embody" the act of riding his bicycle across the surface of a rushing river or through a concrete wall. There *are* real, physical laws that must be obeyed in bicycle riding, and the rider flouts these at his own peril. The fact that the process of riding is intuitive does *not* mean that it is only based in the mind of or entirely subject to the whims of the rider.

On the road to Emmaus, we see the disciples reaching a point of prolepsis in which they intuitively integrate the "subsidiaries" of their experience with the risen Jesus. In the breaking of the bread, "their eyes were opened and they recognized him." This realization is not a process of careful, logical deduction based on empirical sensory perceptions but rather an organic "leap" to a startling, extra-logical conclusion. *Jesus is alive, and he is here with us!* This new knowledge is not a bolt from the blue, however,

10. Colyer, *How to Read Torrance*, 335.
11. Achtemeier, *The Truth of Tradition*, 364.
12. Meek, *Longing to Know*, 77.

but is firmly based on "tradition" in the sense that it is only because of the disciples' past experience with Jesus that they are able to see the risen Christ for who he truly is. Indeed, Jesus himself aids the disciples in this process by reinterpreting Moses and the Prophets to show that the Hebrew Scriptures pointed to his own life, death, resurrection, and glorification. To use the terminology of N. T. Wright, the disciples found that the startling claim that Jesus was alive to be the best explanation (indeed, the *only* explanation) that fits the "story" or the context in which they were dwelling. Thus, the integrative, intuitive, and subjective aspects of knowing are on full display in this encounter.

At least two significant implications for missional discipleship can be drawn from this way of regarding knowledge. First, Polanyi's *prolepsis* can be seen as a kind of conversion experience, in which previously disjointed, nonsensical, or unseen subsidiaries are combined inexplicably into an integrated whole. Many believers speak of a process of coming to faith in which suddenly "everything made sense." The various data points of one's life experiences, intuitions, values, beliefs, and assumptions about the world come together via an extra-logical leap, creating a new vision of reality. While the popular notion of conversion is that of a "leap of faith"—a counterintuitive, anti-intellectual throwing of oneself into the arms of a higher power one fervently *hopes* is real, Polanyi and others have shown that *prolepsis*—an extra-logical (but not illogical) "leap"—is actually an integral component of *all* knowledge, rather than a telltale sign of delusional thinking or wish fulfillment. It is at least worth questioning whether the proliferation of books, websites, radio programs, tracts, and apologetic arguments attempting to prove the existence of God through logical syllogisms or empirical data do not, in fact, fail to fully reflect the ways in which most people tend to make decisions for Christ. As Hiebert declares, "Faith is not simply cognitive affirmation of the truthfulness of a statement. Nor is it simply positive feelings toward God. It is knowledge and feelings that lead us to respond to Christ's call to follow him."[13] This knowledge can and does come about through extra-logical leaps of insight, but it is knowledge all the same.

Another important implication for mission is the attention (or lack thereof) that is paid to story and tradition in the process of disciple-making. The *prolepsis* of conversion, it could be said, is achieved by indwelling the "field" of Christianity—of "trying on the Christian worldview for size with a view to permanent purchase," as N. T. Wright puts it,[14] in the expectation

---

13. Hiebert, *Implications of Epistemological Shifts*, 98.
14. Wright, *New Testament*, 77.

that the claims made by Christianity might best "fit" the story in which a seeker finds herself.

The implication here is twofold. First, it means that missionaries must carefully attend to the stories that spiritual seekers are indwelling and telling. Since the Gospel is always communicated within human contexts, Hiebert contends: "We need to master human exegesis as well as biblical exegesis . . . to study the social, cultural, psychological, and ecological systems in which humans live in order to communicate the gospel in ways that people understand and believe."[15] As we encounter new communities in mission, our priority should be to learn the story of that community, identifying how God has been working, and helping people tell their story in light of God's story.[16] Yet even so, it is important to recognize that missionaries bring their own stories and thus need to be aware of the ways in which their own worldviews impact the stories they are telling about God's work in the world.

While secularism is increasingly the default worldview, it is only Christianity that can provide a fully integrated perspective, the one true story that truly "fits" the present human context. But to disciple persons in such a context, we must teach and preach in a way that "interrogates the dominant, unquestioned narratives of our hearers—on meaning, money, sex, power, politics, gender, and so forth."[17]

Indeed, we have no better example here than Jesus, for he knew the stories of his followers—the narratives that framed their hopes, dreams, longings, and the social-political-cultural context in which their everyday lives were embedded. He immersed himself in their world by listening and learning through hours spent walking, talking, eating, drinking, sitting in homes, and along long dusty journeys from town to town. At the same time, he so thoroughly knew the Scriptures that he could adeptly reframe and reinterpret these in ways that made sense to the hearers. Thus, missional discipleship involves not only learning the stories of those with whom God has called us to minister—as well as our own—but also questioning and transforming them to align with God's true story. In this way, discipleship can be seen as "a convergence of stories."[18]

An integrative, intuitive, and subjective view of knowledge also implies that Christianity is something that often needs to be *practiced* before it is believed. Aspects of the Christian life of prayer, worship, Scripture, liturgy, service, spiritual disciplines and community can—in fact, *should*—be

---

15. Hiebert, *Gospel in Human Contexts*, 12.
16. Myers, *Walking with the Poor*, 205–7.
17. Rishmawy, *Secular Age*, 59.
18. Rishmawy, *Secular Age*, 59.

lived out by those who have not yet fully committed themselves to Christ, as a means of revealing the way to enter into a new story. Indeed, faith communities may be most "seeker sensitive" when they faithfully represent the fullness of the Christian life to outsiders rather than when they most closely mirror the values and practices of the surrounding secular culture. Thus, missional discipleship must be lived out in light of the opportunities, challenges, values, and ethical perspectives that make sense in a particular context.

Practical before Theoretical, Dynamic Rather than Static

To say that all knowledge is practical before it is theoretical is closely tied with the assertion that tradition is integral to knowing. To return again to the example of the toddler learning to speak: a child acquiring a language does not sit down and carefully study verb tenses, subordinate clauses, or the various shades of meaning found in different prepositions. Theories of grammar and syntax can be deduced later, but the actual learning of the language is eminently practical and organic.[19]

In the realm of science, Torrance points to the difference between Newton and Einstein in this regard. Unlike Newton, Einstein did not rely primarily on logical reasoning to arrive at his theories. They were based on years of empirical observation, and he allowed these observations to influence and correct his theoretical constructs. Propelled forward with some intuitive leaps of insight, Einstein's theories emerged more organically than Newton's.[20] Einstein called these intuitive leaps "free creations," pointing to the fact that they emerged "spontaneously" from the data in which the scientist was dwelling and required the scientist to posit a creative conceptual expression of what he was reading in the data.[21]

One is perhaps reminded here of the difference between contextual theology, which emerges from a personal, pastoral, and missional engagement with a particular community rather than, for example, systematic theology, which results more from a rational ordering and prioritizing of discrete bits of propositional truth that can theoretically be assembled "at a distance" from any specific community. In the same way, methods of evangelism and discipleship that consist primarily of systematic, one-size-fits-all approaches may be easier to package and replicate than more organic, contextual approaches, but it is questionable whether they should for that

---

19. Mitchell, *Michael Polanyi*, 65.
20. Torrance, *Reality and Evangelical Theology*, 33.
21. Trainor, *Philosophy and Theology*, 222.

reason be favored over methods which require (admittedly) time-intensive and effort-intensive "indwelling" of particular contexts.

Because it is eminently practical and concerned with making sense of an ever-changing world, knowledge is also dynamic rather than static. As Polanyi explains, each generation approaches the tradition of previous generations with a new set of questions, concerns, and expectations.[22] The questions that any culture in the early twenty-first century asks about the cosmos and humanity's place in it are not the same as the questions that were being asked by the Greeks of the first century, the Europeans of the sixteenth century or even the North Americans of the mid-twentieth century. Thus, each generation and culture leaves its own particular influence on the development of the tradition, based on the questions that concern it most. Knowledge is influenced by what has come before and impacts what comes after; there is definite continuity but also radical and sometimes unpredictable discontinuity.

Torrance grounds this ever-shifting vitality in the dynamic nature of God's self-revelation. Fundamentalists, he says, make the mistake of operating "within a rigid framework of beliefs which have a transcendent origin . . . but these beliefs are not applied in a manner consistent with their dynamic origin and nature."[23] This rigidity leads to the Bible being treated by fundamentalists as "a self-contained corpus of divine truths in propositional form" rather than the living and active Word of God.[24]

In the Emmaus encounter with Jesus, the previous knowledge that the disciples had of Jesus was not sufficient to enable them to recognize him at first. There was radical discontinuity not only in the physical appearance of Jesus before and after the resurrection but also in the very fabric of reality itself. By his death and resurrection, Jesus had fundamentally changed *everything*. God revealed himself at the cross and the empty tomb, not as the result of a rational, inevitable outworking of some chain of causation but rather in an astonishing act of humility, love, and power so unexpected that the disciples failed to grasp its import, even as Jesus himself was explaining it to them. This revelation is indeed the essence of dynamic, living knowledge.

In our current, rapidly secularizing context, the idea of knowledge as a dynamic, changeable force holds some appeal. On a superficial level, this notion seems to mirror the embrace of postmodern, relativistic theories of knowledge and truth. However, unlike popular conceptions

---

22. Mitchell, *Michael Polanyi*, 68.
23. Torrance, *Reality and Evangelical Theology*, 17.
24. Torrance, *Reality and Evangelical Theology*, 17.

of postmodernism, in which each individual "creates his own truth," the epistemology being proposed here honors both continuity and discontinuity with the knowledge of previous generations. One's approach to knowledge and truth—especially the communication thereof in missionary and evangelistic endeavors—may change through time, but this does not mean that each generation simply creates its own truth as it were, "from scratch." Continuity with the past and correspondence with an objective reality are essential ingredients of this epistemology, yet to treat Christian faith as a "self-contained corpus of divine truths in propositional form,"[25] to use Torrance's phrase, is to communicate a culture-bound, inert philosophy incapable of hearing—let alone answering—the questions posed by succeeding generations. Such a philosophy would seem to be the antithesis of a faith instituted by a risen and living Lord, superintended by his Spirit, who is active and moving in the hearts of each believer. Indeed, as Palmer asserts, "Truth is not a concept that 'works' but an incarnation that lives."[26] Thus, our understanding and practice of discipleship communicates truth as embodied in personal relationship.

Incarnational and Interpersonal

The dynamic nature of knowledge, rooted as it is in a God who reveals himself not in static theorems and propositions but rather in a combination of mighty acts and astonishing quietude, leads naturally to our final two points about the incarnational and interpersonal nature of all knowledge. The claim that knowledge is interpersonal can be understood from a number of different angles. Polanyi holds that only *people* can be involved in knowing. Knowledge requires "a responsible participation of the person as an active rational agent . . . but a participation that is controlled from beyond the knowing person by objective reality and universal standards which transcend his subjectivity."[27] Knowledge is neither entirely objective (as the positivist position would hold) nor is it altogether subjective (as a skeptical postmodern account would maintain); instead, it is a melding of both objective and subjective factors into a personal whole. As Meek puts it, "All truth is somebody's truth," but this does not necessarily lead to relativism or skepticism.[28]

---

25. Torrance, *Reality and Evangelical Theology*, 17.
26. Palmer, *To Know As We Are Known*, 14.
27. Palmer, *To Know As We Are Known*, 45.
28. Meek, *Longing to Know*, 58.

T. F. Torrance maintains that an interpersonal knowledge of God has implications not just for theologians or Christian believers specifically, but also that such knowledge of the divine "constitutes the ground on which all truly rational knowledge reposes."[29] He points to the Christian conviction that "since God has irreversibly incarnated his self-revelation in Jesus Christ, the Word made flesh, there cannot be two ways to knowledge of God, one in Jesus Christ and another behind his back, but only one way, through Christ and in his Spirit."[30] Attempts to attain knowledge of God or ultimate reality while circumventing Jesus inevitably fall short, as they disregard the personal, incarnational dimension of God's self-revelation. At best, these attempts can only lead to a fuzzy, confusing, and contradictory picture of God and reality.[31] It is no novel insight that communication of the Gospel must deal head-on with the person and work of Jesus Christ. Approaches to mission that exclude or shy away from a presentation of Jesus, then, are incomplete. This does not mean, of course, that works of compassion, mercy, and justice should be avoided but rather that by themselves, they lack an essential component of a full-orbed picture of truth: a Christo-centric focus.

Within our increasingly secularized context, largely influenced by a disconnected world and life view, contemporary Protestantism has, at times, embraced a more abstract understanding of discipleship—one that is dependent upon logic and propositions or a lock-step process. And sadly, this perspective has been exported to our methods and strategies of discipleship worldwide. In this regard, Smith references Taylor's depiction of "excarnation" (as opposed to incarnation) and the gradual depersonalization of God and his work through the church as an embodied community in this world.[32]

Fundamentally, discipleship is about a relationship with the living Christ. "Jesus did not offer propositions to be tested by logic or data to be tested in the laboratory. He offered himself and his life. Those who sought truth were invited into relationship with him."[33] Moreover, the power of the Gospel message can only be manifest if its messengers embody lives that have a relationship with Jesus.[34]

There is yet a final way in which knowledge is profoundly personal. In light of his Trinitarian being, God's knowledge even of *himself* is

29. Torrance, *Belief in Science*, 3.
30. Torrance, *Reality and Evangelical Theology*, 34.
31. Colyer, *How to Read T. F. Torrance*, 132.
32. Smith, *How (Not) To Be Secular*, 58.
33. Palmer, *Know As We Are Known*, 47.
34. See Myer's discussion of witnessing and the significance of being with Jesus in Myer, *Walking with the Poor*, 318.

interpersonal. According to Torrance, the human correlate of that divine interpersonal self-knowledge is the church. It is within the church and through the communion of the Spirit that "our minds become disposed to apprehend God through profoundly intelligible, although non-formalizable . . . relations and structures of thought."[35] To put it simply, we get to know who God is through living in community with other Christians. The church is indeed the body of Christ, and the depth of our knowledge of Christ is dependent on our healthy functioning as members of that body. It should be of paramount importance that, whenever and wherever possible, one of the chief aims of missional discipleship is to draw believers into community with others. This does not serve merely a sociological function of cementing a change in belief through membership in a likeminded and supportive group, but it is in itself profoundly theological; God chooses to reveal himself in a special way in and through community.

The incarnational and interpersonal aspects of knowing are clear in the Emmaus encounter as well. It is notable that Jesus appears here to a pair of disciples rather than to a single "chosen" follower. This is not a divine apparition to a hermit on a remote mountain but rather a deeply personal, in-the-flesh visit to two friends who are walking and discussing the events that have just transpired. The climactic moment of recognition comes during a meal—that most community-oriented daily ritual—and the two disciples confer with each other, checking their own perceptions with one another ("Were not our hearts burning within us ?" [Luke 24:32a NIV]) before rushing to tell the other disciples. Knowledge here is revealed to, discerned by, and shared with the community of believers.

Conclusion

A note of caution should be raised at this point. We should not assume that, because knowledge is intuitive and interpersonal, it cannot also be rational and empirical, nor should we feel that because knowledge is often an integrative act that therefore deconstruction and classification serve no useful purpose. Christians should avoid the temptation to carve out an irrational, anti-empirical niche in which to shelter themselves from the rest of the world. We should celebrate the fact that our personal, loving Savior "through whom all things were created," who is not constrained by rules of logic himself, has created the beautiful and inexplicably rational universe in which we live, move, and have our being. By the same token, we need not

---

35. Torrance, *Reality and Evangelical Theology*, 49.

eschew missional practices and concepts that have served the Church well throughout the modern period.

However, it is equally true that the Church must take a long, hard look at the presuppositions upon which our faith and practice rests—particularly as it relates to our missional engagement in the world. For much too long, Christians have implicitly accepted epistemological fallacies promoted by the larger, secular culture—that "faith" and "reason" must be at odds with one another, that "objective knowledge" is categorically distinct from and superior to mere "subjective belief," or that discipleship and life transformation are fundamentally a matter of behavior change and correct doctrine. The biblical account, as illustrated in our examination of the road to Emmaus encounter, intimates that knowing is profoundly interpersonal and dynamic, that the lines between faith and reason, knowledge and belief, are not nearly so clear-cut and mutually exclusive as we might assume, and that missional discipleship is a holistic pursuit in which truth—if it is to be apprehended—must be embodied and lived out. Like unsuspecting disciples traveling the road with Jesus, we walk too often with hearts that burn within us but are blind to the truth in front of us. May the church of the twenty-first century, like those disciples on the road to Emmaus, receive what Jesus has to offer so that our eyes may be opened.

Reflection Questions

1. How might the notion of "indwelling" a particular field of inquiry (whether it is particle physics or Christianity), prior to understanding it, inform our concept of mission, evangelism, and discipleship?

2. How have you seen epistemological presuppositions played out in your own ministry context? Consider specific examples and their implications for the understanding and practice of mission and discipleship.

3. How could this proposed "holistic epistemology for missional discipleship" contribute to a fresh approach to discipleship programs and curriculum in our contemporary secular context?

Bibliography

Achtemeier, Paul Mark. "The Truth of Tradition: Critical Realism in the Thought of Alasdair MacIntyre and T. F. Torrance." *Scottish Journal of Theology* 47.3 (1994) 355–74.

Colyer, Elmer M. *How to Read T. F. Torrance: Understanding His Trinitarian and Scientific Theology*. Downers Grove, IL: InterVarsity, 2001.

Hiebert, Paul G. *Missiological Implications of Epistemological Shifts: Affirming Truth in a Modern/Postmodern World*. Harrisburg, PA: Trinity, 1999.

Meek, Esther L. *Longing to Know: The Philosophy of Knowledge for Ordinary People*. Grand Rapids: Brazos, 2003.

Mitchell, Mark T. *Michael Polanyi: The Art of Knowing*. Library of Modern Thinkers. Wilmington, DE: ISI, 2006.

Myers, Bryant L. *Walking with the Poor: Principles and Practices of Transformational Development*. 2nd ed. Maryknoll, NY: Orbis, 2011.

Palmer, Parker. *To Know As We Are Known: A Spirituality of Education*. New York: Harper Collins, 1983.

Polanyi, Michael. *The Tacit Dimension*. London: Routledge & K. Paul, 1967.

Rishmawy, Derek. "Millenial Belief in the Super-Nova." In *Our Secular Age: Ten Years of Reading and Applying Charles Taylor*, edited by Collin Hansen, 49–62. Deerfield, IL: The Gospel Coalition, 2017.

Smith, James K. A. *How (Not) To Be Secular: Reading Charles Taylor*. Grand Rapids: Eerdmans, 2014.

Taylor, Charles. *A Secular Age*. Cambridge: Harvard University Press, 2007.

Torrance, Thomas F. *Belief in Science and in Christian Life: The Relevance of Michael Polanyi's Thought for Christian Faith and Life*. Edinburgh: Handsel, 1980.

———. *Reality and Evangelical Theology*. 1st ed. The 1981 Payton Lectures. Philadelphia: Westminster, 1982.

Trainor, Brian T. "The Divine Undergirding of Human Knowing: Plato and Critical Realism." *Philosophy & Theology* 22.1–2 (2010) 205–34.

Wright, Christopher. *The Mission of God's People: A Biblical Theology of God's Mission*. Grand Rapids: Zondervan, 2010.

Wright, N. T. *The New Testament and the People of God*. 1st North American ed. Christian Origins and the Question of God 1. Minneapolis: Fortress, 1992.

Conclusion

Next Steps for Mission and Evangelism in a Secularizing World

Canadian Perspectives

NARRY F. SANTOS

THE CONTRIBUTORS IN THIS volume have explored how secularism influences church ministry and mission to our community and the world. This concluding chapter proposes some next steps as part of our Canadian missiological response in a secularizing world.

Next Step #1: Discover New Metaphors for Mission Today

We need a creative re-imagination of who we are as the Church and what we can become by adopting metaphors or images[1] that spring out of our new secular realities. DenBok (chapter 2) uses the metaphor of an ecosystem, emphasizing "how seemingly unrelated organisms have a profound effect on one another" and that the "collapse of one part places pressure on the whole." She uses this metaphor for the entire Canadian Church, illustrated by how shifts in the United Church have affected other denominations and networks; churches cannot remain isolated or immune from the actions and decisions of others.

This ecosystem image also incorporates the assembly, agency, and academy and can have a positive application. Churches (assembly) need the mission agencies just as the theological institutions (academy) need the Church. Chaise (chapter 1) re-imagines the outworking of the Church as an ecosystem of missional relationships on which the academy reflects, researches, and theorizes and which the agency applies in practical ways.

---

1. For the importance of images, see Messer, *Contemporary Images*, 19–25.

The even wider ecosystem of the global Church can be imaginatively addressed through Chaise's metaphor of local churches functioning as expert artisans or gardeners. Though the communities have their own unique micro-context, they are linked to influential "non-local and meta-conversations... that take place—through traditional and new media—shaping our future." Thus, on a macro-scale, the global Church can be viewed as a network of community gardens with churches ministering as local gardening experts. Seeing ourselves as connected to others—no matter how different or diverse we may be—can provide courage to face together the challenge of secularism in our neighborhood or city. We are not alone in this journey and we can encourage each other as fellow-gardeners in the whole garden of God called the global Church.

Other stimulating metaphors should be noted. Chaise's proposal that we serve as spiritual tour guides is enhanced by Song's (Response to Chaise) added dimension of the Church being called as a "witness"; thus, we can "behave like tour guides with hearts of a witness." Krause's (response to denBok) image of Christendom being dismantled through secularism like a tapestry unravelled into a pile of threads is also powerful. Reflecting on the distinction between the tapestry (Christendom) and the story that the tapestry tells (Christianity) is a helpful way to address secularism's deconstruction. With discernment from the Spirit, we can discover appropriate missional responses within our location in the deconstruction and trust God for transformation in the people we are called to live with and love. Smither's (chapter 3) picture of mission as history and story through the art of film (*Augustine: Son of Her Eyes*) provides a compelling reason to tell our own faith stories as images of the way of Christ. Franklin's (response to Smither) appeal for "integral" mission extends the "capacity for ongoing transformative experience—like Augustine had—in which a restless heart is exchanged for a heart at peace through a knowledge of God."

These captivating descriptions—ecosystem, expert gardeners, tour guide and witness, tapestry, and integral mission as history and story—help us imagine our place within the local and global context of secularism so that we can boldly engage in evangelism and mission. These new metaphors also encourage us to reimagine our journey of faith as Christ-followers in his Kingdom.

Next Step #2: Embrace the Potential of Multicultural and Next Generation Mission

The contributions of the second part of the book, *Mission to the Next Generation*, invite us to embrace the potential for mission found in three multicultural and next-generation realities:[2] (1) The children of first-generation immigrants ("next generation") may be key to the "reengagement and revitalization of religion in public life and higher education"; (2) Multiculturalism provides opportunity for "engagement, dialogue, and 'incremental' evangelism with the religious 'nones' and 'other-religion' groups"; and (3) An ancient irenic and non-threatening orientation to witness can be a fruitful path to engage millennial Muslims in North America today.

Even while multicultural Canada embraces the narratives of secularism, it also experiences the impact of global migration[3] and the immigration of many who profess ideologies that run counter to secularizing forces. Hsu (chapter 4) calls secularism and multiculturalism the "twin currents of progressivism," which seem, at times, to work in opposition to each other. Secularism "often seeks to marginalize and limit religion," while multiculturalism "offers opportunity for an increased engagement with faith." Hsu's observations at the University of Toronto reveal the potential that "secularism can actually lead to religious regeneration" (as Hsu quotes Lhumann) when children of recent immigrants "push back against the marginalization of religion, using the language of multiculturalism and progressivism. Rather than separating religion from public life, highly multicultural and pluralistic settings may offer a platform for reengagement and revitalization of religion in public life and higher education."

Though Cheung (chapter 5) provides statistical evidence for the decline of church attendance due to what has been called the "silent exodus"[4] of the GXMs (Generation X and Millennials), he also cites studies that demonstrate the growing support of multiculturalism in Canada, concluding that multiculturalism "enjoys 'broad and deep' popular support, having attained the status of 'national aspiration' or the very 'Canadian dream' itself." Related to this multiculturalism are values of inclusivity, diversity, tolerance, equality, civility, peaceful co-existence, acceptance with a non-judgmental attitude, secular pluralism (which theoretically accommodates religion), authenticity, compassion, and pro-minority sympathy. The space for engagement, dialogue, and "incremental" evangelism with the religious

2. See Krause et al., *Margins to the Centre*.

3. See Pocock et al., *Changing Face of World Missions*, and Bramadat and Seljak, *Christianity and Ethnicity*.

4. See Lee, "Silent Exodus."

"nones," "other-religion" groups, "religiously-indifferents," and "religion-rejecters," is therefore a possibility based on the inclusive nature of these values.

Friedman (chapter 6) suggests that the juxtaposition of millennial Islam with secularization may be an opportunity for witness to the next generation of Muslims. He observes that "US Muslims—roughly 60 percent of whom are under 40—are going through a process of . . . finding new, diverse, self-constructed identities in their faith, ranging from fully secular to deeply pious." In response, Friedman proposes to use Ramon Llull's "irenic rational-mystical witness" to engage secularizing Muslim communities in North America through "dialogue and witness." Could the irenic and non-threatening approach of an earlier era be an effective way to reach those who are also struggling within a secularizing environment?

Next Step #3: Learn from the Global Church and Missionaries

The third part of the book, *Mission in Global Christianity*, calls us to humbly learn from what is happening in Global Christianity and the positive impact of missionary work. In his first of two chapters in this volume, Martin (chapter 7) demonstrates that the secularizing trend in the Western world is not reflected in Africa, where "over 99 percent of the population" self-identify with religion. Not only is this orientation projected to remain stable, but Africa's "higher-than-average birthrate also increases the significance—not only statistically—of its relative resistance to secularization." The increasing influence of African Christianity is also expected—a decentralized, spontaneously adaptive, oral, holistic, conservative, and supernaturalist Christianity.[5] What can we learn from what God is doing through African Christians who are holding firm against secularism in the Global North? Can we gain insights from our African brothers and sisters so that we can continue to advance God's global mission with hope and confidence?

Pepper (chapter 8) explores the harsh challenge rising from a secularizing narrative, "Do missionaries destroy culture?" While acknowledging that "some have" and "some do," she presents some important biblical principles that guided appropriate missions practice in the past and will continue to do so. She affirms first that God "is the author of culture" and because "his image is present in every person," each human being is given an intrinsic value. Based on this, she then stresses that the role of the missionary is to "live

---

5. See Mugambi, "Migration and Human Dislocation," 50–56, and Walls, "Towards a Theology of Migration," 414–17.

exemplary lives *in terms of the virtues and social norms stressed by the people group* among whom they live" (emphasis added). She also warns against imposed change, claiming that "change is best when it is self-initiated and not a result of external pressure." This implies that we can learn from both positive and negative experiences of missionaries in relation to long-term culture change. The challenge from the secularizing narrative cautions us to treat culture with care and respect. The three culture-change lessons—living out the values and social norms of the people group that they serve, pursuing ongoing relationships, and avoiding external pressure to elicit change—are essential since we continue to be evaluated through a critical, secularizing lens.

Next Step #4: Experiment with New Mission Expressions

The last part of the book, *Mission and Strategy in a Changing Context*, encourages us to courageously initiate missional and strategic experiments[6] in the areas of bivocational ministry, use of technology, and missional discipleship.

Watson and Santos (chapter 9) explore the viable and countervailing impact of starting new churches through Christian immigrants, the majority of whom self-identify as Christian. They cite three experimental models for congregational mission—missional groups, small church plants, and larger church initiatives—that can be used to connect with Canada's religious nones. Such initiatives can be pioneering or emergent expressions of Christianity in our secularizing context. Watson and Santos also consider the benefit of incorporating bivocational ministry (or tentmaking) that mobilizes "networks of relationships that allow for creative contextualization." Such pioneering and emerging expressions have the potential to break down the "sacred-secular," "clergy-laity," and "church-community" dichotomies in local and global mission. Can we envision new expressions of church and Christianity that will not only reach new Canadians but also the younger generation of religious nones?

In his second contribution, Martin (chapter 10) discusses the complicated relationship of technology and secularization with a focus on their impact on mission and evangelism. Though he sees downsides to the increasing influence of technology, Martin affirms that technology can be a handmaid to the advance of the Gospel in today's secularizing world. He foresees the Gospel of Jesus Christ to continue in its "relentless spread"

---

6. For examples, of these missional experiments, see Stiller, *Going Missional*, and Barrett, *Treasures in Jars*.

through the use of available technologies that includes "mission mobilization." This encourages us to "leverage" technology and social media because "friendship with people unlike us may build bridges toward unprecedented global harvest and may potentially counteract some of technology's arguably inherent bent toward secularization." How can we use technology to create connections with and to understand the world of nones? How can we use social media as a bridge to face-to-face contacts?

Shetterly and McEwen provide the last experiment in our secularizing Canada—missional discipleship. These co-authors define missional discipleship as the "whole-life transformation of individuals into the likeness of Christ through active participation in a community of believers devoted to cooperating with God in the *missio Dei*." This kind of discipleship involves a process that is integrative, intuitive, subjective, and based on a holistic epistemology that knowledge is revealed to, discerned by, and shared with a community of believers. Missional discipleship challenges secular culture in the form of three holistic affirmations: faith and reason go together; subjective and objective beliefs are both needed; discipleship and life transformation involve behavior change and correct doctrine. In other words, missional discipleship demands a "holistic pursuit in which truth must be embodied and lived out." What would it take to cultivate missional discipleship so that relationships in community are developed with people steeped in secular culture, resulting in a transformation toward Christlikeness?

Taking Steps with Hope

The next steps we listed in this concluding chapter are baby steps, compared to the protracted extent of the journey and the ongoing challenge of creatively responding to our secularizing Canadian context. But we can take these steps with hope, knowing that we have a God who is on mission, who is committed to fulfilling that mission for the sake of the world he loves and to whom he sent Jesus Christ in love. We can commit to travel the journey together, confident that "God's mission has been accomplished, is being accomplished, and will be accomplished."

Bibliography

Barrett, Lois. *Treasure in Clay Jars: Patterns in Missional Faithfulness*. Grand Rapids: Eerdmans, 2004.

Bramadat, Paul, and David Seljak, eds. *Christianity and Ethnicity in Canada*. Toronto: University of Toronto Press, 2008.

Krause, Michael, et al. *From the Margins to the Centre: The Diaspora Effect*. Toronto: Tyndale Academic, 2018.

Lee, Helen. "Silent Exodus: Can the East Asian Church in America Reverse the Flight of its Next Generation?" *Christianity Today* 40.9 (1996) 50–53.

Messer, Donald. *Contemporary Images of Christian Ministry*. Nashville: Abingdon, 1989.

Mugambi, Jesse N. K. "Migration and Human Dislocation: Accountability in Christian Missions from an African Perspective." In *People Disrupted: Doing Mission Responsibly among Refugees and Migrants*, edited by Jinbong Kim, et al., 48–61. Pasadena, CA: William Carey, 2018.

Pocock, Michael, et al. *The Changing Face of World Missions: Engaging Contemporary Issues and Trends*. Ada: Baker Academic, 2005.

Stiller, Karen, and Willard Metzger. *Going Missional: Conversations with 13 Canadian Churches who Have Embraced Missional Life*. Winnipeg: Word Alive, 2010.

Walls, Andrew F. "Towards a Theology of Migration." In *African Christian Presence in the West: New Immigrant Congregations and Transnational Networks in North America and Europe*, edited by Frieder Ludwig and J. Kwaena Asamoah-Gyadu, 407–17. Trenton: Africa World, 2011.

www.ingramcontent.com/pod-product-compliance
Lightning Source LLC
Chambersburg PA
CBHW070328230426
43663CB00011B/2252